Dialogical Community Development

Dialogical
Community Development

with depth, hospitality and solidarity

Peter Westoby and Gerard Dowling

Tafina Press

First published in Australia, 2009
Reprinted 2010

Published by
Tafina Press
PO Box 5519
West End, Q. 4101
Australia

ISBN: 978-0-9757658-3-8

Typeset in Dante
Printed and bound by
Lightning Source UK

Contents

Preface

You'll read a lot about the inner Brisbane neighbourhood of West End in this book. That's because we met in West End in 1987, and it's where we still live. We had moved into the area to be part of an experiment in radical Christian discipleship and intentional community, which later came to be known as the West End Waiters Union. We were responding to an invitation from Dave Andrews to join him in getting to know our neighbours, going out of our way to get involved with those whom we perceived as being on the margins, reflecting with others on the intended and unintended outcomes, and learning to change our little bit of the world.

You'll also read a fair amount about the year 1988 in West End—a watershed year in our experience as Brisbane hosted World Expo 88, and its impact on our neighbourhood fast-tracked the emergence of our critical consciousness and got us involved in defending our community through many place-based activities and actions.

This book is a reflection on our twenty years of shared and separate experience of community life and community development practice since that formative time. In reflecting on our practice, we have often struggled with questions such as 'What is it that we see?', 'How do others experience it?', 'What are we trying to achieve?' and 'What is it that we actually do?' In answering those questions we have articulated the *implicate method* in our work—the practice that we have built on intuition, embodied experience and the integration of our selves into the community development practice. It has been a challenge to put words to express ways of thinking and acting that seem to come naturally, that we share easily, that we take for granted. Moments of agreement between us were a sure sign that we were articulating something significant for us that might also be of use to others.

Acknowledgments

We are keen to acknowledge the people with whom we have shared the journey. We are both attentive to process, and have learned much practice wisdom in living, working and playing alongside others. The approach to community development we are describing is not something we have made up—it is an approach that we have co-created and co-discovered with many others in multiple processes of dialogue over twenty years. This book is a reflection on the community and the work that we have shared with many very different people. If you have been our companion, the chances are you may recognise your own insights here—if not in specific phrases, then in a familiarity with perspectives, values, principles and ideas that we have distilled from a shared history of practice.

As first-time authors, we feel a bit like first-time Academy Award winners making acceptance speeches: they get a bit emotional, want to thank everyone, and inevitably leave out someone really important. We would like to acknowledge some of the many people whom have made important contributions to our understanding of community and our practice of community development:

- *West End past and present fellow-travellers:* Johnny Glover, Ruth and Chris Todd, Dave and Angie Andrews, Judy and Steve Collins-Haynes, Matthew Leggett, Greg Daley, Wendy Webster, Wendy Moore, Jim Dowling, Trevor and Theresa Jordan, Nigel and Sue Lewin, Carmel Rosella, Jenny Alford, Jenny Nash, Lisa Westoby, Jimmy DeCouto, Michael O'Brien, Kimberley Williams, Faye Lovett and all the crews at the West End Reading and Writing Group and the West End Partisans Football Club.
- *Those who have journeyed with us, with refugees:* Carlos and Roberto Monterosa, Dionisio and Oscar, John Diew, Russell Eggins, Domingo Montenegro, Marco and Elvia Ramirez, Paula Peterson, Donata Rossi, Keithia Wilson, Renae Mann, Nermina (Nera) Komaric, Ally Wakefield, Lois Wiseman, Robyn Sheptooha, Danijel Kis, Saba Abrahams and Catalina Hernandez.

- *Colleagues who have shared, amongst many other things, the ongoing experiment that is Community Praxis Co-op:* Jason McLeod, Chris Brown, Betty Chapelle, Noritta Morseu-Diop, Helen Beazley, Polly Walker, Athena Lathouras, Ken Morris, Neil Barringham and Howard Buckley.
- *Brisbane colleagues we have learned from:* Maria Tenant, Deirdre Coghlan, Janelle Scognamilglio, Erna Hayward, Juanita Phillips, Ian Schmidt, Julie Ling, Maria Brennan, Morrie O'Connor, Paul Toon, Paul Donatiu, Bea Rogan, Fiona Caniglia, Anna Spencer, Colleen Kelly, Lisa Price, Anthony Esposito, Karen Walsh, Phil Crane, Mark Young, Jeremy Liyanage, Wally Dethlefs, Jon Eastgate, Liz Upham, Roberta Bonnin, Pam Bourke and Ken Butler.
- *Some of those Peter has journeyed with from around the world:* South Africa: Sipho Sokhela, Verne and Kerry Harris, Mike Cuthbert, Nick Lindner, Caroline Skinner, Mpume Zama, Treven Hendricks, Lucius Botes.
  Vanuatu: Anne Brown, Paul Jensen, Charles Vatu, Selwyn Garu and Dickinson.
  Papua New Guinea: Landy, Joe and Louise.
  Philippines: Therese, Digna, Jose, Stuart and the rest of the "gang".
- *Colleagues of Gerard in Brisbane City Council:* Steve Capelin, Ryan Foster, Kerry O'Connor, the Kelly's Rivas and Nelson, Tim Graham, Deanna Borland-Sentinella, Nina Bowbridge, Theresa Godbee, Frances Missen, Julie Chenery, Scotia Monkovitch, Chris Gibbings, Ewen Heathdale and Donna Bowe.
- *Students who have taught us by challenging our practice:* Denise Foley, Anna Strandring, Helen Abbott, San-Marie Esterhuysen, James Douglas, Fiona Murray and Gabby Denning-Cotter.
- *Those who sat with Gerard in the playground and imagined a vibrant community around our children at Buranda Primary School—for all those 'what if . . .' conversations:* Julie, Mark, Lyn, Lynne, Kath, Don,

Miriam, Sue, Mark, Maaritt, Lynne, Carlos, John, Lynne, Ivy and Corena.

- *Gerard's colleagues from the early days of the Tenants' Union of Queensland:* Janice Jordan, Lurline Comerford, Robyn Cochrane, Gary Penfold, Tim Seelig, Tim Wilson, Peter See, Louise Villanova, Lillian Lawson-Geddes and Rebecca Foote.
- *University teachers and colleagues:* Allan Halladay, Ann Ingamells, Mary Graham, Lilla Watson, David Massey, Jayne Clapton, Patricia Harrison, Tony Kelly and David Ip.
- *Our families who have seen less of us this year:* Iris, Michael, Lisa, Jim, Ella, Kaiya, Ross, Ciaron, Jack, Dot and Pat, Sharon, David, Marilyn, Ross, Tamma, Maurie, Dorothy and Peter. And of course as fellow-journeyers and also supporters in the writing task we'd like to thank our partners: Larah Seivl-Keevers and Lyn Dowling.

Finally, we'd like to acknowledge those who have given indispensable help with this book. Thanks to Polly Walker and John Owen for giving it a thorough read, risking strong feedback, challenging our assumptions, and wielding the red pen. Thanks to Dave Andrews for encouragement to 'go for it', and to Tim, Corrine, Howard, Deanna and Ryan for comments, questions and enthusiasm. Roland at Tafina Press for advice, companionship, and publishing know-how—it has been great to have a publisher who is into community work himself.

A note on authorship

Peter is the primary author. The book started as *A Soulful Approach to Community Development*, a paper written when he was living in South Africa, published by an organisation called OLIVE. Gerard has always been a fan of that paper, and was thrilled when Pete came to him with a book-length expanded draft, saying "While I'm overseas I'd like to leave this with you—to go through with a red pen, edit and give me critical feedback." As we chatted Pete eventually made this invitation: "if you really get into it, you could become a co-author and we could finalise it together." We agreed that this was probably a reasonable thing, given the old 80/20 rule:

that even though Pete had the guts of the book 80% written, he had probably only done 20% of the work needed to get it to press, and we could share the 80% of work that would be required to finish it.

Gerard has taken a co-author role, working as a critical friend, reflecting on shared experiences, questioning, developing a collaborative analysis, articulating a shared practice framework, and testing it against our shared and independent histories of practice. Gerard has also worked in dialogue with an evolving text: refining the expression, unpacking unfamiliar terminology and grounding it in practice, and relentlessly shortening and lightening sentences and paragraphs.

Introduction

We love community work. Both of us have spent many years trying to live in a community orientation in our own neighbourhoods and workplaces, while also working professionally as practitioners of community development. During that time we have learnt much about community life and community work. Our lives have been deeply enriched as a result of this private, personal and public work. We have had the privilege of working with amazing people, been a part of creative community processes, and lived in sometimes challenging and often beautiful places. In reflecting on those years we find that there is much to celebrate.

However, as well as being a celebration of such people, processes and places, this is also a critical reflection on several concerns that have led us to re-think community development in particular ways. These concerns may simply reflect what is going on within us—an internal dialogue which involves our personal struggles to maintain the praxis of solidarity with the poor and marginalised—rather than a potential crisis in the profession itself. Some of the reflections and propositions shared here will ring true for other practitioners. We also hope that our concerns are shared public and professional concerns rather than mere personal problems. This is an invitation to a dialogue about the future of community development practice.

A legitimation crisis in community development

At the core of this analysis of current practice in community development is the observation that during the past few years the tradition we had learnt about as young practitioners has become increasingly influenced and perhaps co-opted by a modernist approach to philosophy, work and technique. In common with Jacques Ellul (1965), we maintain that in this 'modernising' process, community development work has lost something of its depth and soul, and therefore its capacity for genuine solidarity with the poor and marginalised. In losing that capacity, we argue that community development work could lose its basis for legitimacy.

Jurgen Habermas (1976) describes the contemporary state as being in a condition of 'legitimation crises'—lurching from problem to problem developing new *techniques* to solve society's problems. However, many of these problems require social solutions rather than technical solutions. Community development practice is falling into the same crisis of legitimation. In much current discourse, an approach to community development co-opted by modernist philosophy is heralded as one of the latest techniques to solving community problems. If the practice continues down this road, it is possible that technical approaches to community development will enter into their own crisis of legitimation. For a technical approach, this crisis would be welcome; however, the real danger is that in so doing we sideline the rich tradition of dialogical community development, full of depth, hospitality and solidarity. It is the shallow community development technique that needs to be critiqued.

We are making a distinction between *tradition* and *technique* in community development. Technique is seen as being co-opted by the modernist approach to philosophy and work. This approach sees the 'ills of society' as problems that need urgent solutions, in much the same way as some versions of modern medicine see the unhealthy body as problematic, requiring some form of medicine to fix it. In the modernist paradigm the ideal healthy body is one without sickness. In the same way, the modernist worldview sees an unhealthy society as a problem requiring a technique-based solution. However we should imagine a healthy society as one not without problems, but rather as aware of its problems, learning to live creatively and imaginatively with them, and engaging them socially.

It is with such an analysis in mind that we articulate a dialogical approach to community development. Allied to the analysis of Jacques

Ellul is the argument that a particular approach to community development has become one of the latest techniques that can apparently solve the problem of what is perceived to be an 'ill society'. The government has for a long time been expected to *fix* things; it has tried all its techniques—techniques of the right, the left and the centre. For many people such techniques have failed or seem to be failing. Yet in recent years there has been an almighty shift in the role of the state, the market, and civil society—a shift with both negative and positive consequences. One of these consequences, for better or worse, is the maxim that 'the community must take responsibility'. We hear politicians argue that 'the community must and can solve many problems', and even 'let's make people responsible through community membership'.

The government and 'the community' may have to learn afresh what each of them can and cannot do. In advocating that the community must solve its problems, key organisational stakeholders, usually wielding substantial institutional power, often look to the technique of community development, as defined according to a modernist paradigm, to facilitate the community to fix it. Such an approach is an impossible task. The 'stuff' of community and development requires work that is deeper than what technique alone can offer.

It is worth saying at this point that a critique of the technique of community development is in no way meant to imply that techniques are unimportant. On the contrary, techniques are essential; but they must be put in their right context. Any use of technique must be informed by an understanding of the tradition of community development work.

One useful way of imagining the loss that comes with an over-emphasis on technique is to imagine it is as a shallow-ing approach to community development. This shallowness is contrasted with the idea of *depth* articulated in Manfred Max-Neef's (1992) groundbreaking *From the Outside Looking In*. In the introductory section he argues that development "requires a study in *depth*; a penetration of the hidden relationships of existence". He goes on to argue that "the person who can really help in the solution of even such apparently strictly material problems as economic development, is therefore the philosopher rather than the mere specialist and technician" (1992, p12, emphasis added). In the same vein one of our key propositions is that community work practitioners require depth.

Depth can re-emerge from shifts in thinking, being and doing. This added depth is critical in utilising a dialogical approach to community development. A dialogical approach requires engaging with 'others'—other ideas, other perspectives, other people, horizons, hopes, analyses and so on. This requires us to resist the shallow-ing temptations of technically oriented work, and instead to orient our work towards *dialoguing* by:

- Embracing depth.
- Re-imagining community as hospitality.
- Enfolding community development within a commitment to solidarity.
- Infusing our practice with a soulful orientation.
- Opening ourselves to deconstructive movements.
- Reconstituting our work as a social practice.

These orientations embody our proposals for re-thinking community development. The proposals represent six concepts or dimensions of our framework that offer a way forward for dialogical community development. However, in naming them in this particular way we have included a number of significant verbs—infusing, reconstituting, opening, enfolding, re-imagining and embracing. As verbs they imply actions that we can participate in. While it is a call to enter a dialogue, this book is also a call to action—actions that can be embodied in daily life, and also our deeply connected private, personal and public worlds.

We hope to open up new ideas and analysis that you can embrace, to infuse you with new attention and awareness about possibilities, to enable you to re-imagine community life, and to provide a perspective for reconstituting your community practice and enfolding it within a commitment to solidarity.

Dialogical community development: the framework

When we started out as practitioners in the late 1980s, we were introduced to a tradition of community development. Colleagues like Ann Ingamells, Dave Andrews, Morrie O'Connor and Anthony Kelly introduced us to authors such as Martin Buber, Paulo Freire and Mahatma Gandhi. Their work has seeped deep into our bones. In the past few years we have been attempting to distil how we might name our approach. We have called it *dialogical community development*.

Dialogue: the challenging engagement of 'other'

At the centre of the tradition we learned, is the notion of dialogue. When watching our colleagues, we observed a practice of dialogue. When we immersed ourselves in the works of Buber, Freire and Gandhi, and travelled further into the worlds of those such as David Bohm, Ronald Arnett, and John Paul Lederach, we learnt more about the theory and practice of dialogue. We have come to understand dialogue as a deep, challenging and enriching conversation, a mutual process of building shared understanding, meaning, communication and creative action. It has become central to our practice.

We believe that a dialogical approach to community development is infused with hopes about means and ends. The hope, as end, is for *community as dialogue*. In this sense, community is an experience of dialogue, both in everyday practices of being present to one another, and also in extra-ordinary events when we experience 'deep presence' with one another (Buber, 1947, 1958).

The hope of community development as a *process* is that it is intentionally and purposefully dialogical. Firstly, we can consider our practice through the idea of the movements of dialogue in working relationally with people (Buber, 1947; Bohm, 1996). Relational community work focuses on the subtle and dynamic processes of valuing and nurturing relationships between people. Such valuing and nurturing requires an orientation toward *learning*, "withholding the impulse to tell until one understands the context, topic, and the persons" (Arnett et al., 2009, p. xiii). In this sense our community development practice engages people with a commitment to *our own* agenda of solidarity, hospitality, and depth, but holds that agenda lightly as we intentionally listen to people's stories, understand their concerns and therefore engage with *their* agendas. The dialogical process ensures that we can somehow find a common agenda that emerges in the relational space between us.

Secondly, our community development practice very deliberately and carefully fosters the transformational space of dialogue, where people set out to do what Paulo Freire (1972) calls "naming the word and the world"—thereby being able to ask strategic questions and challenge de-humanising social relations. In this sense dialogical practice is not only about listening and finding shared agendas. It is also about practitioners eliciting a mandate from the people they are engaging with: a mandate to do analysis together, pushing the boundaries of how we together interpret our shared world—into 'other' spaces of awareness and possible action. Dialogue requires a process of questioning.

Finally, dialogical community development points in the direction of practices that transform community conflict and foster deep respect (Lederach, 2005). Dialogue centres a practice of tackling some of the deepest challenges of contemporary social life—namely, how do people live together and overcome their propensity for violence? Dialogue offers a radical alternative to the clumsy ways conflict is currently dealt with in community settings.

We have only drawn on a few of the disciplines that explore the potential of and imperative for dialogue. For those who would like to know more, we would recommend contemporary authors such as Kwame Anthony Appiah (2008) and William Isaacs (1999).

Embracing depth

We use *depth* as a metaphor that calls for a movement beyond over-simplified and shallow approaches to community development. Our world can be characterised as complex (Rihani, 2002). Any approach to community development that is not cognisant of such complexity is bound to do harm. A depth approach invites workers to bring philosophy and attentiveness to the practice. It requires a resistance to the shallow-ing of practice, the product of an age of speed, spin, quick-fixes and amnesia. Our colleagues and the quoted authors were consistent in modelling a depth approach. Since our initiation into community development work, we have constantly been told 'it takes time', 'slow down', 'first watch, and then listen and learn'. Such mantras invite a depth approach that opens up the possibilities of counter-cultural practice.

Dialogue implies depth: firstly to listen deeply to what the other has to say, and secondly to make oneself present to the other. One cannot do this with a shallow orientation that filters out the unwanted responses and that does not take time to build connections and understand the other.

Re-imagining community as hospitality

In the early days of our community work we learnt about the practice of *hospitality* from the likes of Jean Vanier and Henri Nouwen. These authors invited us to reflect on collective spiritual life. However it has been more recent reading of philosophers like Gustavo Esteva and Jacques Derrida that have enabled us to identify hospitality as central to our tradition of community development work. Hospitality orients towards relationship and a welcoming of the 'other'. Strangers and intruders are welcome into the kind of community that we advocate.

Re-imagining community as hospitality involves considering the way in which ends and means are enfolded within one another—as destinations, and as processes of moving towards those destinations. For Derrida "community is hospitality". The term 'community' describes the ends being worked to-wards—the kind of community dreamt of and yearned for. Community is a space where people have created a climate and culture of hospitality. When people close themselves, their groups, their spaces from others, then they are no longer experiencing a Derridean community, but some other kind of collectivity. Hospitality as means, invites practitioners to consider the experi-ence of community along the journey—the process of building community within the work. Hospitality refers to the process of welcoming other peo-ple, other ideas, and other ways of thinking about community life—living together, naming and solving community problems. It is an orientation that ensures people do not close minds, souls, and hearts to the 'other'.

The Mexican Gustavo Esteva also shares a perspective on post-devel-opment as hospitality, arguing that hospitality orients towards the princi-ple of non-intervention and 'co-motion'. The in-hospitable practices of intervention and 'pro-motion' tend to mean that many professional development practitioners have pre-determined what they are going to do with and for people. Hospitality guided by the principles and practices of non-intervention and co-motion balances the other imperatives of our framework, such as depth and solidarity (Esteva, 1987, p. 149). It calls for an opening up of spaces with people and to be part of the people, not only with them, but *amongst* them, and to move together. This kind of hospitality involves the creative regeneration of spaces where people can interact and find common ground.

These insights lead to a deeper understanding of community, and of the role of hospitality as a cornerstone for a dialogical approach to community development. In re-imagining community as hospitality, we recognise that dialogue, community and hospitality are enfolded within one another. Dialogue requires welcoming the stranger, the other. In turn, hospitality requires a willingness to enter into dialogue, to learn about the other. Both are oriented towards the other, embracing difference, strangers and potentially intruders.

Enfolding community development within a commitment to solidarity

Solidarity is the fourth cornerstone to the framework of community development that we are describing. This concept is informed by the likes of the Polish union movement *Solidarity*, by mutual aid philosophers such as Peter Kropotkin and Pierre Joseph Proudhon, and by the injunction of liberation theologies towards a preferential option for the poor. The idea of solidarity ensures that while community work practitioners are willing to relate to everyone with hospitality, the primary orientation is towards the poor. The commitment is with those experiencing poverty and disempowerment. The work of community development enfolded within a tradition of solidarity is also committed to the principles and practices of mutual aid, and to a tradition of communitarian anarchism that fosters people's associations and co-operative structures.

We make the connection between solidarity and a dialogical approach because it requires entering into particular kinds of committed relationship with the poor. "This solidarity is born only when leaders witness to it by their humble, loving and courageous encounter with the people" (Freire, 1972, p100). Such solidarity requires movement out of our comfort zones, and engagement not only with the other, but with the particular 'other' of those who are marginalised from society. Community development is committed to the poor and disadvantaged. Solidarity requires entering into dialogue with those people, listening to them, and learning about their social, political, economic, ecological, cultural and spiritual realities. It requires working together for social change—for example, in building community associations, and in working through co-operative and federated structures that provide a vehicle to articulate the voice of the poor and disadvantaged in the broader democratic process.

In summary, we have introduced dialogical community development as a practice of dialogue that embraces depth, re-imagines community as hospitality, and enfolds the work within a commitment to solidarity. In later chapters, we shall explore in more detail the ways that these ideas relate to everyday community development practice.

Widening the framework

We can create this quality of dialogue by infusing our practice with a soulful orientation, opening ourselves to deconstructive movements, and re-constituting our work as a social practice. These three ideas add a further level of thinking about the practice of dialogical community development rooted in depth, hospitality and solidarity. Together they complete the development of a framework that holds seven dimensions. See Figure 1.

Infusing our practice with a soulful orientation

A genealogy of soul would require a book in itself, but for the moment we are content to begin with the singer Ray Charles, who calls soulfulness "the ability to respond from our deepest place".

A *soulful approach* invites awareness, attention and imagination that are directed at our relations to one another, our relations to place, to practice, to economics, culture, earth, politics and the traces of history and so forth. We draw on the likes of psychologist Thomas Moore (1992), pro-

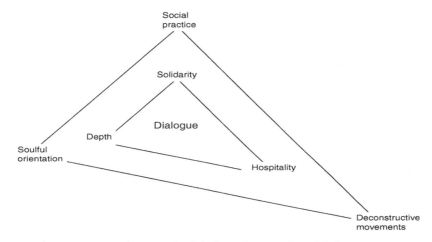

Figure 1. The framework of dialogical community development

posing that soul is a quality, a dimension, a movement towards experiencing life in a way that adds depth, value, relatedness, heart and substance to our community development practice. A soulful orientation invites hospitality towards other people and places and other ways of being, doing and imagining. It requires community practitioners to be both attentive to and engaged with community in 'another' way, one that demands heart, emotion, and will.

Reconstituting our work as a social practice

A *social practice* signifies a movement towards reclaiming our world as a social world. Solutions to human problems will be primarily social and only secondarily technical. Social practice means reconstituting 'development work' in terms of social agency and political contestation. A social practice also gives life to particular processes purposeful to a tradition of work that (i) fosters social relationships; (ii) invokes agency not just in private and personal relationships, but also in public relationships, and (iii) strives to reclaim and re-inhabit places as spaces of social activity rather than speculative economic activity. We learned to value this tradition of the social through two beautiful, simple volumes of home-grown community development case studies: *People working together,* volumes II and III (Kelly et al., 1986 and 1997).

This idea of community development as social practice will recur throughout the book. Freire (1972) has most clearly articulated such a social practice in the context of literacy programs. He argued that literacy programs cannot be just technical processes of enabling people to understand the word; they also need to be a social practice in enabling people to transform their world, through dialogue and co-investigation. Community work cannot be simply reduced to a deterministic process such as, for example, 'toolkits' for community consultation and recipes for 'building social capital', but must include the social practice of solidarity and political contestation.

Opening ourselves to deconstructive movements

Finally, the idea of *deconstructive movements* provides an opportunity to remain open to complexity, refusing to practise the tyranny of simplifying techniques. The notion of deconstructive movement also invites pulling apart or destabilising simplistic ways of thinking that are usually expressed through dualisms such as us–them, centre–periphery, top–bottom, land-lord–tenant and rich–poor. It ensures that our thinking about community development is more nuanced by an awareness of the complexity of human relations.

The idea of deconstructive movement also marks the importance of always challenging given assumptions, ensuring that people remain open, humble and uncertain social beings and therefore always hospitable to the 'other' (Kapuscinski, 2008; Levinas, 1999). When referring to the other we are drawing on a social science tradition that alludes to the 'stranger' that disrupts our world in some way. A particularly common practice in today's world is to think of strangers as "difficult and dangerous classes" (Young 1999, p59). In contrast, for us 'other' is not about the difficult or dangerous, but simply about the disruptive—with all its positive as well as negative implications.

In many ways this book represents an attempt to destabilise the current discourse of community development that is technically oriented, and to reconstruct it in the light of an approach to being, living and working which brings a different attention, awareness and imagination to our social lives and social practice. This deconstructive movement requires what Jacques Derrida calls *alterity*, a focus on the 'other'—not the obvious, the surface, the given, the assumed, but an-other way of thinking and imagining community life and community development work.

A *dialogical* approach is central to the framework. The other six dimensions are connected through the core theme of dialogue, but also with one another in different ways. Depth is connected to a soulful orientation: the contribution of these two qualities to the framework is like looking at two sides of the one coin. Depth encourages going deeper and looking below the 'surface' or the superficial appearance of community, and a soulful orientation enables the deepening process, with the practice of attention, awareness and imagination. Similarly with hospitality and deconstructive movements: hospitality alludes to welcoming the 'other', and deconstructive movements are the destabilising process that frees us to do just that. So also with solidarity and social practices—solidarity orients towards the poor, disadvantaged and marginalised, but the social practice underpins the everyday work.

An overview of the book

This introduction has described our induction into a tradition of community development, and our analysis of a looming legitimation crisis as this kind of work becomes captive to modernism. We have then articulated a framework for dialogical community development that provides a way forward for practitioners. The remainder of the book is an exploration of how that framework relates to everyday challenges of community development practice.

Everyday community development work involves re-imagining community life, facilitating transformative community processes, building and holding an analysis, caring for different spheres of community life and transformational training of change agents. Each of these is considered in turn in the five chapters that follow.

Chapter One, *Re-imagining community life and community work,* aims to support community workers to re-imagine community and our work within it. In re-imagining community as the context for our work, we begin to deconstruct contemporary community work, and to explore alternative approaches that are soulful, social, have a critical edge, and draw us into the depths of our professional and life experience.

- *Awakening love* observes that community can only be born if there is some transformation that shifts awareness and attention towards an other-orientation—a journey from *I* to *we* through dialogue and hospitality. We explore how love animates a sociality of connecting, belonging, yearning, creating and caring that is the life-blood of soulful, deep community work.
- *The alchemy of poetic participation* explores the soulful transformation that comes when people genuinely participate in community life as an intimate engagement of their creative imaginations.
- *Emplacing* alerts us to the dangers of seeing community primarily as an objectified 'site', and explores the dialogical nature of community as a process of ongoing place-making that requires people's daily creative endeavours.
- *Welcoming problems* observes that modernist community development techniques try to fix social problems, whereas dialogical community development values them as gifts that can invoke depth in our practice—as voices calling us into hospitality and dialogue.
- *Dancing with the shadow* offers a fresh perspective on social issues as shadows that we can dance with—facing ourselves and our communities as we truly are in an acknowledgment of culpability that leads to a profound humility and depth of practice, and can reveal gifts that bring about a healing social transformation.

Chapter Two, *Transformational community processes,* explores how community can become a vehicle for social change in which people find their own paths towards development as freedom.

- *The discerning and gentling of method* introduces a systematic way of doing dialogical community development work, and explores the push and pull of a gentle approach which requires discernment and carefully negotiates mandate.

- *Widening analysis* considers a staged process of building a dialogical, community-owned analysis that gives people a way forward—a sense of what to do and why they are doing it.
- *Transforming our power* unravels the complexity of power within the work, exploring a relational practice that nurtures supportive co-responsibility, practices of power-with, co-operative power, and the wielding of skilful and soulful power.
- *Careful conflicting* explores how we might carefully conflict in our practice, recognising that escalation of conflict where necessary might be important for transformational work.
- *Structuring without strangling* discusses the need to build place-based, community-oriented, democratic people's organisations, creating a new sociality of power that enables people to structure their own initiatives.

Chapter Three, ***Practitioner analysis: challenges and ways forward,*** examines what we consider to be several of the most significant trends that undermine a dialogical approach to community development practice.

- *Objectification* explores thought processes that reduce people, creatures, land, indeed all things, to a subject–object kind of binary relationship—without chance of mutuality or dialogue. We offer a way forward through an understanding of inter-subjectivity and an embracing of deconstructive movements.
- *Ideological positions* identifies ideology as a key challenge for dialogue, and offers an alternative way of thinking that takes an appreciative attitude towards 'other' ideals, expands conceptual frameworks, and delights in mystery.
- *Disenchantment* considers how particular contemporary discourses of secularism undermine pluralism, fuel a limited materialistic 'development' vision, and support the expansion of modernity with its accompanying by-product of human waste. In their place, we advocate a community development approach that appreciates

both spiritual and secular sensibilities, and re-enchants our communities with sacred wisdom, ritual and attunement.

- *Addictive consumerism* explores how people increasingly substitute the sociality of embodied community life for consumption as the primary means of meeting their need for belonging.

- *Therapeutic culture* argues that people and professionals increasingly collude to find solutions to social problems via technically oriented therapeutic interventions that focus on coping with the distress at an individual level. We offer a way forward through examining social processes of healing.

- *Collusion with a garrison state* considers the danger of contemporary movements away from a social contract and towards a garrison state, in which citizens give legitimacy to the government in exchange for security. We explore ways forward that require both social engagement with our fears, and efforts to fight back for a social state.

Chapter Four, ***Caring about different spheres of community life,*** suggests that our role as community development workers changes remarkably if we think about it as ongoing care rather than the modernist quest for a cure. We identify *caring* as a core imperative of dialogical community development.

- *Caring for the ordinary* explores valuing the mundane, the commonplace, and the everyday events that form the social glue connecting ordinary people with one another.

- *Caring for a social ecology of diversity* looks at nurturing diversity in the fragile web of social relationships that are at the heart of community—cultivating an ethic of plurality and fostering centripetal dynamics of connection that bring people together.

- *Caring for a relational economy* considers the impact of growth-oriented, free-market capitalism on our communities, and explores the building of alternative, local, human-scale, relational economies with social and ecological objectives.

- *Caring for democratic political processes* outlines dialogical processes for democratising our social, cultural, economic and political contexts and ensuring people "connected as community" are able to collectively take their private concerns into public assemblies.

- *Earth care* considers the urgent imperative to restore health to the planet through people working together both locally and globally—changing our behaviours as households; creating alternative institutions that model new ways of consuming, growing, producing, commuting, working, and travelling; changing hearts and minds; and holding environmental sites as the local and global commons.

Chapter Five, *Training for transformation: the possibilitators,* reflects on our experience that the key to community development is the quality and creativity of the people who dream of a better world for their communities and want to take some kind of public, communal, transformational action. Such people are *possibilitators*: change agents, organic intellectuals in their communities. As dialogical community development workers we have a key role in providing a training space where they can learn transformational skills and strategies.

- *Creating space to re-imagine* starts with our observation that many people can no longer imagine a community or society based on anything other than what is. The media has dominated our dreams and there is too little space to create a society in which we care for the earth, economy and *polis* in a new way. We reflect on the work of creating space for imaginative literacy and creating spaces that support imaginative literacy.
- *Sparking re-imagination* identifies *stories* as a vital resource that provide a soulful counter to modern infotainment—evoking depth, integrity, passion and insight in the imaginations of people working together to change their worlds.
- *The exchange of inspiration not information* argues that for people to experience empowerment, they need to feel inspired to be involved in processes of change that relate to their real, lived experiences, and they need to believe that change can happen and that they can make it happen. We reflect on our experience of resisting the seduction of content-focused technologies, such as presentation

software, which are destroying the role of dialogue in the learning space; and we explore the importance of understanding inspiration as taking new ideas and new energy deep into ourselves.

- *The process of deconstructive conversation* explores the social journey of deconstructive conversation, preferably shared by our cadre of colleagues, as we together destabilise the *mythos* of our social, cultural, ecological, economic and political worlds.

- *The logic of wishing, willing and acting* argues that the learning process is a failure if it does not inspire action. We explore the journey from wishing, to willing, to acting: regaining our ability to wish for a better world; unlocking our willingness that is captive to despair; and asserting our response-ability through action.

The Conclusion, **Enfolding community development within a tradition of solidarity,** invites people to consider whose interests, sympathies and aspirations they connect themselves to. It calls for a stand with the most disadvantaged, marginalised and vulnerable people in our communities. A vocation of solidarity calls people to be attentive to their own mortality. It invites people into a tradition of practice wisdom that infuses the work with love, humility, courage and passion. It requires nurturing a vision that brings life, energy and depth to practice, and cultivating a 'passion of not knowing' that is hospitable to dialogue.

Invitation to dialogue

We hope this book will engage readers in a dialogue. We hope you take to this text with a vigorous pen that captures your own reflections, questions and critique. We hope that those who reject parts of our analysis will not dismiss the whole book—but instead take up an engaged critical dialogue. We would love to hear from you! We welcome dissent. We look forward to hearing your other perspectives. Welcome to the dialogue.

CHAPTER

One

Re-imagining community life and community work

This chapter reflects on the experience of twenty years of re-imagining our role as community workers. Critical questions are asked about contemporary trends in community development practice, and fresh perspectives are offered on relationship, place, participation, community problems and social issues. In re-imagining community as the context for our work, we begin to deconstruct contemporary community work and to explore alternative approaches that are soulful, social, have a critical edge, and draw us into the depths of our professional and life experience.

This chapter supports practitioners to re-imagine community. A daily re-imagining of community life helps resist the seduction of taking it for granted. We understand community as a dynamic process and dialogue as a transformational space. At the heart of dialogical community development, then, is the intersection between dialogue and the dynamic of community—a deep, challenging and enriching conversation with the idea, the ideal, and the reality of community. Practitioners encounter many manifestations of community that change over time, among different groups of people and in different places. People bring a curiosity to these encounters, and engage each new expression of community in a process of building shared meaning—a re-imagining of the possibilities of community life.

1.1 Awakening love

Anyone who has lost someone they loved dearly has reflected on sayings such as "It is better to have loved and lost, than never to have loved at all".

Such a saying is infused with emotions of fear, anxiety, grief, hope, relief, wonder, and delight. It implies that love requires risking and overcoming the ever-spectral fear of loss that accompanies deep loving. In many ways these generative words—love, risk and fear—describe things that are central to community life. They cannot be avoided in community work.

An invitation to re-claim love in our practice

Love is not a fashionable idea in the contexts of community work. Only recently Peter was asked to remove the word *love* from a journal article he had written about community development. For many it is too closely associated with Hollywood or Bollywood and with romance, with shallow 'new age' personal development, or with abuse and misuse of trust in professional or pastoral relationships. However, while acknowledging the concerns, we need to reclaim love within our work and our re-imagining of community life.

In some ways the invitation to re-centre dialogue within community work is an invitation to re-claim love in social practice. While authors have made a powerful case about the demise of love within social lives, such as Zygmunt Bauman in his book *Liquid Love* (2003), we remain hopeful that it can be reclaimed and re-practised. Bauman might have argued that 'togetherness' has been dismantled by the current social conditions of life, but he has overstated people's loss of a commitment to truly love. Our sense is that love, connectedness and community are central needs in people's lives. Without them, people wither.

In 2007 Peter was travelling in India. He decided to use some of that time to re-read Paulo Freire's classic, *Pedagogy of the Oppressed* (1972). The reading reminded him of a critique, analysis and method of work that is still highly relevant to community development practitioners. But the striking feature of this re-reading was Freire's constant and unembarrassed use of the word 'love' in relation to his work, and more particularly in relation to dialogue. For example, he states

> dialogue cannot exist however, in the absence of a profound love for the world and [men]. The naming of the world, which is an act of creation and re-creation, is not possible if it is not infused with love. Love is at

the same time the foundation of dialogue and dialogue itself (Freire 1972, p62).

Freire not only articulates a wonderful method of social change, but also had a soulful practice infused by a profound understanding of humanity. Freire drew heavily on the works of Eric Fromm and their dialogue gives valuable insight into the place of love within community work.

Cultivating a capacity for love

Love, as described by the likes of Freire, is transformative. Community work without love will become technical, routinised, shallow and exploitative. While Freire reminds practitioners of the significance of reclaiming love, it is Eric Fromm (1957) who provides an invitation to re-learn the art and practice of love. There is no point in reclaiming it without re-learning to practise it.

For Fromm, learning the art of love requires engagement in the challenge of overcoming ego-centricity, and moving towards a position where the needs of the other become as important as our own. Here is a central point in arguing for the reclamation of love—people move towards a position of *mutuality* whereby their legitimate needs as a human being are levelled alongside awareness and attention to other people's needs. Without this mutual consideration of one another's needs, community as dialogue or hospitality is impossible.

As psychotherapist David Yalom (1980, p371) points out, drawing on Fromm's work, people can then move from a state of needing to be loved to that of loving as an "effective potent state". For Fromm, love is an active state of being, that requires giving. Yalom argues that mature love implies other practices: concern, responsivity, respect and knowledge. We could therefore say that to reclaim love as an integral part of community life, people must foster the attitudes within themselves and one another that ensure an attitude of concern about others, are responsive to the needs of others, and are respectful of the uniqueness of the other. To adopt these attitudes is to know the other deeply. For Fromm "true knowledge of the other is possible only when one transcends one's self-concern and sees the other person in the other's own terms" (Yalom, p372).

ı a dialogical approach to community development, practitioners ııссu to awaken this kind of love. Awakening this kind of love requires a fundamental, counter-cultural shift towards the 'other'. Much of the way people live is now based on fear and risk aversion—building fences and gated communities, retreating from public spaces and public transport, and relating only to others of similar class, race, education, sexuality, and sub-culture. There is a kind of 'bunkering down'. Even when with people with whom we are comfortable, more often than not we merely pass the time in superficial chatter—a process of making a point, providing our perspective, rehearsing our opinion. In short, people get stuck in their own story. By reclaiming love such trends can be destabilised.

Dialogue invites movement out of the bunker, movement into public spaces, engagement with people who are different, and movement away from the habits of chatter. Instead it cultivates a commitment to the other person's story. It is easy to live a shallow life that never takes the time to enter the world of those around us. Maybe you have been hanging out with someone for a while, but did not take the time to ask, 'What is your story?' 'Where do you come from?', 'How did you get to be here?', 'What are the deep concerns in your life?', 'What are your passions and hopes?', 'What are your everyday concerns?', or 'What are your fears in life?'

To take the time to hear someone's story means responsibly gaining knowledge about them, their lives and their concerns. It is the respectful willingness to be responsive to this story that is the key movement in community as dialogue and community as hospitality. Community-builders move from their own story (which is important) towards the other person's story. This involves holding their own agenda less tightly, acknowledging the other's agenda, and hopefully together building a shared agenda—something Martin Buber (1947) called an 'in-between space'. This is community infused with love.

At the heart of Freire's unapologetic use of the word 'love' was his deep knowledge that it is impossible to engage in dialogue without cultivating a capacity to deeply listen to other people's stories. And he knew that deep listening, unless it is simply reduced to a manipulative technique, requires love.

The profoundly humanising process of co-creation

Another who can provide guidance in this awakening and practice of love is Martin Buber (1947, 1958). Buber talks of the experience of community as requiring a shift between two people from what he described as an *I-It* encounter—crudely understood as a subject-object kind of relationship, to an *I-Thou* encounter—understood as a subject-subject kind of relationship. This shift is critical to experiencing a dialogical or hospitable community. The shift can be illustrated by the following story from Peter.

> I was recently 'teaching' some Master of Development Practice students from Vietnam. They were telling me how they felt 'tortured' by a feeling that their four years of work on a large AusAID-funded[1] project in Northern Vietnam had failed. Independent evaluations had shown how the local indigenous people had hardly gained anything from the multi-million dollar initiative. In talking with the students about their sense of failure, we started to reflect on how the project workers had engaged the villagers. After some discussion, one of the Vietnamese students had an 'aha!' moment and shared it with the class. She realised that "what we did wrong is that we didn't really approach these villagers as people equal to us; we didn't go and sit with them around their village fires, hear their stories and understand their world. We didn't create the project together". I asked her what they did do. She thought about the question for some time and then reflected back to us how the project workers would turn up in four-wheel drives, facilitate meetings, talk about the importance of participation, empowerment and natural resource management, then draw up a list of activities and actions for local people, and leave.

In the classroom Buber's contrast between I-It and I-Thou was used to reflect on the worker's unintentional but disastrous process and the sad story's outcome. The student realised that the project workers as subjects (that is, as active agents making decisions, using their creativity, resources,

---

1 Australian Agency for International Development, the Australian government's overseas aid program

relationship and intelligence) related to the villagers only as objects—in a sense the villagers become people to whom a project could be done *to* or *for* rather than *with*. There was no sense of the villagers as equal participants, as equal subjects in a process of dialogue and co-creation.

The student's 'aha!' moment also incorporated a renewed vision of what awakening love could offer to such a project. She recognised that awakening love could reorient everyone towards subject-subject and co-creative kinds of relationship—an I-Thou relationship in which a space for relationship building, for story telling, for deep listening, and for building a shared commitment to change could be activated. As Peter went around the class reflecting on this student's analysis of their participation in a failed project, others started to realise that many of their 'failed' attempts at development work came down to this failure to truly love the people they were working with. There was a recognition that this failure to love blinded them to the possibility of dialogue and therefore to the profoundly humanising process of co-creation as development work.

Some challenges in developing a practice built on love

Such I-Thou kinds of relationship are not easy to imagine in contemporary society. One might challenge the analysis developed in reflection on the above story by arguing that it is unreasonable to expect such project workers to take the time to build loving relationships with the villagers. You could argue that there are simply too many villagers or that the project schedule itself would not allow for it. But there is a fallacy in arguing that I-Thou relationships take more time. Love develops from the very beginning of an encounter; and if community workers are going to spend minutes, hours or days with someone, then surely they invest in the quality of relationship for those minutes, hours or days. It does not take more time to be loving, but it does take more attentiveness, and rebuilding dialogical and hospitable community may require a re-orientation towards 'slow and less'—in the above story, fewer villages; and in most of our lives fewer connections, but deeper ones.

Some people could argue that contemporary life is too fast, relationships are too many and there are too many needs. However, the irony is that while for many there is a sense of 'too fast, too many', there is also a sense that relationships are lacking in deep connection, friendship, solidarity and meaning. Many of us are so overloaded with diverse kinds of relationships that we have lost our capacity to discern a moment of true, genuine encounter with the other (characterised by I-Thou qualities); or if we do discern it, we move on so fast that we fail to cherish or celebrate it, and then build on it. In this process the opportunity for a more meaningful sociality which is the foundation for community development is missed.

It is worth pointing out that those who are on that journey from the I-It to I-Thou often find that there is a central paradox. To make the shift towards 'others' requires a reflexive journey in which the depth of our own capacity for hospitality not only towards other people but towards ourselves needs exploring—the complexity associated with 'I'. While it implies a movement away from egocentricity, I-Thou in no way means a movement away from the self. It may require a confrontation, or put more gently, a dialogue with the ego; it might require the painful suffering of re-socialisation; it most certainly does require an ongoing encounter with our complex and dynamic selves. This encounter requires us to move away from ego-centricity towards other-orientedness.

A dialogical approach to community development can in no way move to simply a *collectively oriented* consciousness devoid of love for people. This is what has been disastrous about revolutions—they inspired collective action devoid of love. People were sacrificed for collective ideologies. While being concerned about community, dialogical community development is also acutely aware of, and concerned with, individuals. Buber (1947) carefully argues that collectivity is in many ways the antithesis of community—"collectivity is based on an organised atrophy of personal existence . . . it is a flight from community's testing and consecration of the personal, a flight from the vital dialogue, demanding the staking of the self, which is at the heart of the world". For Buber, in contrast "community is where community happens". Community is a "dynamic facing of the other, a flowing from *I* to *Thou*" (Buber, 1947, p37)—in other words, a dynamic of awakened love invoked through a soulful movement.

Transformation of the ordinary into the extra-ordinary

In exploring the place of love in community life and work, it would be easy to simply dismiss romantic love or *eros* as irrelevant and to focus more on the place of love as described by the likes of Fromm, Freire and Buber. However, in arguing for the reclamation of love, romantic love or the erotic can teach us something important about community.

Plato called this kind of love 'divine madness'; he recognised the great archetypal world of gods and legends lying deep within our psyches, that are unlocked when 'in love'. Students of romantic love have observed that in some way such love seems to unleash the great powers of these gods and legends. When people 'fall in love' they are usually transformed by such gods. You can see it in their dreamy eyes, the music that is played, the way they float around the house or the office. This transformation can be said to bring both a kind of new life and a new death—even if for only a short period of time. There is a new aliveness that emerges due to the encounter with the supposed god or goddess, and a death to the pragmatic, rational world where so many of our waking but un-awakened lives are spent. When in love, people are animated; the world is full of a whole new sense of wonder, meaning and beauty. At the same time love's dark sides are entered, with its complexities of fears, wounds and pains. Many of the concerns and efforts that previously claimed their energies—at work, in homes, and their ideals—suddenly shrink from the centre to the periphery. A new dance is being danced!

Some observers of such love interpret it as not so much about relationships (such a huge concern of modern society when thinking of love) but as about 'soul'. Romantic love is often an initiation into soul. It is the grand opportunity to enter life's inner dramas and mysteries; it is an invitation to explore those inner parts that have remained dormant, quiet and asleep. It is often the first opportunity to encounter other dimensions of our selves in all their grandeur and complexity—as well as to encounter the 'other' person.

This kind of love can illuminate the process of re-imagining community work, as it transforms the ordinary into something 'other'. Life becomes animated. What was previously dreary takes on a dreamy quality. This is partly what a soulful orientation is all about—the animating transformation of the ordinary into the extra-ordinary. Awakening love as *eros* can introduce people to a soulful orientation in a way that is potentially transformational to community life. With this soulful orientation people bring a new awareness, attention and imagination to their lives, to others and to the world around them.

In *The Re-Enchantment of Everyday Life* (1996), Thomas Moore goes even further and argues that to reclaim erotic love into community life, the world needs to be re-sexualised. His analysis is that *eros* has been banished to either the bedroom or to the pornographic underground and the result is (amongst other things) that public spaces are dominated by branded advertising and ugly architecture, and discussions about sexuality are vulgar, moralistic or fearful. The potential transformation can be imagined through considering Hanif Kureshi's comment that "pornography is the junk food of love" (2008, p179). In the same way that junk food is soul-less food devoid of any creative culinary process, cooking reduced to quick techniques, so pornography is symptomatic of a loss of love from the social world. As erotic love becomes diminished, so people find technical ways of reintroducing it—through DVDs and sex shops. *Eros* becomes a technologically mediated process devoid of social relationships.

Moore argues that we need to rediscover *eros* in community life and culture—in the context of real everyday relationships. This can be imagined through life-giving carnival, festival and other rituals, through beautiful and provocative architecture, through public art and performance that expresses creativity, through a re-introduction of life-giving, pulsating love into everyday social lives. People might no longer literally make love in the fields as a way of invoking the gods to provide a plentiful harvest, but the equivalent kind of erotic attention to community hopes and desires can be sparked through new kinds of ritual and action.

Destabilising our habitual perceptions

Such erotic transformation is also destabilising, transformative and animating. There is a potential deconstructive movement at work in which previous essentials and habits are shaken, their contradictions revealed. At an inter-personal level, people in love notice details, they observe imaginatively, they are aware and attentive, and they change their habits. Of course there is a shadow side to this sudden awareness—the acute perception of love can often be complemented by a kind of blind madness. At a social level, the ancient Carnivals in which marriage vows were put aside for a day and a night to engage in orgiastic release, or the pre-Lent festivals in early nineteenth-century Italy, were certainly destabilising.

Laura Esquivel in her mythical novel *Like Water for Chocolate* (1989) draws a beautiful picture of the nature of such transformation and animation, and warns of the tragic consequences of that never happening:

> As you see, within our bodies each of us has the elements needed to produce phosphorus . . .each of us is born with a box of matches inside us but we can't strike them all by ourselves; just as in an experiment, we need oxygen and a candle to help. In this case, the oxygen, for example, would come from the breath of the person you love; the candle could be any kind of food, music, caress, word or sound that engenders that explosion that lights one of the matches. For a moment we are dazzled by an intense emotion. A pleasant warmth grows within us, fading slowly as time goes by, until a new explosion comes along to revive it. Each person has to discover what will set off those explosions in order to live, since the combustion that occurs when one of them is ignited is what nourishes the soul. That fire, in short, is its food. If one doesn't find out in time what will set off these explosions, the box of matches dampens, and not a single match will ever be lit. *(p104)*

This is a call: to find out what sets off those 'explosions' that will awaken and nourish a soulful orientation that then leaves people dissatisfied with an everyday life *without* erotic love.

This potential transformation from the ordinary to the extra-ordinary is the daily concern of dialogical community work infused with soul that is awakened by love. It is this transformation of awareness, attention and imagination that animates community as dialogue—a sociality that destabilises habits of the ordinary gaze and re-infuses everyday life with the gaze of the extra-ordinary. The dialogical approach to community work therefore requires an attention to people in a way that pays attention to detail, an orientation to openness and people's story, and an awakening of different kinds of love. Here is an example from Gerard's reflections:

> Every day of my working life is filled with conversations. Many are important, but most are superficial. They don't touch either of us, the group is not moved; there is no sense of the extraordinary. However, I know when I am having an intimate conversation with someone—my heart rate changes, the pores of my skin open, I am holding their eyes. I know when I am being hospitable—I am alert to every nuance, I listen deeply and in silence, and my body language communicates a profound respect for the moment and the other. All these things are familiar to me ever since I was about ten and in love for the first time!
>
> I vividly remember one interagency network meeting among the dozens I have attended in recent years. There was the usual exchange of information, some fun personal disclosure, and the gentle ribbing that builds collegiality in Australia (where no-one is allowed to take themselves too seriously). Then one of our colleagues strayed into a personal reflection on the recent tragic deaths in a police car chase of two young men whom many in the network had worked with. Others told the stories about what had happened, the agenda was suspended, and for twenty extraordinary minutes the network became an intimate space and the nature of the relationships between us was transformed—we experienced extra-ordinary community as dialogue and hospitality.

We do not want to pretend that this is easy. Freire admonishes people who engage in work for social change without love, and his warning is a daily challenge to our own community work practice. While we do not often experience love as terrifying any more—maybe we're just dulled by habit—we do find it constantly challenging.

What we do know is that we want to live, work and play in communities where people are alive, in love with life and skilled in this animated dance called community as dialogue and hospitality. And we want to work with colleagues who are alive—the kinds of fools who continually fall in love with life, and who are alert to the potential transformation of the ordinary to the extra-ordinary that is the daily concern of soulful community work.

1.2 The alchemy of poetic participation

To be co-creators of dialogical community, we must be soulful people, people who have been awakened by love. Yet the paradoxical converse of this is that such soulful people are 'made' through participating in the everyday and ordinary things of life with a particular attentiveness, awareness and imagination. The kinds of love proposed as central to re-imagining community life, alongside the emergence of other social practices, will emerge from participating with 'others' within a particular kind of dialogical or hospitable community. Love cannot be separated from the social, and it is this invitation into a particular kind of loving sociality that is critical for community work.

This loving sociality can be illuminated through the idea of *the alchemy of poetic participation*. Participation is a significant key in understanding community life and community work processes; but it is a particular kind of participation that is required. In community work, both the plain concerns of participation in everyday life, and the particular concerns related to people's suffering, can be the raw material (the *prima material*, as the alchemist would call it) of a process of alchemy that can transform soul and sociality. According to Thomas Moore (1992),

> Alchemy was a process in which raw material was placed in a vessel where it was heated, observed closely, heated some more, passed through various operations and observed once again. In the end, the result was an arcane product imagined mysteriously to be gold, the stone of the philosophers, or a potent elixir. In Jung's view, however, alchemy was a spiritual practice carried out for the benefits of the soul. Its play with chemicals, heat, and distillation was a poetic project in which substances, colours and other material qualities offered an external imagery for a hidden parallel process of the soul. (p184)

Here Moore is drawing on Carl Jung to provide an insight into re-imagining participation. Jung calls this process of working the stuff of soul the *opus*, that is, 'the work'. Just as the alchemist's opus was central to the individual's process of soul-making, so it is potentially the opus of social life that can invoke soul and feed poetic participation.

The limitations of participation techniques

For many involved in community work, there is an awareness that participation is one of the keys to development 'successes' (Craig & Mayo, 1995, Botes & Rensburg 2000). Authors such as Robert Chambers (2005), Somesh Kumar (2002b) and Amartya Sen (1999, p19) have helpfully emphasised the substantive and instrumental importance of people exercising their own social agency—articulating the importance of participation both as a means to and an end of development work. Conversely, countless evaluations point out the failure of many activities, projects, programmes and plans due to a lack of participation. Many community workers have seen buildings sitting in impoverished communities, a potential resource, but empty, unused, wasted. Some workers have also seen well-funded programs achieve little or nothing. Why? Development practitioners generally think they have the answer—it is a lack of participation, or at least particular kinds of participation. They trace failed development processes back to an agent or 'facilitator', making the decisions—about a building or a project—without involving the intended beneficiaries.

But this does not provide a complete answer. Many activities, projects, community programs and planning processes have also been full of participation—yet there is no life, no creativity, and no animation of people's awareness, imagination, hospitality or collective power. Jung would suggest that the root of the problem is that there has been no opus, no alchemy. In much community work, participation has become a mere shallow technique and has lost its philosophical roots, or its alchemic roots.

The potential of poetic participation

In contrast to shallow participation, there is potential for poetic participation, drawing on Jung's notion of the opus but also drawing on Rabindranath Tagore's analysis of the importance of the *poetic*. Jung, as quoted by Moore above, describes the opus as a work of attention and imagination that leads to the unlocking of "hidden processes of the soul". In some way opus implies that there is a hidden yet creative internal process at work. Tagore reminds us, "it is the poetic that rescues people from the *ennui* which is the desert haze of inactive imagination" (Gupta 2006, p26). A useful way forward in re-thinking participation might be to consider it as a process of using the poetic as a trigger for unlocking hidden resources of creativity and imagination within individuals and groups. Put another way, unless the participation of people evokes within them a poetic sensibility that unlocks their creativity and imagination, then community processes seem doomed to fail, or at least to become meaningless, empty, routinised and boring.

Shallow forms of technically oriented participation will not be a catalyst for the kind of social agency that is required for people to creatively transform themselves, their groups, their places and societies. Only when the process of participatory community development consists of poetic participation where a group of people do the work/opus, will social change be sustained. The work/opus is the actual engagement of creative imaginations, the deep loving listening to one another, the hospitality to one another's ideas and perspectives, and the giving of attention and care to the analysis that enables people to discover creative options together.

For Jung, opus is the work that an individual does within the process of individuation, which is the conscious movement towards psychological wholeness. It is not work that anyone else can do; it can only be done by the person concerned, with her/his own self. The outcome is individuation, the process was the opus. This approach to the parallel 'developmental' notion of poetic participation is informed by the perspectives of what Raff Carmen calls autonomous development (1996) and Amartya Sen calls development as freedom (1997). It is not participation based on the perspective of fitting people into projects or empowering people in the 'we must help them' or 'we must enable them' mode. Empowerment is not something that anyone can do to anyone else. Empowerment (parallel to individuation) is the outcome of poetic participation (parallel to the alchemic opus). Put in a slightly different way, empowerment is the outcome of a process whereby people gain confidence, new information, relationships, resources and information, as a result of poetic participation.

In this sense, then, it is not the opus of "being reached, being intervened in, being fitted (to projects), being appraised, rapidly or otherwise; in a word, being developed" (Carmen 1996, p51). It is participation that is genuinely about power and freedom—the power of groups of people to be creative and imaginative together in seeking and creating their path of development, and the power to expand freedoms and overcome "under-development as un-freedoms" (Sen 1997, p86). In this sense the opus of poetic participation is about groups of people being creative in places, and building organisations that enable the transformation of personal power into collective power which in turn enables people to challenge their marginalisation.

It is important to be clear here that we are making the distinction between community and collectivity, a distinction discussed briefly in the previous reflection. When discussing poetic participation, we are not talking for example about 'community as a neighbourhood or a village'— some kind of collective entity—implying that everyone in a village or neighbourhood should be participating; rather we are talking about Buber's notion that 'community is where community happens' within our understanding of community as dialogue and hospitality.

The implication of this is that community work often takes place at the level of groups, where the focus of 'community' and community work is not a whole village or neighbourhood, but a network of people who have come together, heard one another's stories and are willing to join in the struggle for social change. Community as dialogue and hospitality has been activated; a group of people have become animated in their experience of one another. For the purposes of understanding community work, the opus of poetic participation needs to be activated at this level—for example, a group of women, young people, or people with disability issues. It is often such a group of people, on the margins of their village or neighbourhood (in terms of access to decision-making processes and resources) who will engage in the opus of poetic participation. It might not end there, but it will often start there.

Enabling poetic forms of expression

Furthering our ideas about the opus, we also like to think more explicitly about *poetic* forms of expression that are required within this kind of participation. According to the architect Anthony Antoniades, "poetics comes from a Greek verb that simply means 'to make'" (1992, p3). He goes on to discuss the importance of imagination and creativity within design. It is in this sense that we are also interested in the poetics—the role of imagination and creativity in people making the kinds of projects and places where they want to live and be involved. This kind of 'making' with a poetic edge requires expression of insight, the risk of personal vulnerability and an invitation to intimacy among participants. It arises in the moment when an individual or group sees within themselves some insight or wisdom that needs to be expressed to get to the heart of the matter at hand, and takes the risk of putting their innermost selves on the line.

This expression of the poetical is an invitation to intimacy, and to a vulnerability and depth of participation between people that invokes creativity and therefore stronger developmental outcomes. Tagore's proposal, that the poetic is the key to thwarting people's *ennui*, was infused with an idea that poetry itself is profoundly intimate; it invites people into the poet's deepest fears, hopes, longings and sufferings. Poetry infused with such intimacy has a way of transcending a certain shallowness that is characteristic of a purely rational world. Within the social world, intimacy requires the transcendence of purely rational interactions—it requires a caressing of touch, listening and attention. If participation can be infused with this kind of intimacy, an unfolding power will emerge that is grounded in strong community ties. This poetic resource of intimacy will pay the dividends of deep connections and correspondingly creative ideas. In such spaces people start to envisage new worlds of possibility in their midst. People start to dream again. When they feel alone, people hardly dare to dream; but when they are experiencing intimacy with others, when they are involved in the opus of what we are describing as poetic participation, they start to re-think: 'maybe we can dream together'. People together recover what Paulo Freire called literary imagination. Here is a story illustrating the role of intimacy in practice:

Kate was a resident in a public housing estate where we were doing some training. Along with about twelve other residents she attended a weekly three-hour 'training' session designed to explore community work. After some weeks of dialogue discussing the kinds of communities we wanted to live in, the barriers to building those kinds of communities and consideration of some ways forward in building community, Kate started to regain a sense that something could be different in the street where she lived. For years she had felt like a lone voice in her community, but through the dialogical process of the community training, she realised she could be creative in trying to change the situation. Others in the group encouraged her. The intimacy of the group, created through people's vulnerabilities (people had shared their hopes and sadness about community) brought people together in a way that made the space safe. Ideas could be generated, experiments could be considered.

At the same time as the training course was running, the State Government had set up a formal community reference group in the neighbourhood to consider actions for renewing the community. Kate was a member of this formal group but was disheartened by the lack of involvement of other local people. When she asked other locals why they didn't get involved, they told her it was too formal and they couldn't understand the 'government speak' and didn't want to look stupid asking for clarification all the time. Kate had an idea. She decided to open her home for a morning tea at which she would invite residents in her street and let them know what was happening at the community reference group. At first a couple of people turned up and they had a discussion about issues in their community. The morning tea became a regular event and it grew and grew as more and more people in her community wanted a safe space to discuss issues and to hear about the initiatives of the 'government group'. It wasn't long until Kate's Cuppa, as it became named, had more people involved than the formal group! Kate had become a conduit for people to share their concerns. Soon others felt more confident to attend the formal meetings as well. The experiment to connect with others through a simple means of having a cuppa together had not only become an expression of 'community as hospitality' but also gave voice to people who were not being heard.

The approach to development that supports the kind of poetic participation Kate was practising, requires balancing the notions of *objectives* and *dreams*. Clear objectives are needed, within which community workers can think strategically and plan in a participative way. In our work with Kate's group, we were clear that our strategic objectives were to nurture people through a process of re-thinking community, and then to engage in dialogue about community-building skills. Yet when committed to a dialogical approach that creates intimacy and unlocks people's creativity, it is important not to let the objectives get in the way of the process. Management by clear objectives is often the agenda of the worker—but it must be held lightly so it can create supportive space for a complementary approach that supports people's dreaming, experimentation and co-discovery. In Kate's story, the outcomes were not pre-determined. The framework of development created an intimate space for participants to dream of and create the kinds of initiatives that they wanted to experiment with. Kate created her own experiment. She, along with the others in the group, did the *opus*—and community was awakened.

1.3 Emplacing

One of the most interesting and yet perplexing issues in relation to community life is that of people's relationship to place. It is easy to think about community primarily in terms of geographical space, site or territory. For many, the concept of community is associated with place. People ask questions such as 'what community do you come from?', referring to a physical place. This is an important perspective in people's social lives. Every day people relate to family, friends and neighbours in significant ways that are connected to place—we recognise people in our streets, people we share our parks with, local shopkeepers and traders, and many others. If community development as a social practice works to reclaim and re-inhabit places, then community can be grounded physically in place.

However, an understanding of community that is too focused on place, or that associates community with place, can provide a rationale for superficial and technical notions of community development. Within such per-spectives the 'community' can become objectified as merely a space, site or territory, targeted by professionally designed and driven interventions, usually to deal with perceived deficiencies or problems going on in that particular locality. From this perspective 'community as place' becomes an object to observe in a detached way and think about as something sepa-rate from social relations. 'The community' becomes an objectified site that needs more development, more investment in services, roads, foot-paths and so forth. When community workers inadvertently find them-selves co-opted into this perspective, they tend to see themselves, not as part of the social relations that make up community, but as something separate to 'the community'—and hospitality becomes impossible.

Community as a process of ongoing place-making

An alternative, re-imagined approach can see dialogical community as a process of on-going *place-making* that requires people's daily creative en-deavours in purposefully inhabiting space. Community then becomes not only the 'result' or experience of people being in dialogue with one an-other, as in the previous reflections on Martin Buber, but also a result or 'emergent property' of social interactions between people and place.

For Kelly and Sewell (1988, p42ff) such creative endeavours invite a transformation of the ways people relate to *space, place* and *base*. Within this perspective *space* is historically considered to be a physical space. This can now be conceived in broader ways: for example, cyberspace. The first transformational shift to understanding space as a *place* occurs when peo-ple develop some kind of belonging to that space—and in turn it imparts a sense of identity. The space becomes 'my or our place'. The second trans-formational movement towards *base* occurs when the social processes of inhabiting place not only create a sense of belonging and identity, but also evoke a sense of responsibility. To make a place one's base is to take some responsibility for purposefully inhabiting it with particular intentions.

In a dialogical approach to community development, part of the work of nurturing community requires paying attention to place-making social processes that people participate in. Community workers give attention to inhabiting a space, transforming it into at least a place and hopefully a base. In making a space and place into their base, people are making a commitment to inhabiting space in particular ways, that is a space inhabited for community as dialogue and hospitality, and sometimes in opposition to others who intend to inhabit spaces for different purposes, for example purely profit-driven or speculative purposes.

Building a relationship with place

Such processes require on-going creativity and imagination. Firstly there is a shift in the consciousness of space. People come to recognise that they can develop a relationship to space—a relationship that, like all relationships, is *potentially* hospitable. This shift of consciousness then invites an awareness and attention to the creative social practices that enable people to inhabit spaces, transforming them into places and bases. David Turton (2004), an anthropologist who has worked for many years in the Horn of Africa, usefully describes this social process as *emplacement*—hence the title of this reflection. Within dialogical community development, part of the challenge is to awaken people's consciousness and release their creative juices, so that they can actively engage in the processes of emplacing.

The American author Kurt Vonnegut wrote his delightful final book at the age of eighty-four—*A Man Without Country* (2005). He tells the following story that also illustrates the importance of emplacing his New York streets:

> . . . not long ago, I used to type. And, after I had about twenty pages, I would mark them up with pencil, making corrections. Then I would call Carol Atkins, who was a typist . . . we would chat away, and finally I say 'Hey, you know I got some pages. Are you still typing?' And she sure is. And I know it will be so neat, it will look like it was done by a computer. And I say, 'I hope it doesn't get lost in the mail.' And she says, 'Nothing ever gets lost in the mail' . . .
>
> Anyway, I take pages . . . I go downstairs to take off . . . and this is on 48th Street in New York City between Second Avenue and Third, and I go out to this newsstand across the street where they sell magazines and

lottery tickets and stationery. And I know their stock very well, and so I get an envelope, a manila envelope. It is as though whoever made that envelope knew what size of paper I'm using. I get in line because there are people buying lottery tickets, candy, and that sort of thing, and I chat with them. I say 'Do you know anybody who ever won the lottery?' And, 'What happened to your foot?'

Finally I get up to the head of the line. The people who own this store are Hindus. The woman behind the counter has a jewel between her eyes. Now isn't that worth the trip? I ask her, 'Have there been any big lottery winners lately?' Then I pay for the envelope. I take the manuscript and put it inside.

I go next to the postal convenience centre down the block at the corner of 47th Street and Second Avenue. This is very close to the United Nations, so there are funny looking people from all over the world. I go in there and we are all lined up again. I'm secretly in love with the woman behind the counter. She doesn't know it. My wife knows it. I am not about to do anything about it. She is so nice. All I have ever seen of her is from the waist up because she is always behind the counter. But every day she will do something with herself above her waist to cheer us up. Sometimes her hair will be all frizzy. Sometimes she will have ironed it flat . . .

So I wait in line, and I say, 'Hey what was the language you were talking? Was it Urdu?' I have nice chats. Sometimes not. There is also, 'If you don't like it here, why don't you go back to your tinhorn dictatorship where you came from?' One time I had my pocket picked there and got to meet a cop and tell him about it. Anyway, I finally I get up to the head of the line. I don't reveal to her that I love her. I keep poker-faced. She might as well be looking at a cantaloupe, there is so little information in my face, but my heart is beating. And I give her the envelope, and she weighs it . . .

Then I go outside and there is a mailbox . . .

And I go home. And I have had one hell of a good time.

Electronic communities build nothing. You wind up with nothing.

How beautiful it is to get up and go out and do something. (pp57ff)

Sandgate is a neighbourhood within the city of Brisbane. In a project with the Sandgate Affordable Housing Network, we facilitated a place-based organisational development process. These soulful colleagues expressed their vision for the organisation as a fable, enabling them to evoke the sense of place that was at the heart of their work together. It begins like this:

> As the ibis flies from the tall grasses of the wetland she circles the surrounding places. The glow of indigenous pride warms the air as she glides over the lagoons and follows a creek flowing to the bay.
>
> Below she sees a diverse community—busy, colourful and leafy. Under tinned and tiled roofs of many shapes and sizes simple, attractive homes seem to huddle together as if enjoying one another's company.
>
> In these neighbourhoods people move easily in the spill of gardens from yard to yard. Common spaces are shared. In communal gardens, work-sheds, studios, kitchens and parks people share their resources, skills and interests with the comfort of old friends.
>
> The ibis watches familiar faces as they mill in the streets and front yards. Some are on their way somewhere, others just out to greet one another. Tolerance and inclusiveness characterise all interactions. People are concerned about what's going on around them. There is a strong sense of pride, and of common identity among those who call Sandgate home.

Locality as an inherently fragile social achievement

Many contemporary social commentators focus on place-related 'problems' such as mobility, migration and displacement. While they are real phenomena that pose particular challenges to contemporary social life, a community development perspective infused with deconstructive movements can transform this focus. The key challenge instead becomes one of understanding and nurturing processes of emplacement. For example:

> We have used simple things like community film nights to awaken a community's attention, awareness and imagination to the process of place-making. During the 1988 Expo eviction crisis in West End, Bris-

bane we showed *The Milagro Beanfield War*, a David-and-Goliath story from New Mexico that resonated with our own traditional, inner-city community, experiencing invasion by economic rationalism and vandalism. After the film, people spoke of their passion for the neighbourhood, and hatched plans for creative, grassroots ways of defending it!

In Vanuatu, people talk about emplacement through the metaphor of the 'tree and the canoe'. The tree represents the social processes of people making connections to their local place—the site of their ancestors, their kin, and their land. The canoe represents the social processes of making connections to other places, usually other islands, where they exchange goods: kava, fish, shells, mats and tusks. Emplacement then occurs locally and across the islands, weaving a web of reciprocal relationships that invokes a sense of place, base and trans-local community.

Within Brisbane we have been involved in a process whereby new groups of refugees and migrants are emplacing a neighbourhood—which brings new challenges:

In one of our Brisbane neighbourhoods called Moorooka—dubbed 'our little Morocco' by the local Australian-Africans—there has been a recent substantial change to the demography. There has been a significant influx of African migrants and refugees into the area, both as residents and as business people. The local shopping streetscape is now dominated by Sudanese, Egyptian, Eritrean, Ethiopian and Somali shop-fronts. Many older residents—both multi-generational Australians and more recent migrants and refugees, Serbian, Croatian, Bosnian, Polish and so forth—are struggling to deal with this change process. There is a sense of displacement and disorientation. We have started working with the Brisbane City Council's community relations workers to re-think how to engage dialogically with people in this neighbourhood, so as to make everyone more hospitable to one another and re-imagine a sense of place. The way forward requires moving from a focus on displacement and disorientation towards creating new processes of emplacement. The idea of Moorooka/Morocco becoming an African precinct in the city—a particular neighbourhood full of street life, music, diverse foods, colours, and languages—could revitalise the place and bring people back to the streets. The focus of the work becomes the process of imagining new ways of consciously and creatively inhabiting the place to build a new sense of place and base.

Arjun Appadurai (1996) reminds us that "locality is an inherently fragile social achievement. Even in the most intimate, spatially confined, geographically isolated situations, locality must be maintained carefully against various kinds of odds". He goes on to argue that the work of locality production is always and everywhere a constant struggle to keep at bay "an endemic sense of anxiety and instability in social life" (p179). The social production of place has always been a fragile thing, as the story of Moorooka illustrates. Anxiety and instability threaten to undo people's creative energies and shrink their imaginative capacity. Place can easily become a space where racisms and other forms of exclusion and violence manifest themselves.

Processes of ongoing place-making

Ethnographic records of traditional societies reveal that "hard and regular work is needed to produce and maintain a sense of place. This work includes everything from the building of houses and settlements to rituals of all kinds" (Turton 2004, p13).

> On the Vanuatu island of Pentecost each village is centered by a local *nakamal*—a meeting house as a hub of social activity. The nakamal is upon or close to sacred ground called the *nasara*. The nasara is a key place for rituals that continue to revitalise the web of relationships between those presently alive, and also between these and the ancestors. Without the on-going rituals, the web of relationships, the order to community life and the land itself would suffer. Attention is given to this soulful, sacred social process of on-going place-making in which place is alive, infused with the need to be danced upon, sung to, and toiled within.

These insights from Vanuatu echo the insights in Deborah Rose's *Country of the Heart* (2002), a story of homeland in Australian indigenous life. She illuminates the creative dialogical processes of place-making within indigenous social life, which involve people relating to country and also listening to country as it relates to them. Many indigenous world-views illuminate this mutual process of place-making—people creating place in country and country 'singing it up' to people. This is a profound process of weaving webs of relationship between people, the cosmos, other creatures, and ancestors—a community as hospitality that stretches far beyond many Western conceptions of community.

The lesson from indigenous worldviews is the genuinely dialogical nature of the social process of place-making. While dialogue for Buber entails transformation of *human* encounters from I-It (subject-object) to I-Thou (subject-subject) kinds of relationships, indigenous worldviews remind us that I-Thou kinds of relationship can also be forged between people *and* places. The ground can also be a subject, rather than just an object that we act upon and try to control. Places can become subjects that are related to dialogically, with which people develop a profound relationship characterised by love, care, attention, deep listening and mutual learning. Dialogical community development invites this kind of place-making.

Listening to the language of the streets

If place-making can be dialogical, or more simply, if places can talk to people, it should be possible to listen to the language of the streets. Peter reflects on an experience of how a fresh encounter with an exotic location can amplify this street language:

> . . . I am captivated as I wander down the narrow alleyways of Zanzibar's Old Town. The streets are talking to me of their history (slavery, liberation, life). I catch glimpses of people's hidden lives through arching doorways. Even the doors captivate me—they are creative endeavours in themselves. As I stroll different streets I weave my ways through diverse neighbourhoods. I come across ancient churches, mosques, fishing markets, castles, city walls—I start to find myself on the outskirts and I am amongst spice gardens.

In the classic book *A Pattern Language* (1977) Christopher Alexander and his colleagues provide insights into place-making processes for those of us living within modern urban contexts. They articulate and illustrate the ways in which strong identity and deep connections can be reinforced by *archetypal patterns* of place-design. While most places that people live in are already designed, and mostly badly, people can still weave their own patterns in the street. Peter reflecting on place-making in his street tells how:

> My street is long—there are many people living on it. I would struggle to relate to everyone, but I can relate to those around me. Occasionally my partner and I invite the neighbours over for drinks on the back deck. We love getting together and sharing stories of other neighbours, holidays, how the kids are doing and so forth. One neighbour, two doors up, hosts a chicken co-operative that a number of households participate in—people put in money for chicken feed, do their turn in cleaning and everyone in turn receives eggs. Each of the neighbours in turn have created holes in their fences so we can move back and forth between back-yards—the children are free to play across at least four gardens. It's a street in an urban centre but we are place-making.

Creating holes in fences has become an experience of place design for some of the neighbours, giving an understanding the possible shapes of the street and opportunities to create connections.

In the same way, Christopher Day in *Places of the Soul* (1990) specifically addresses the importance of architecture and environmental design in place-making processes. More recently Alain de Botton's *The Architecture of Happiness* (2006) reflects on people's relationship to things, objects and particularly buildings. His thesis is that buildings speak to people, but they only speak to those who listen—again, a quality of soul and a practice of dialogue not only with people, but with 'things'. In being attentive to the way buildings, streets, streetscapes, parks, sculptures, shops, and cafés speak to them, people can engage in more creative dialogical processes of place-making.

These authors are delighted that people who are attentive to their environment—a quality of soulful awakening—can understand the languages of built form and urban design. For example, in the centre of Brisbane's West End stands a lizard, a sculpture that inhabits the edge of a key intersection. It has become a meeting and gathering place for local residents. The design element in placing the sculpture at that location is critical in imagining how to weave community into emplacement processes.

Place as a site for hospitality

Strong communities emerge from places where there is a great deal of hospitable place-making going on. In a neighbourhood, emplacement becomes a daily activity of people walking streets, drinking in bars, conversing in cafés, bumping into one another at the shops, or picking up children. People develop a 'footprint' through both the everyday tracks: travel to and from work, home, or school, or walking to the corner store; and the 'off-tracks' of attentively exploring side-streets and shortcuts during walks and rides. The social practice of emplacing involves getting to know the neighbours, greeting shopkeepers by name, waving to friends in the street and smiling at acquaintances in passing. Peter reflects on living in our own neighbourhood:

> I have lived in the neighbourhood of West End on and off for some 18 years. I moved into the space having never lived in the same place for more than five years. I am part of a migrant family and so the whole place of Australia seemed somehow alien or inhospitable. However, I set out to make this West End my home, to emplace it. After 18 years I have inhabited the space making it 'my place'. My footprint is indelible—I have walked all of its streets, climbed up and down a street with a backpack full of books training for walks in Nepal, and slept on the streets in protests against ruthless landlords. I've drunk in most of the coffee shops, am almost addicted to the local bookshops, have been part of a local football club—until I had to hang up those boots with aging feet—and I've danced and celebrated at many of the local festivals. The *I* is aware of being welcomed by others and in turn I feel the need to be hospitable to other newcomers.

However, when reflecting on the neighbourhood, it becomes increasingly obvious that while many local people constantly engage in these processes of inhabitation, there is the ever-present anti-emplacing spectre of global capital. We see it on our daily horizon: in new flats or pubs that are the same as the ones in every gentrifying neighbourhood; in threats of bridges, tunnels, and new freeways making the community hospitable only to cars, not people; in the undermining of local business as multinational companies move into the area. Politicians in local government imagine the city only in terms of Real Estate—for them space is nothing but a commodity. Capital wants to carve up and colonise. 'We' are hospitable, but we are also engaged in contestation. While engaged in the fragile work of emplacement for hospitable ends, we sometimes also need to stand our ground.

In much of modern society, emplacement occurs around sites of commerce and exchange, which become the locus of contestation. Soul seeps away and people become marginalised when places become merely functional sites for consumption or property speculation. People in wheelchairs cannot access the pavements as they are literally colonised by cafés; poor people cannot enter the new super-glossy pubs. People on lower incomes can no longer afford to live in their beloved neighbourhoods. We have all been in places where attention and imagination are geared towards profit, not soulful living. If the place has been created, or is being re-created by speculative rather than soulful social processes, people have less investment—their greater selves are symbolically submerged within the concrete. They do not make the space 'their' place or base; they will probably just join the ever-increasing trend towards 'moving on' when they feel like it or when a better job is offered.

The social practice within dialogical community development illuminates places not only as places for emplacement, but also as social sites of contestation. Where some might be trying to inhabit a space as a site for hospitality—to ourselves, to others, and to the land—other people, organisations and institutions might be working to colonise the space for economic or political purposes. So while a deepening awareness of the process of emplacement alerts people to the possibilities of hospitality, it also warns of the dangers of people who have no understanding of a hospitable relationship to space and place.

One of the key challenges of community development is contesting the efforts of those who would enclose what many people have called 'the commons' (Shiva, 2005) rather than inhabit it hospitably. In the above reflection on our neighbourhood the footpaths should remain as commons: a place for all, not just for people who can constantly afford to consume. The pub should be a place where all common people can gather and have a 'common' drink, instead of a place monitored by ever-present security guards making it very clear who is and is not welcome. The mix of housing should ensure that there are options for all kinds of people.

A dialogical approach to community development is engaged with powerful dynamics: not only struggling against global capital's weapons of profit, not only struggling for significant issues such as affordable housing, but also struggling for soulful places with strong identities and deep connections. Contemporary community development as social practice is therefore purposeful in that it is oriented to supporting people to inhabit and transform places that are also being shaped destructively by the 'project of globalisation'. Where there are creative and dialogical social processes of place-making, the soulful parts of selves are awakened. People feel motivated to engage in difficult struggles. They fight for something they love—a place where they have invested something of themselves.

1.4 Welcoming problems

From the perspective of re-imagining how to think about community problems, we have found great value in the philosopher Michel Foucault's analysis of how populations came to be talked and thought about in different ways through history. Foucault's thesis is that with the emergence of modern bureaucracy, populations increasingly came to be acted upon as objects. In the same way that populations were acted upon, so community problems were also to be *fixed* by these modern bureaucracies. A science developed in which the collection of data and the manipulation of sectors of population became central. The population with its accompanying problems was seen as 'out there', to be acted upon as object, rather than being something 'we' are a part of. In *Powers of Freedom* (1999), Nikolas Rose, drawing on the analysis of Foucault, has called this a process of *territorialisation*.

Historically people were all part of communities, but now the community is often imagined to be 'out there', a distinct entity from the people who make it up. For many professionals, *the people* are no longer subjects of their own transformation dealing with their local problems, but objects to be acted upon. Following this kind of logic, the *technique* of community development engages in territorialising processes such as mapping a 'community', 'targeting' groups, collecting data, designing initiatives to solve problems and eliciting shallow-participation. Such a technocratic framework of community development gives ample opportunities for contractors and consultants, all given particular tasks from the above list and a brief to 'go, do and deliver'. This type of framework can indeed provide useful data, and occasionally, good processes and projects. However, the fundamental assumptions behind such a paradigm are open to serious question. This reflection asks the questions, and explores some ideas that might provide renewed wisdom.

Attending to the details of social life

The dialogical approach to community development is a continuous process that concerns itself not so much with 'fixing' problems—a prime concern of modernity—as with attending to the details of social life. At the risk of nostalgia, it is worth reflecting that such attention may have been easier within traditional or pre-modern societies. Clear and relatively unchanging rules and traditions maintained the rhythm of social life, although this is not to say that some people were not deeply unhappy, or were not marginalised from decision-making processes. People had to give close attention to the intricate web of relationships that were infused with commitments and obligations to kin, ancestors, place and the cosmos. In the midst of this web of relationships were clear processes or customs for dealing with social or community problems.

Such processes and customs are no longer so clear. Even in more traditional societies, the tentacles of modernity have penetrated deep into rural contexts. People have developed a different consciousness, moving away from an understanding of their lives and choices as governed by norms, roles, customs and traditions; they have entered a new age of options and choices which require more thinking and feeling about the strategic choices to be made in individual and collective lives.

Community problems as potential gifts

A focus on problems can reflect an inability to imagine community with depth. Social problems can be imagined as voices calling people back to a renewed dialogue. Community workers have to look with depth beneath the obvious manifestations of problems in particular places, and open a new dialogue starting with the question: 'What are the manifest problems really saying?' or 'What do these problems articulate about the condition of our places?' Within dialogical community development the 'problems' are symptoms, but also gifts, calling people to look deeper into themselves as individuals and groups. They are an invitation into what Jacques Derrida calls alterity: another, often hidden dimension of social life that needs to be considered.

A soulful orientation will see a problem as a potential gift that offers a quality or dimension of life in a way that adds value, relatedness, heart and substance. As practitioners we may be tempted to see our role as that of an exterminator attempting to eradicate particular problems, or alternatively we may easily collude with other people who themselves want to see a problem exterminated. But we would be passing up a gift—an opportunity to develop an approach that gives back what is problematic to 'people as community' in a way that uncovers its value and invites people to give it attention within a broader sense of the whole.

Many parts of Australian society only have eyes to see their Aboriginal and Torres Strait Islander brothers and sisters as 'community problems'. This might be a generalised problematic gaze, with words such as 'bloody Aboriginals', or it might focus on some of the more difficult Aboriginal people who are misusing alcohol, with resulting violent behaviour in public spaces. Historically the goal for many people has been either literal extermination ('shoot the buggers') or symbolic extermination ('move them on' from our neighbourhood). For others, however, getting to know Aboriginal and Torres Strait Islander people has been a gift, an invitation to discover whole new ways of being and living in the world. The 'gift' of getting to know such people isn't always pleasant—it can be deeply challenging. One comes to realise that the 'community problem', that is, difficult Aboriginals and Torres Strait Islanders, is often a symptom of much deeper racisms within Australia and within one's self. Receiving this problem back is confronting and requires deep reflection and renewed action to swim against deep currents within our society.

Hospitality towards our problems

Paulo Freire's critique of community development was that it often focused on a particular problem without understanding the whole social context. He made the case that this produced a *focalised* view of problems which disconnected the community development workers' analysis from the *totality* of the situation (1972, p111). One of the most significant dysfunctions of most technically oriented community development work is its continued focus on particular problems and even particular places. In this focus on fragments, an understanding of the whole is lost.

Conversely, when people in places and social relationships begin to observe the ways in which problems are manifesting themselves, they can be enriched rather than impoverished. They can receive back what is theirs—the very things that they assumed were so horrible and thought they needed to be rid of. It follows that a dialogical approach to community requires practitioners to develop a new approach towards problems with a view to understanding the whole. When regarding social problems holistically, with an open mind, people begin to find the messages that lie within the apparent social sickness, the corrections that are prompted by remorse and other uncomfortable feelings, and the necessary changes demanded by violence and intolerance.

For some time I have been training youth and community workers in inter-cultural youth work practice. In many of the workshop discussions the challenge of working with 'problem youth' kept coming up. Initial discussions focused around the problem of these young people, and some of their ways of being and interacting, particularly the way they would hang around in groups, perceived by the wider community as gangs. Gradually the discussions would start to move in another direction. Questions would start to arise along the lines of 'why we are thinking of these youth as a problem?'. There was a gradual recognition that these problems are much more complex—sometimes tied up with young people being excluded from school and work opportunities; or with perceptions of race and ethnicity in relation to refugee, Pacific Islander or indigenous young people. Sometimes the issues involved perceptions of legitimate uses of contested public space. Participants started to consider the need for hospitality towards the perceived problem. In fact many started to recognise that the problem was one of 'community as inhospitality'—the setting up of many dynamics of antagonism (for example, Australian vs. African vs. Muslim) that are damaging personally, inter-personally, culturally and socially on a local, national and international level. People started to realise that a dialogical approach to community development invites an open mind and a dialogical engagement with the issues, with fresh perspectives and questions.

If you were asked the question: 'Is your picture of a healthy, well-developed neighbourhood simply one that has no problems?' your answer should be 'No!' Many of us want to live in a place that is filled with the rough and tumble of challenging social life (as well as the pleasures of a sometimes less hectic social life). Most people don't want to live shallow lives in a sanitised place. A community is much more than simply the absence of problems. From a dialogical perspective a community is more likely to come alive where people together are able to remain open and hospitable towards their perceived problems.

From a perspective informed by depth and soul, problems are signposts that make people reconsider the whole. If a particular group is perceived to be dysfunctional, then from a dialogical perspective this problem group simply highlights a critical contradiction in the configuration of social relations in that place or society. Problems viewed this way ensure community workers remain attentive to the whole and that they keep on working towards transformation. Any attempts to remove a 'problem group' without a consideration of the whole usually indicates the choice of a pathway oriented towards sanitation rather than soul, towards further injustice rather than love and justice.

1.5 Dancing with the shadow

It is a perilous thing to ignore symptoms. This is true of our bodies, our relationships, our local places and our societies. Communities often lack awareness of 'problems' as indicators of deeper troubles or social contradictions, and then experience manifestations of those problems in other shadowy forms.

The notion of *shadow* is again drawn from the work of Carl Jung. Psychologically it simply means that issues not consciously acknowledged and dealt with will be pushed into the shadow or unconscious realm, only to manifest themselves at a later stage—usually in a more destructive way than the original problem. This pattern of psychological behaviour can be transferred into the social, inter-personal realm. For example, our own intolerance towards some particular 'others' may eventually be manifest in that other group expressing a learned intolerance towards us, even more violently than our own intolerance. If people refuse to acknowledge a particular social problem and understand its deeper implications for the whole, this will usually manifest itself in a greater destructive social dynamic. Destructive race relations and unemployment are ignored in the suburbs of Paris, or the Cronulla or Redfern areas of Sydney, and boom! there is a riot. The task is to acknowledge and understand individual and collective shadows, to welcome all our shadow selves into soulful communities, and to learn to dance with them.

Our shadows invite humility

A dialogical approach to community development invites us to acknowledge the shadow (such as destructive race relations) both personally and collectively. Such an approach requires the courage to face ourselves and our society, warts and all—full of racism, sexism, greed, homophobia, guilt and violence. Soulfulness and depth require openness and authenticity. Here is the starting point for creative intervention and transformation. Such acknowledgment of personal and collective shadow leads to a humility that crosses barriers of class, education, sexuality, gender, disability and race. We can then start unravelling shadow symptoms in neighbourhoods by unravelling the shadow in ourselves, rather than looking straight away for the shadow 'out there'.

Shifting the starting place can lead to a different ethos, strategy and outcome. Let's imagine that while working in a community, we identify a major problem as young people engaging in vandalism. A typical response would be to simply mobilise resources to remove the young people from the community and clean up the mess. The traders and power-brokers would put pressure on the police and courts to take tougher action against young people now labelled as vandals. A conventional community development approach would hopefully be more progressive, in that it would engage in a process of relationship-building and participation to develop a program that channelled the potentially destructive energy of vandalism into creative energies of art, recreation, education and job creation.

However, a dialogical approach would go a step further and work with other stakeholders within the community to develop a sense of solidarity with the young people. It should facilitate a soulful acknowledgment of how our individual and collective compulsions and fears have caused young people to lose hope and feel marginalised from our families and society. Within this acknowledgment and awareness of our own 'shadow' lies the possibility of an imaginative, long-term process of generating transformation together—not just amongst the young people (maybe through projects of art, recreation, education and job creation) but also amongst ourselves (through spending less time in compulsive work and giving time to our children, less time in front of the TV and more time eating a meal together or playing football in the local park).

How does shadow develop and thrive in a community?

It is often the very individuals, groups, or neighbourhoods that look squeaky clean that are experiencing the most destructive energies at a hidden, unconscious or subterranean level. These are the soulless modernist collectivities that masquerade as communities—people who come together without a capacity for hospitality to those who are 'other'. They refuse to dance with their own shadows and therefore project shadows onto other problems. We have worked in one place, which won a Tidy Town Award and appears to have few social problems, but which in fact has a very high rate of incest and domestic violence. From the outside you would never imagine such violence was happening. In contrast, places that look more chaotic—where the issues are out in the open—may be the ones that are struggling to develop a more authentic approach infused with soulful attention, creativity and imagination.

There are many people within neighbourhoods that wish there were no problems; they do their best to either remove or conceal the symptom. Rhetoric develops: 'We do not have homeless youth in our neighbourhood' or 'we are not racist'. Of course there are good reasons why such rhetoric develops; people do not wish tourists to be afraid, or do not wish investors to leave the area. However, these good reasons do not legitimise rhetoric or strategy that is colluding with shadow, or failing to acknowledge and confront it.

A school with an investment in the claim that 'we do not have bullying in our school' creates a myth of well-being that at a superficial level may be enjoyed by most students, parents and teachers. But what of the student who experiences what she thinks is bullying? She is not likely to find a sympathetic ear. She may encounter otherwise good people who, in not listening, are acting out of their own investment in the myth— their own desire to preserve or defend what they see as the good in their school community. In their determination to stay deaf and blind, they collude with a small injustice and create a much bigger injustice: a student who feels not only bullied by a fellow student but also by an uncompromising administration. She may feel forced to leave the school, depriving it of the ongoing benefit of her sensitivity.

In the long term the rhetoric and repression may lead to a shadow problem that explodes with much greater destructive impact than could have been previously imagined; or it may simply push the shadow into some other place. The ethics of this 'nimbyism'[2] are highly questionable.

---

2   'Not in my backyard"

Shadows as possibilities that have not yet been realised

Jung identified two kinds of shadow. The first kind as already discussed is shadow as repressed, negative, destructive energy. The second kind consists of possibilities that have not yet been realised. Jung advocated that there are gifts locked deep within shadow compartments of each of our psyches. In the same way there are gifts that are repressed into the hidden shadow compartments of social life. If unlocked, and welcomed into our communities, these gifts can bring about healing transformation.

In Australia for many years the Health Department adopted a policy of institutionalising people suffering from mental health problems. Those classified as sick were simply placed in psychiatric wards of hospitals. This policy was well suited to suburban neighbourhoods. There was a clear definition of who was sick and who was healthy; the 'problem' or 'sick' could be removed and put into institutions; our notions of mental irrationality could be projected onto those who were hidden and we could continue living in our neighbourhoods with an illusion of rationality and well-being. In the process our own sickness became shadow. If we are not defined by the system or society as sick, then we must be well.

Then, due to many pressures (primarily budget), the policy changed. A de-institutionalisation policy was adopted, and people who had been previously defined as sick and removed from neighbourhoods were suddenly relocated into hostels in neighbourhoods. There were and still are many ramifications of such a shift in policy. People in the neighbourhoods were scared; people in hostels were still isolated, un-welcomed and medicated.

However, I was fortunate as a young community development worker in West End to get involved in a community development process where several people in our neighbourhood who defined themselves as 'mentally healthy' started building bridges with those defined as 'mentally sick'. These groups met for dinner on Friday evenings, then for picnics on Tuesdays; a few of us started a self-help mental health group—for all of us—using the methods of GROW, an international self-help movement. What amazed us through this process was how similar in essence were the problems we all struggled with. Those of us defined as 'well' or 'rational' experienced as much inner chaos and irrationality as did those who were defined as unhealthy. We suddenly all had a safe space to explore what was obvious for some (who had been told for years by psychiatrists), and what had become shadow for the rest of us—our repressed feelings of self-doubt, delusion, paranoia and neurosis.

The policy shift led to a community of people coming face to face with a group who had been removed from our consciousness. In the process of encountering one another we were given a safe place to engage with our own shadows. This is the gift of shadow.

Dancing with the shadow invites possibilities, ignoring shadow is dangerous. A dialogical approach to community development requires practitioners to attend to the shadow with new questions, a fresh perspective, a purposeful interrogation of given rhetoric, alertness to collusion, and a deconstructive orientation that destabilises community analysis as it exists. A dialogical approach to dancing with the shadow holds the promise that what some people see as bad and unhealthy—problematic youth, racism, intolerance, people with mental health problems—can be welcomed into spaces and places. Such an approach can reawaken a fresh sense of community as hospitality.

Summing up

The first reflection of this Chapter was a call to re-awaken *love* in community work practice. In the same way that being in love ignites the archetypal mysteries of our psyches, so love animates a sociality of connecting, belonging, yearning, creating and caring that is the life-blood of vibrant, deep community work. Community can only be born if there is some transformation that shifts awareness and attention towards an other-orientation, a journey from *I* to *we* through dialogue and hospitality. We want to work with colleagues who are alive—the kinds of fools who continually 'fall in love' with life, and who are alert to the potential transformation of the ordinary to the extra-ordinary that is the daily concern of soulful community work.

The second reflection explored what we call the alchemy of *poetic participation*. To be co-creators of dialogical community, soulful people are needed—people who have been awakened by love. Yet the paradoxical converse of this is that such soulful people are 'made' through participating in the everyday and ordinary things of life, albeit with a particular attentiveness, awareness, animation and imagination. The stuff of soul is made by genuinely participating in initiatives emerging from people's shared sufferings and concerns, a work we have called poetic participation. Poetic participation invites people into an intimate engagement of their creative imaginations, hospitality towards one another's ideas and perspectives, and the giving of attention and care to building a shared analysis of ways forward.

The third reflection alerted practitioners to the dangers of seeing community primarily as an objectified site or 'place'. Soul seeps away when places become simply functional sites for consumption, property speculation and professionally designed and driven interventions. A re-imagined approach can see community as a process of ongoing place-making that requires people's daily creative endeavours. An approach to dialogical community development awakens people's conscious and purposeful processes of *emplacing*.

The fourth reflection was a call to welcome community problems as gifts that can invoke depth in our practice. Modernist community development techniques try to fix social problems. The approach to community development presented in this book concerns itself not so much with 'fixing' a particular flaw, as it does with attending to the details of social life. Community problems are voices calling forward into a dialogue and back to depth—and a deep response begins with developing a new hospitality towards community problems.

The fifth reflection introduced the Jungian idea of *shadow* which illuminates social issues with a fresh perspective. This perspective reveals that social issues not consciously acknowledged and worked with, will be pushed into the shadow or unconscious realm, only to manifest themselves at a later stage. A dialogical approach to community development requires acknowledging shadow both personally and collectively. It requires the courage to face ourselves and our communities as we truly are: full of racism, sexism, greed, homophobia, guilt, and violence. This acknowledgment of culpability leads to a profound humility and depth of practice that crosses barriers of class, education, gender, sexuality, disability and race. In doing this people find they can dance with the shadow, and reveal gifts that bring about a healing social transformation.

We hope that this brief excursion into re-imagining community life and community work has challenged previously un-thought about 'givens', has destabilised habits of perspective, and has invited you into a reconsideration of community development practice. This Chapter has laid the foundation for re-thinking transformational community processes in the next chapter. We invite you to continue with us in the dialogue.

Transformational community processes

Community development is a process of transformation. While the previous chapter considered the transformative process of re-imagining community and community work, this chapter considers transformation in terms of more orthodox understandings of community development. We explore a dialogical approach that involves a discerning approach to methodology; community-owned analysis; practices of power-with and co-operative power; careful conflicting; and structuring the work through place-based, community-oriented, democratic people's organisations.

These five reflections provide a mud-map for how a dialogical approach to community development can transform our social world. They explore the role of a skilled and soulful worker in supporting 'community' to become a vehicle for social change in which people find their own paths towards development as freedom.

2.1 The discerning and gentling of method

In the late 1980s we both started getting involved as unpaid community workers in West End. This meant getting to know our neighbours along with some more experienced community workers, and getting involved in a variety of community activities and projects—with refugee groups, indigenous people, and people suffering mental illness. It was clear that many interesting and good things were happening. In the midst of all this Peter asked one of his key mentors Dave Andrews, 'How do you make sense of all this activity?' A part of his answer was 'I know it all looks a bit mad, but there is a method within the madness'. Learning the method in our own neighbourhood has been a key part of our journey of community practice over the subsequent years.

A methodical and rhythmic approach: bonding, banding, building and bridging

One of the most useful ways of thinking about the social method of community development has been developed by our Queensland colleagues in dialogue with Tony Kelly (2008). For them, 'method' signifies a way of ordering and structuring the community development process in levels: *micro, mezzo, macro* and *meta* levels.

The focus of the micro level is *bonding*—nurturing purposeful interpersonal relationships through dialogue. In many ways it involves many of the practices discussed in the preceding chapter. It requires the loving practice of hearing a person or people's stories, articulating with them an understanding of the key issues that they are struggling with, and exploring with them the possibility of sharing their story and trying to do something public about it.

This level of the process requires practitioners to be conscious of their own agenda—this may be 'doing a worthwhile project', 'fulfilling a funding obligation', or 'delivering some outcome'—but to hold it lightly, or put it on hold, so the concerns and therefore the potential agenda of other people in the community can be clearly understood.

The bonding process requires a movement towards others and hospitality towards their concerns. Within therapeutic or counselling approaches, this concern would be directed towards finding a therapeutic solution: for example, someone might be concerned about the ever-present noise pollution in their neighbourhood, and a therapeutic solution would be to find new ways of 'coping with the noise' without getting overly angry. A community development approach moves the hospitable conversation or dialogue towards an agreement to do something about this concern publicly—that is, it asks the question "Are other people suffering the same problem or feeling the same concern? If they are, can we get together and do something that makes it a collective public process of action?"

The mezzo level involves *banding*: working with these people whose stories have been heard, linking them together, and working with them to move what might have previously been felt as a private concern into collective public action. Neighbourhoods are complex webs of relationship and some people may already be linked together in different ways; but banding is about coming together around a common purpose.

The shift from micro to mezzo requires a movement from purposeful relationships to purposeful and participatory action groups. This level involves people sitting down together in relationships of mutual trust, agreeing to do something public together as a group, conducting analysis of what are the issues, the issues behind the issues, the players/stakeholders, the possibilities, and the tactics and strategies that might best reach their objectives. This can seem chaotic and disjointed, but the method in the madness is to be purposeful about facilitating a process of weaving relationships and moving towards clarity of analysis.

In a noisy neighbourhood, this level might bring together local residents who share the same concern, forming some purposeful bonds and agreeing, for example, that 'we want to do something about noise in our neighbourhood'. That agreement is built upon a mutual trust in one another's ability and desire to journey together. It then requires the group to sit down and consider questions like 'What might we envisage a neighbourhood with less noise to look like or feel like?' and 'Who is making the noise?', to 'Who might be our allies in reducing noise?' and 'Who will try and hinder us bringing change?' Strategies will be chosen—for example, campaigning to stop trucks driving down small streets (a campaigning strategy), or agreeing as a group of neighbours that we will not do renovations on Sunday afternoons (a mutual co-operative strategy).

The macro level of the method requires *building*—working with these people who are now involved in purposeful and participatory public action, to form and stabilise groups and organisations that can carry the work on in a sustainable way. Sugata Dasgupta (1968) argues that it is the democratic nature of these grassroots people's organisations that is critical for this level of the work. They must be built and owned by the people for the people. They are community-based organisations (CBOs) with their 'base', their impetus, their whole rationale grounded in the community. The shift from mezzo to macro level work then entails moving from participatory *action groups* to democratic, and therefore still participatory, *community organisations*.

For the practitioner supporting this work of the people, a particular kind of leadership is required. The preferred approach is to pay gentle attention to both process and structure in a group. Many groups, because they do not pay close enough attention to process, find themselves under threat of fracture as the emergent group leadership just wants to 'get on with it'. Returning to the noise pollution example, this level of the work might see the group of active residents form a non-incorporated organisation 'Locals Against Noise Pollution' and build a link with the local neighbourhood centre to work under their auspices for insurance and financial reasons.

The final level of method is described as the meta dimension which involves *bridging*: linking stable community-based organisations into alliances, coalitions, co-operative arrangements, networks or federations that enable people to tackle trans-local issues or global issues. Within the example, the now-formed local group might want to create alliances with groups doing similar work in other localities—in the recognition that it is no good stopping trucks driving through one neighbourhood if it simply means they drive through the adjacent one. A local problem might require a regional solution. In Brisbane in the 1980s, a local residents' group concerned about traffic in their street ended up developing an analysis of traffic planning and roads infrastructure, and became a regional alliance across several suburbs called *Citizens Against Route Twenty*. There is more discussion of this level in the reflection below, *Structuring not strangling*.

A gentle and discerning approach to method

One of the key skills in dialogical community development is to be aware of the level reached by an individual person or group, and to facilitate their engagement with the process at that level. To move too quickly usually leads to an unravelling of the process: either relationships are not strong enough, analysis has not been considered well enough, or groups are not stable. To move too slowly could mean that momentum is lost, or actions and activities become too localised and unable to connect with broader movements tackling international or national forces.

Groups and practitioners need to discern carefully where they are in the process. This discernment is central to an approach to method infused with depth and soul. Reflective questions need to be considered:

- How strong and solid are relationships between people, groups and organisations?
- How coherent is the community analysis? Does it take into account both obvious and subtle forces and dynamics?
- How stable is the structuring of public action? Is it vulnerable to undercurrents of personality, power or politics?
- Is there movement towards strong organisational forms? Is there sufficient leadership to move this along?

We refer to this skill as *gentling*—a skill requiring discernment. In the gentling process, a practitioner needs to know when to push people to try something new, to trust the power of the group, to 'walk their talk'. Yet gentling also requires knowing when to back off, letting go of untimely opportunities, giving people a break, hinting at potentials, or holding an idea or initiative lightly. It involves discernment to know that maybe the group is not yet strong enough to tackle a big issue, and needs to build strength by tackling a smaller one.

One of our Brisbane colleagues, Morrie O'Connor, introduced a useful idea that we call a 'bonding and banding task'. This is a task that a practitioner might facilitate, not for the outcome of the task itself, but for the value of the process to the group. For example, a newly forming group that has come together to do something about noise might decide to organise a raffle to raise funds, or to hold a Christmas party, or to have a stall at a school fete. It may not really matter what the task is. The important thing is that the initiative matches the whole group's stage of development, so as many people as possible can participate, and that the group learns more about working together from the experience. Smaller examples might be asking two quieter members of a group to go to the shop together to get some milk for morning tea—giving them a different kind of one-on-one opportunity for a chat—or washing up with someone who you know has something on their mind, to open up a space for them to raise it if they want to.

> One morning in about 1989 our friend and neighbour Chris Todd, recently settled into a new home, had an argument with his wife. Wanting to keep his distance from the house, he found himself in the furthest corner of the backyard, building a chook run. Curious neighbours came and asked what he was doing, and briefly lent a hand. Through the course of the day an idea emerged, perhaps with the original aim of justifying the size of the run, and the local 'chook co-op' was born where members shared costs and tasks like collecting and packing eggs and buying feed. Of course we got fresh eggs and shared a barbecue when the hens went off the lay, but the chook co-op was more than that—it was a gentle shared adventure between a diverse bunch of people who otherwise would have had little in common. A couple of years later this web of quiet but by then reasonably strong neighbourly relationships was galvanised into public action when an accident on their street sparked a small, local campaign to get something done about traffic speed.

A dialogical approach to method

The dialogical approach pushes community workers to practise a social method that is aware of and hospitable to those 'others' not usually invited into the community development process. This approach to community development holds to a tradition of solidarity with the poor and marginalised, and therefore would start the micro-method through entering into dialogue with the invisible or disenfranchised on the edge of a 'community'. However it does not mean that practitioners cannot also enter into hospitable dialogue with those considered to be at the economic, political or cultural centre of power.

The degree of separation between the centre and the margins is often less than we suppose. People at the centre often have at least one relationship with those on the margins—it may be a disabled relative, an abusive uncle, a son or daughter whose behaviour they find challenging or a cousin they have visited in jail. Sometimes an encounter can happen in unexpected ways, and if it is not crowded by unforgiving expectations or strident demands (that is if it provides a hospitable space for the humanity of people in power) can have unexpected results.

It was the height of the Expo 88 housing crisis in West End. Local residents and community groups had been campaigning for months, raising public awareness of the issues for local people being evicted from their homes or facing big rent hikes. We had convened the Expo Social Impact Summit, held press conferences, and had stories in national magazines, TV news, and local papers—but with no response from the Queensland government. Then the story was picked up by a journalist from the Catholic Leader, who was interested in the social justice angle and happened to know the state housing minister through family and church connections. One morning we got a phone call, saying she had convinced him to have a look for himself, and they were about to leave—where should she take him?

Gerard gave her a few addresses, and could do nothing else but wait and trust the process. We heard later that he visited a couple of boarding houses, and was moved by what he saw and the people he met telling their own stories, probably much more eloquent and graphic than the community advocates who had been speaking on their behalf. He was so appalled by the conditions at one place that he wanted it closed down immediately, until the journalist gently asked him where he thought the people would go. Within weeks the state housing department had agreed to fund one of the state's first housing workers, to be based at the local neighbourhood centre for twelve months. Twenty years later someone is still doing good work in that role.

An over-simplified dichotomy of centre-periphery can be challenged by deconstructive movements. While maintaining a social commitment to those on the edge, we do engage respectfully with those deemed to be at the centre, as shown by the above story. A subtle *geometry of practice* can build purposeful relationships with those on all points of the spectrum between the periphery and the centre, the bottom and top, the inside and outside.

 The starting place must be dialogue with everyone. Dialogue unlocks the possibility of story, and story unlocks the possibility of genuine exchange of ideas and perspectives, leading to potential change of all parties to the dialogue. As mentioned in the Introduction, the deconstructive dimension of this book destabilises a simplistic centre–periphery, top–bottom, landlord–tenant and rich–poor view of the world.

Mandate within the method

Community practitioners often discuss the importance of building trust within relational work. 'Trusting relationships' can become the mantra that defines the work. Without trust it is very difficult to move forward within any level of the method. Within the micro (bonding) level, there is the need to cultivate trust between practitioners and the person or people with whose story they are engaged. At the mezzo (banding) level it is critical to cultivate trust between people who are travelling together on a journey of community work.

One of the key practices in building this trust is 'gaining a mandate'. This refers to the process of a practitioner constantly checking back with people about what 'we' have agreed to do—in terms of analysis, goals, objectives and strategies—and getting active consent to move forward together.

For example, you as a practitioner might have been talking with someone in a wheelchair, about their constant problems in accessing transport options in the neighbourhood. This is the micro level of the method. You hear their story and you might respond, "Do you know anyone else living around here who also has a disability or is supportively concerned about people living with disabilities, who could come together with us? We could have a coffee together and talk about it". You might also say something like, "I know someone else who has a similar story to you, would you mind if I shared your story with that person—maybe we could then get together; what do you think?" In both cases there is a potential movement from the micro to the mezzo level of the method. The point is that permission has been sought from that person, or more accurately the decision-making process has been moved from yourself—an *I*—to include the person you've been talking with—a *We*. The mandate to move forward is legitimised within the dialogical relationship. Trust building is strengthened if this process takes place as often as possible.

> Peter was recently in Vanuatu working with a group of thirty newly elected chiefs. The task at hand was to consider the problem of conflict within a particular locality. People were drawing a mud map of the local issues, building an analysis of the causes of conflict. After some 30 minutes of the group discussing conflict, Peter sensed that people were missing some key elements of the analysis. They had got stuck on the issue of a land conflict, obscuring other sources of conflict to do with overpopulation, lack of family planning services and so forth. So Peter chose a moment to interject and sought permission to introduce some new ideas. He didn't just bring new ideas; he firstly sought a mandate from the group to 'shake the analysis up'.

In the process of negotiating that mandate the group was able to engage dialogically with the new ideas. New strategies were considered, and trust was reinforced between the facilitator and participants. The mezzo method was strengthened through the clarity of the analysis developed by the participatory group.

2.2 Widening analysis

Many of the previous reflections have engaged implicitly with the issue of analysis. The story at the end of previous reflection is about analysis: a group of chiefs building an understanding of their situation and a facilitator gaining a mandate to support a group in widening their thinking. This reflection considers a process of widening analysis, so that it can become a key transformational process in which people find their own paths towards development as freedom.

Analysis is central to any process of community development, ensuring that people have a way forward, a sense of what to do and why they are doing it. It ensures people become aware of the forces that are acting upon and within their spaces and places, and requires people to become conscious of the ways that such forces are shaping the way they are living. This is Freire's 'naming of the word and the world'—literacy as a process of being able not just to read and write words, but to understand the forces impacting and shaping us in the world. Analysis makes conscious or visible these forces—local, regional, national and increasingly global.

Within Vanuatu some of the key complexities of development are to do with land. Currently there is an intense social struggle related to diverse visions of how land should be owned. Traditionally land has been used to support activities such as subsistence living (gardens, livestock) and ceremony. However, in recent years there are significant pressures at play to change the way local people relate to their land. Customary practices are feeling many pressures.

Within an initiative Peter has been working on, chiefs are trying to make sense of the forces at work around them in relation to land. Locally, population pressures have made it difficult for kin groups to keep allocating enough land to new young families to ensure a sustainable subsistence living. Families are therefore under increased competitive pressure when trying to access good land for food growing. Young people also have new aspirations as a result of global media that expose them to other lifestyle and livelihood options. Sometimes young people do not want to stay on the land. To make it even more complex, land can be claimed by different groups. Some groups that left land decades ago, maybe as a result of colonisation processes, may return and claim a connection to the land.

At the same time there is a push by the national government to develop an income base to pay salaries and provide services, so they promote tourism and other forms of income-generating investment. Such pressure plays itself out in changes to land legislation, allowing families to lease land to foreigners. Internationally, foreign capital aligns with or influences local elites in demanding new forms of land tenure, so they can build large resorts or sell off subdivided plots to aspiring middle class foreigners.

We see from the reflection above that analysis is complex—it demands that local people become aware of all these inter-twining forces exerting pressure on their lives. However, within transformational community work the process of analysis goes further than building this kind of under-standing. Analysis does not just privilege thinking. It also refers to action: to consideration of tactics and strategies for moving forward. Combined with thoughtful analysis of the situation, there is also a need to develop an action analysis of what to do.

Referring to the Vanuatu case, such tactical and strategic questions might be: "Do we engage in active non-violent struggle against real estate agents, local elites within the Land Department, and international agents such as the Asian Development Bank and Australian Government?" or "Should we just get pragmatic and learn to get the best deal for our land through leasing and sub-leasing?" or "Do we then try to use the money we earn to educate our children and young people in Western forms of liv-ing, giving them the chance to find a cash-earning job?" It can be difficult to make these distinctions and decisions between alternative analyses.

Holding the practitioner analysis lightly

Practitioners engaged in community processes bring well-developed personal and professional skills of what we would call *practitioner analy-sis*—the use of traditional analytical skills (sorting, sifting, questioning, collating and so forth) to the understanding of a problem with the goal of devising a solution. Peter's reflection on the complexities of land in Vanuatu is an example of good practitioner analysis. He sat down with a sheet of blank paper and considered all the economic, political and social forces that are at play within Vanuatu, collecting information and sifting and sorting into an analysis of some of the key issues and potential strate-gies. Practitioner analysis aims to be accurate and astute, and workers need to use all their analytical skills and their acumen in social and politi-cal science to understand a situation. However, while a worker might be conducting this practitioner analysis within themselves, they will usually put the analysis 'on hold' or at least hold it lightly, to create space for a group to develop their analysis.

Building a group analysis

A group analysis is enfolded within a participatory process, actively con-
ducted by people who are affected by particular concerns. It is a group
analysis, because as discussed in our reflection on poetic participation
(Chapter 1.2), it will not usually include everyone within a neighbourhood, village, or other kind of place. Usually it will start with a group of
people on the 'edge' of a space—women, young people, or some other
marginalised group.

Within the process of group analysis the practitioner enables people
to collect data, sit with a paper and marker pens, and try to 'connect the
dots' themselves, building their own understanding of the relationships
between issues, problems and actors, in such a way that they discover a
way forward. A practitioner may intercede and gain a mandate from the
people to add to the analysis, or suggest that the group invite an 'expert'
to share information that might be critical to building the analysis. The
point is that the group analysis aims to be accurate, astute and informed,
and to involve the group of people *themselves* in designing actions that are
effective and have a high level of ownership and commitment.

We do not want to imply that the 'data' is merely information. Of
course, it will be infused with meaning for each participant, and it is important that within the participatory process of group analysis the practitioner creates a space where there is a high level of intimacy and vulnerability that enables all people's views to be expressed.

Another of the key processes in both the thinking and the acting dimensions of group analysis is to separate the technical tasks. On the one hand,
the 'dot-connecting' part of analysis requires that somewhere—maybe on
a whiteboard, a piece of butcher's paper, or in the sand—the practitioner
gather what we call the 'data' emerging from people's stories and their
perspectives.

However, there is a different process that must move on from generating
data and connecting the dots. This second process involves developing a joint
agreement about what to do as a result of examining the patterns of data. It
is one thing for a participatory group to make sense of what is going on; it
is quite another to agree on what to do (tactics, strategies, actions, activities)

and how to do it (who, where, and when). We refer to the two processes as *data generation* and *agreement generation*. They are both part of the process of analysis, but it is helpful to think of them as distinct processes that are enfolded within one another. Once the group has embarked on both processes then it is moving ahead—it has taken the next step in public work.

Building the other into a dialogical community analysis

In reflecting on transformational community practice, the question arises: how does a dialogical approach to community development enrich, or inform, an understanding of this process of doing group analysis? The question can be usefully explored through an identification of movements that widen our analysis beyond the normative gaze of practitioners and usual suspects that overlooks the 'other'. The task of building a dialogical group analysis is to include the 'other' in three distinct ways. These widening movements help us to consider and build a dialogue with 'other' within an emerging analysis.

The first widening movement simply is to ensure that 'other' people, who are not usually considered important, are invited into the process of moving from a group to a wider-community analysis. People's conception of community usually includes people more 'like us'—people easier to relate to or easier to access. The 'other' dimension of the movement ensures that we consider the invisible people:

- the poorest
- the rural—those on marginal land within rural settings
- the homeless—therefore unable to respond to a letter-box or door-knock survey
- out-of-school young people—not at school and therefore we are required to get onto the streets to find them
- sufferers of domestic violence—who often are not able to go to meetings because their partner exercises control over their lives
- future generations—who have no voice.

A dialogical group analysis ensures hospitality towards that 'other-community' often considered not so easy to include. The accuracy, authentic-

ty of the analysis will be determined by the degree to which
an participate.

d widening movement involves thinking about those usu-
ther' in terms of 'enemy' or adversary—people or organisations that are often purposefully excluded. Most community development work is engaged with conflictual kinds of relationships, in which
there are conflicts and concerns over people's divergent agendas. This
is not to deny that solidarity with the poor is the primary factor. However, in thinking about the other as 'enemy', community workers can
diminish the possibility of finding common ground. For example, in the
Vanuatu case study, how do we think about the commercial banks oper-
ating in Vanuatu? Do we consider Westpac Bank (one of the major banks
involved in financing loans for investment purposes) as an enemy, and
therefore should we reconsider our attitude towards it?

A dialogical approach, while at times advocating actions against others, does not start with them. A dialogical approach initiates a process
by at least engaging in dialogue with the traditional 'other'—politicians,
bureaucrats, corporate leaders, chambers of commerce, multinationals.
Within this commitment to dialogue, it is important to acknowledge the
complex deliberative democratic processes that are often required to bring
lasting social change.

During 1988, people in West End were upset with the pre-Expo 88 development. Many were made homeless both by the loss of dwellings,
knocked down for development, and by the spiralling pressures of ris-
ing rents. In this context, some colleagues organised a large gathering
of local residents who came together to watch the movie *The Milagro
Beanfield War*, a fictional story about a local struggle against global corporate power.

At the end of the movie people started discussing and debating what
they could do in their neighbourhood as a response to the making of
homelessness. A community analysis was starting to develop. However, it became clear that this analysis was underpinned by a framework
where landlords, as 'other', were being perceived as enemies—as 'bad'

people. One person in the meeting eventually stood up and challenged this, advocating that we conduct an action that publicly rewarded landlords who were not putting up the rent and therefore not evicting local people, while also confronting those who were evicting local people for the primary purpose of profit.

Within this emerging dialogical analysis the 'other' was not considered enemy, and strategies or tactics were chosen that reflected this analysis. The chosen strategies included (i) a group going on a hunger strike until 50 local landlords could be found who would declare that they were either maintaining the rent as it was or decreasing it in the light of people's economic hardships. These landlords were then presented with bouquets of flowers in a public ceremony; (ii) groups of people sleeping on the street outside the houses of landlords who were evicting local people to cash in on Expo—primarily a symbolic action to confront these landlords with the reality of their actions in creating local homelessness. Such landlords were not sneered at or abused—they were silently and symbolically challenged to confront their own greed.

Jesus
3rd way

The story illustrates the importance of re-thinking our habitual way of framing the other as enemy, and invites reflection on assumptions about them.

The third widening movement invites consideration of the 'other' in terms of what is included within the analysis. Usually this is limited to the most visible elements—economic and political dynamics and forces. People are also increasingly aware of the importance of social, psychological and maybe even cultural dynamics and forces. However, the perspective outlined here invites engagement with *all* the dynamics and forces at work within a given space and also pays soulful attention to intuition, energies, and creativities when considering a way forward. Awareness of these interconnections requires the nurturing of practitioners' own inner/outer connections through integrating thinking, feeling and doing. This is Peter's reflection on how he engages this process:

> I meditate daily for approximately half an hour. This process of meditation attunes me to my body and feelings as well as the many thoughts

that make up my 'monkey mind'. One of the key feeling dimensions of this meditation is to become conscious of my connection to land. I feel the earth when I do a walking meditation. This feeling of connection to earth in turn sits within my gut when I am involved in discussions about the loss of people's land in Vanuatu. People are displaced from their land which is an economic (livelihood), political (who has the power to do the displacing) and cultural concern (people lose access to sacred sites), but it is also a spiritual and personal concern.

We find it useful to think of these movements as a shift in self-perception of the group, from recognising that it represents a limited perspective *within* the community to an acknowledgement that it represents a limited perspective that is *alongside/among* and in dialogue with other perspectives in the wider community.

Valuing unresolved tension and contested understanding

Let's go a little deeper into analysing the second widening movement. Taken to its logical extreme, dialogical analysis challenges community workers to include the very people who are identified as the 'problem' within a group analysis, and to build a new analysis *with them* that informs a shared, if not a collaborative, agenda of action. This is the tough bit—what happens when you sit down with the enemy and attempt to build a shared wider community analysis? It brings to mind the cartoon in which environmentalists advocating sustainable development negotiate with multinationals advocating rapacious exploitation—and end up with sustainable exploitation. It is important to guard against the dangers of being co-opted. Of course any polarisation of analysis—friend or enemy, sustainable or exploitative—is antithetical to dialogue, which is best informed by a diversity of perspectives.

Peter and Gerard are part of a collegial community of interest, the South East Queensland Intercultural Cities Forum (SEQICF), which aims to encourage deep intercultural dialogue and engagement across the region. In 2007 SEQICF designed and facilitated a dialogical community analysis process, *Out of the Shadows*, which aimed to identify new and emerging intercultural issues in south-east Queensland; document differing perspectives on these emerging issues and options to address these; and be a catalyst for coordinated responses too preventing inter- and intra- cultural conflict.

The *Out of the Shadows* process created a safe space for dialogue, where people from different religious and cultural backgrounds, with a variety of ways of understanding inter-cultural conflict and different roles and responsibilities, could meet and hear one another's experiences and perspectives. Participants included families, young victims, young perpetrators, cultural elders, community representatives, frontline workers, academics, policy analysts, and government workers in multicultural affairs, police, social policy, community development and community safety.

There was a whole process of community engagement in the months before the event, and an invitation to participants that explicitly stated 'principles of dialogue' that they accepted as a condition of participating. The main activities through the two-day event were 'fishbowl sessions', a series of facilitated dialogues between 8-10 key informants in the centre of the room, with another 60 or so people watching and listening from rows of seats on either side. These sessions were interspersed with lighter times of musical and dance performances, short films, good food, and plenty of time for informal chat in breaks.

In terms of outcomes, the analysis provided a rich depth of material that is informing new directions in policy and practice. Some of these more promising directions emerge precisely from the points of unresolved tension and contested understanding that were highlighted in the dialogue.

In *Out of the Shadows* and other formalised dialogue processes, it is necessary to set ground rules or principles of dialogue to frame the nature of the discussion. These may include practices such as speaking and listening from the heart, honouring silence, suspending judgment, listening with perception, looking within one's self, identifying assumptions, and maintaining an attitude of learning and a spirit of enquiry. Facilitators negotiate an agreement with participants to work from these principles. This gives the group a point of reference to guide the process when people depart from the agreement—a frequent occurrence, because people are not used to this way of relating to one another in contested territory.

Dialogical community analysis requires an appreciation of the dynamic of *affirmation* and *scepticism*. Affirmation consists of validating the perspectives expressed. The assumption is that a view expressed is not only valid from the participant's point of view, but that it also expresses something significant about the whole of the matter. Colin Peile's (1994) holographic paradigm suggests that the sharpest focus in an analysis will come from assembling, legitimating and attending to as many views as possible at the same time. In this context scepticism means working from the assumption that a perspective emerges from a particular point of view, from a particular horizon, and therefore is less likely to express the whole of the truth about a situation, and more likely to express insight, agenda and potential.

A key challenge is not just to hear different perspectives and incorporate them into a more holistic understanding, but also to value the dialogue between unresolved tensions and contested analysis. It is often the voices that are considered 'problematic' that open up new possibilities. It is often in the intensity of energised disagreement that people are pushed beyond the recycling of preference, ideology, habit and disappointment.

The challenge for the practitioner-facilitator is to value dissent, hold the tension and keep the dialogue open by maintaining goodwill and an inquisitive 'community of enquiry'. John Forester in *The Deliberative Practitioner* (1999) argues that "much more is at stake in dialogic and argumentative processes . . . At stake too are issues of political membership and identity, memory and hope, confidence and competence, appreciation and respect, acknowledgement and the ability to act together" (p115-116). The careful engagement in dialogical and deliberative processes amongst people of difference is transformational—it can create community.

Shared insight dawns on a group's life when a creative synthesis opens up a surprising potential at the heart of an apparently implacable contradiction or contention. The moment is often characterised by a pause in the discussion, silence, a deep listening to something said that would usually not have been heard, the realisation of the significance of the suggestion, and the unspoken resolve of the group to take the risk involved and move forward together.

> At *Out of the Shadows* one young participant said "For the Muslims, when we see our indigenous brothers and sisters, and they are still experiencing straight-out racism, both covertly and overtly, it is our community that says 'well, what chance do we have?'" This insight led to an analysis that the poor treatment of indigenous people sets the standard for ways in which diverse groups feel they are being treated, and to a new resolve to make "addressing the legacy of colonialism for all Australians" a priority in the ongoing work of the South East Queensland Intercultural Cities Forum.

This emergent analysis linked the experiences of Muslim and indigenous young people in ways previously not considered by the leaders of each of those cultural communities. This linking created new relationships and a sense of solidarity between previously isolated struggles for justice.

2.3 Empowerment: transforming our power

Sites of community life are full of different interest groups and entrenched conflicts. Any notion of community development that implies transformation requires an understanding of power and the dynamics of power relationships within social spaces. A dialogical approach does not imply voluntary change or transformation without the possibility of conflict and confrontation. On the contrary, it is often some form of violent experience, something that the psyche experiences as shocking, that leads to the start of recovery and healing. This is also true within community development—change may come about through the shock of conflict or crisis and a sudden manifestation of different agendas and power dynamics.

> World Expo 88 was a huge international affair requiring a large area of land to build exhibition tents for display of culture from around the world. Contrary to recommendations from a government research re-

port, the state government of Queensland decided to locate the Expo in the centre of Brisbane city—the neighbourhood of South Brisbane. The report made it clear that this option would lead to the creation of many homeless people, and transport and construction chaos. However, the politics of inner city-gentrification and financial and speculative capital sidelined the report. For those of us living in the neighbourhood, it was this shock that mobilised action and generated a coming together of people in a transformative experience of belonging and empowerment.

This type of situation seems to be becoming more common. As community workers we desire to become hospitable to our selves and to 'others'. But what are practitioners to do if other people in the neighbourhood do not share the same wishes? What if those in power refuse to acknowledge the reality of the poor? Revisiting the Expo 88 story, what should be done when the state government sidelines recommendations in reports based on concerns for people rather than concerns for profit? What should be done when some people in the neighbourhood support the process as a chance for some private landlords to make heaps of cash, and for some local traders to finally get rid of the poor? These points create the need for personal and communal power—a power that can annoy, confront and persuade.

Relational work and supportive co-responsibility

Let's start with personal power. Poverty is intimately connected to power; our analysis sees powerlessness as a primary cause of poverty. It can then be useful to consider powerlessness broadly and think about it in terms of:

- Cultural powerlessness—for example, people who are marginalised or excluded from access and opportunities because of their cultural, ethnic, or sub-cultural markers, or through lack of education.
- Social powerlessness—for example, people whose experience is deeply connected to their social location of gender, disability, age/generation, health or illness, and their lack of social connections to people who can "help them get ahead".

- Economic powerlessness—related to class and economic strati-
fication; insufficient financial capital, poor access to credit and so
forth.
- Political powerlessness—disenfranchisement, statelessness, youth,
age, lack of connections to people who have influence.
- Spiritual powerlessness—a loss of identity, a lack of self-mastery
and confidence.

All of these different experiences of powerlessness are destructive to life
chances and opportunities. Dialogical community development works
with people's experience of powerlessness through engaging people's
stories and then inviting people to join with others to work for change.
Someone's story could be about their experience of social powerlessness
("I'm in a wheelchair and don't have access to transport in my neighbourhood") or economic powerlessness ("I'm stuck living in this caravan park
because I cannot afford the rent for a house"); however the beginning point
of moving towards empowerment involves the interplay between personal
responsibility ("I want to do something about this") and supportive *co-responsibility*—a practitioner, a neighbour, a colleague, or someone living the
same experience saying "shall we do something about this together?" Enfolded within both these notions of personal responsibility and co-responsibility are rights—which are really about some 'other' person's responsibility: maybe the local council needs to take responsibility for making
existing buses more accessible to someone in a wheelchair.

Personal power starts with the (co-)responsibility to act. It cannot be
avoided by invoking social or structural perspectives on poverty and its
causes. However, a critical point from the perspective of dialogical community work is that such personal power—initially expressed as something like "I want to do something about my situation"—can be activated
through someone else engaging *relationally* with that person who is struggling with a sense of personal powerlessness. The change process is not
some individual cognitive process of shaking oneself and saying 'I can do
this', or 'pulling oneself up by the bootstraps'; it is a relational process.

As Fritz Schumacher (1974, p161) reminds us, poverty can be understood as a condition of someone being "destroyed by the inner conviction

of uselessness". Overcoming this conviction of uselessness requires something other than just positive thinking. Gaining personal power, which involves overcoming such a conviction, can be triggered through relational processes that are experienced as supportive co-responsibility. The dialogical and hospitable engagement with someone's story is often critical in their personal transformation—a shift from seeing themselves as worthless, to seeing in the loving attention of a comrade that they are 'worthy'. This relational experience can be the catalyst for transformational processes that involve confidence building, the restoring of self-worth, and daring to dream again.

Power-with and co-operative power

This relational approach to empowerment is a practical way of working with communal power within community development. This approach exposes the contrasts between *power-with* and *power-over* (Butcher et al., 2007). The idea of power-with focuses on not trying to control others. While community workers are committed to supportive co-responsibility, the gaze always remains focused on controlling ourselves. It is easy for discussions of responsibility and change to move towards manipulation and changing others—'trying to make others more responsible'. However, in controlling ourselves, community workers can enter into co-operative mutual loving relationships that are at the heart of empowering community.

In a dialogical community development process, this coming together provides a degree of communal power that is a critical next step in empowerment. Empowerment is partly a result of the opus of people working together, of experiencing poetic participation. One of the challenges within this work is how to facilitate a cultural transformation towards a co-operative understanding of power (Andrews, 2007) and away from the hegemonic wielding of coercive power (the 'power of the stick') and co-opting power (the 'power of the carrot'), which are the common ways of experiencing and expressing power in our social systems.

In the earlier reflection on participation, we advocated that 'people's participation' needs to be informed by the perspective of autonomous development—that is, autonomous human agency and people's power. Participation is not about people aligning themselves with outsider-initiated developmental interventions, and neither is empowerment about people 'being empowered'. It is about people moving from dependency to co-operative control, where people control the process of defining their own needs and satisfiers. Community development involves building democratic people's organisations that disperse power across a group—creating a new sociality of power that enables them to structure their own initiatives. A co-operative approach to power infuses the on-going process of building and maintaining relationships within such groups and organisations. It also shapes co-operative partnership with other organisations.

Autonomous development pathways in no way imply that the state is exempt from participation. On the contrary, empowerment requires a partnership between an effective state and people's movements (Mayo 1999, p4; Green, 2008). Part of the outcome of empowerment is people finding their voice, building an analysis of who is responsible, and building the organisational ability to assert their democratic will. The state often becomes the target of this analysis and will.

Skilled and soulful power

We now turn to consider power in more depth. How can community practitioners reflect more carefully on attempts to engage in power-with and co-operative types of relationships? What conceptual tools do community workers have to ensure the dialogical process remains consistent with the call to love?

Thomas Moore and Jack Kornfield provide some useful ways of thinking about this through two contrasting types of power. For Moore (1992), heroic-egotistical power is in opposition to soulful power, while Kornfield (1993) contrasts unskilled-painful power with skilled power. The qualities of heroic-egotistical and unskilled-painful types of power are grasping, greed, longing and inadequacy; while the qualities of soulful, skilled types of power are those of creativity, wisdom, vitality, love and compassion. Such soulful power could be understood as closely related to Gandhi's notion of soul-force—essentially a moral-spiritual power.

It is important to recognise that conceptualising power in these dualistic ways is not about a moral choice of one over the other. The actual substantive forms of power will be more or less the same, but there will be a subtle shift in the nature of the power exercised, the energy behind the power. People have options within the power exercised; the need is to bring an acute attention to this process.

In providing names for two types of power, we are simply examining what lies beneath our actions, whether it is the relational level of micro-method, or the mezzo, macro or meta levels of joining people together, forming organisations or linking groups.

One of our colleagues in West End, Carmel, has taught us a lot about the experience of people in our neighbourhood who can't read and write very well. When she became involved in the community, she started getting to know people in hostels and boarding houses. When some of them learned that she wasn't good at reading and writing either, they opened up to her about how they found it hard to look after their money, shopping and medicine.

Carmel started the West End Reading and Writing Group on Wednesday mornings in a local community centre—in contrast to the local TAFE Literacy and Numeracy Course that people couldn't join because they didn't understand the timetable and couldn't fill in the enrolment forms! She took on the role of group co-ordinator, and Gerard supported her to access state government funding to pay for her work (sometimes), buy some resources and hire a teacher. We linked with a local community group who auspiced the grants in a supportive way and let Carmel get on with what she did best—helping people to learn to read and write better by getting alongside them as a trusted companion. Her work in this role was a delightfully subtle, relational form of supportive co-responsibility infused with wisdom, love and compassion. With Carmel as their role-model, others in the group took on responsibility for things like morning tea, washing up, supporting one another to get there, and so on. Over the last fifteen years the vagaries of government funding have some and gone, but the West End Reading and Writing Group continues to meet.

Carmel found the experience transformational, to the extent that at one time she ran a project that she called 'Easy Words are Better', where she visited community groups and suggested ways for them to improve their communication with people who couldn't read and write very well.

The exercise of skilled and soulful power calls for moral examination—not a moralistic desire for pure motives, but a desire for awareness and depth, that can promote clarity and transform choice. Such an examination will enable a shift in the energy behind transformational work, bringing depth to people's power which will result in greater, sustained energy and resilience.

Dangers of unskilled and soul-less power

In bringing this kind of attentiveness to the exercise of power, it can be helpful to name some of the dangers that lie within unskilled and heroic power that can easily trip community workers up.

The first danger is *narcissism*. This danger reflects the problem of heroic self-interest as individuals or a group become mobilised—but with a mobilisation not grounded in love, nor informed by a wider analysis, and lacking a moral commitment. There is a risk that practitioners become attached to the image or collective *persona* of being activists rather than being motivated by care for people. The collective ideology becomes primary and the being or making of community secondary. Gandhi's greatest triumph was in recognising that the human social dynamic of love must remain primary and the political outcome secondary.

The second danger is that *we become what we hate*. Within the exercising of power there lies a powerful shadow. As mentioned previously, community development work while committed to dialogical processes may also engage in conflict with 'others'. In using energy against people seen as adversary, opponent or enemy there is a risk of becoming in many ways the same as the adversary or enemy. This is true of psychological dynamics; for example, an alcoholic who fights against being an alcoholic can actually give energy to the addiction. The 'hating of the alcoholic within' leads down the road of alcoholism. Walter Wink (1992), in his groundbreaking theological treatise *Engaging the Powers*, demonstrates how this process is equally true in the social world. Wink discusses in depth an example of how the Allies, during World War II, became as 'hateful' as the German army, climaxing in the abominable bombing of Dresden. The warning here is to be very careful in exercising power. We need to ask ourselves: what are the motivations and energies feeding our work, our participation, and our confrontations with the 'other' powers?

The third danger is *passivity*. Egotistically oriented acts of power may reflect a deep inner passivity. The outer energy can have a shadow of inner emptiness. Soulfully inspired action is goal-orientated—action filled with passion and vitality. In contrast, an action that is simply an attempt to flee our own passivity is unskilled. People simply jump on a band-wagon, and their involvement in action brings the danger of bypassing the inner *opus* and alchemy of connection with deep values and commitments.

Identifying these dangers enables community workers to take precautions. We can question the energy behind our use of power in a particular situation. Are our desires, which legitimise our exercise of power, simply rationalisations for narcissism? Are they simply heroic attempts to escape our passivity rather than soulful, passionate attempts to build community? Is the power exercised transforming us into the images of our enemies?

Reflective practice requires an understanding of our own innocence, denial and belief. We may believe we are too innocent to become like the enemy. We deny our own shadows and hold to the belief that our crusade or exercise of power is grounded in truth. We need to stop and reflect with honesty that acknowledges not only the energy of compassion, anger and wisdom, but the possible energies of narcissism, violence and longing. We might not be so different from the enemy; in their position we could well do the same. But our entry into an awareness that enables us to debunk our own innocence and be free from our denials will enable us to transform the kind of power we exercise.

2.4 Structuring not strangling

In the previous reflection we argued that a key part of the work is building democratic people's organisations that disperse power across a group, creating a new sociality of power that enables people to structure their own initiatives. We also alluded to this organisation-building process when discussing the macro and meta levels of the method. This reflection discusses in more depth the importance of building place-based community-oriented structures within transformational community work, a process that we have called *structuring the work*.

Innovative structures

One of the key transitions within transformational community work is the shift from a participatory action group, characterised by informal relationships based on mutual interest—what we call non-formal work—to an organisational *structure* in which a group's relationships become characterised by roles and responsibilities and are defined not in relation to one another but in relation to the group as an entity.

There are many reasons for this kind of transition. Sometimes the number of people involved in a group has grown to the point where they can no longer make decisions by involving all members in a discussion around a table. Once a group has grown to more than about twelve people, it becomes almost impossible to maintain informal processes, and necessary to set up more democratic ones. Sometimes a group is taking public action or making public statements, and needs a name as an entity in its own right; people may call for more formal, accountable and transparent processes of decision making; or a group needs to engage with the formal system and structures, usually of the state, for the purposes of grant acquisition, management, insurance, audits and so forth. Authors such as Henderson and Thomas (2002) have written extensively about what groups should consider when choosing to make this transition.

People often make the mistake of thinking that they have to become a legally incorporated organisation. But there is real value in formalising organised structure, *without* becoming a legal entity. A group might take on a name for itself, assign simple non-hierarchical roles such as convenor, and have a rotating chair and minute-taker to facilitate and record meetings. Of course, people might also choose to form a formal legally based organisation—usually in the form of a not-for-profit association, a co-operative or company structure. However, one of the key problems for community-based work is that people tend to move too quickly from being an informal or non-formal participatory action group to becoming a formalised legal structure. The leap is made without considering both the risks of making that shift and also the alternative options, such as the one illustrated below.

> We were angry. We had formed the West End Refugee Support Group—a non-formal organisation with roles, rules and procedures, but without the legal trappings (we were not incorporated in any way). We had been welcoming and working with newly arrived refugee families for several years. However, as our work expanded we found that we needed a legal entity to act as auspice, to take care of some financial grants that we were accessing, for example to employ a tutor to run home-based language classes for refugee women. Every time we approached an organisation as a potential legal auspice, it seemed that they wanted 20% of the grant money and also wanted to control at least some of our activities. For example, one organisation that we approached said 'yes' on the condition that they could decide who should be the project worker.
>
> We were not happy with these conditions and the impact on our work. So we started thinking about turning the West End Refugee Support Group from a non-formal organisation into a formalised legal structure, so that we would no longer need an auspice, but we could just do it ourselves—which is what many groups do at that stage in their life. But in considering this option we started to recognise some of the risks: the main one being that our organic grassroots energy would become focused on the organisation—setting it up, maintaining it, finding money to pay for insurance and audits and so on. So a few of us started to consider what alternative options we had.
>
> Peter and Gerard started talking about setting up a new community-based organisation that could act as a local formal structure, to auspice the work not only of the West End Refugee Support Group, but also a whole heap of other organic grassroots work that was occurring in the neighbourhood. We could see the potential nightmare of every participatory action group structuring their own work through forming their own legally incorporated organisation—a proliferation of organisations

all requiring voluntary management committee members, insurance, and audit fees. We had seen it happen in other contexts. We decided there must be another way.

After some deliberation we considered that we needed a minimalist model—a formal incorporated association that would provide the necessary legal and official cover, but would exert minimal control over the community-based activities. The idea was that the West End Refugee Support Group and any other local group would be able to utilise this non-controlling auspice for their purposes of interacting with more formal systems.

In May 1994 the Community Initiatives Resource Association (CIRA) was incorporated under the Associations Incorporation Act. The minimalist model was encapsulated in the principles of CIRA. It was like a two-dollar shelf company, set up to resource community initiatives, with a management committee that had vowed that the organisation as a whole would never actually run any of its own community projects. The idea was that any members who wanted to do something had to form their own working group to organise and manage their initiative. We were clear that the business of the management committee was to manage the organisation as a whole, but not to micro-manage these working groups and projects—it would delegate authority and responsibility to the people doing the work. Through this innovative, minimalist model CIRA fulfils the contracting, insurance, accounting, auditing, and reporting needs of many local and some non-local groups. It continues to this day and has auspiced well over 100 local initiatives and hundreds of thousands of dollars in cash flow (Barringham, 2003).

Those of us involved in CIRA have reflected for many years on the beauty of setting up this local structure. We realised that the other options for these grassroots groups had included becoming either reliant on a larger organisation that would auspice our local work, with all the associated risks mentioned—such as overcharging on an auspice fee, or wanting to control the work; or every action group setting up their own legal structure, which would exhaust people sitting on multiple committees, finding money for insurance and audits and so on. CIRA was based upon a different paradigm, where the local structure was to be a shared legal auspice working in a parallel structure with community groups and projects. It only needed one management committee and one annual audit. It enabled many organic grassroots groups to engage with the formal system of legality and finance (grants, accounts, audits, insurance) without having to worry too much about it. Such groups could focus on what they did best and were set up to do: the work of participatory action. This kind of structuring of the work releases local energy, imagination and action. When we reflected on the work after the first ten years, someone coined the phrase 'structuring not strangling', which seemed to describe the process beautifully.

Small and accountable structures

However, this kind of structuring of the work is becoming increasingly difficult. More and more regulation by state structures, combined with more and more interest in neo-liberal logics of efficiencies and economies of scale, have led to the decimation of place-based community-oriented structures. Small is no longer beautiful in the eyes of the powerful. Gerard reflects on this shift:

> When I started in the field, in the early 1990s, you could still get funding for small local initiatives. I remember talking with elderly residents who couldn't get to the shops, doctor or hospital. I wrote a funding submission and got $3,000 to organise a church mini-bus driven by unemployed local young people to pick up residents of three local retirement units twice a week. If I put together the same submission today, any funding body I know would want it to be a $50,000 'regional partnership initiative' meeting 'complex needs' across a 'corridor of disadvantage'.

One of our colleagues, Howard Buckley (2007), has provided a succinct analysis of what is going on within our home state of Queensland, Australia. He argues that that there are several syndromes that have become endemic within community settings:

- The *'bigger is better' syndrome* in which larger national bodies, such as church organisations, have positioned themselves to attract funds for human service delivery due to their perceived efficiencies *and* capacity to deliver through economies of scale. This syndrome also includes organisations aspiring to function as large corporate entities despite having started as small locality-based, community-based organisations. It is fuelled by Commonwealth Government funding programs that offer funding for regional-scale programs in response to national needs analysis.

- The *'absorption' syndrome* in which smaller community-based organisations become absorbed by larger organisations, losing their autonomy and legal status as they amalgamate with the larger entity.

- The *'go it alone' syndrome* in which smaller community-based organisations attempt to find their place in this changing environment, but find they are unable to compete with the larger entities, particularly for sub-regional and regional funding programs, thereby eroding their capacity to grow their services.

There is an increasing proliferation of structures that are not community–based organisations. They soak up resources and space, and demand attention in localities. Yet from the perspective of dialogical community development, they are fundamentally flawed because they have not emerged from people's place-based struggles to build community or tackle community issues—that is, from people's own analysis of their situation. Instead the authority for the work comes from bureaucratic 'needs analysis' and allocations of government money. Within such logics, when the money moves the work will move. Such organisations only relate to space; they have not done the work of emplacement and made a place their base. They therefore remain unaccountable to people in those places.

One of the most significant consequences of this kind of shift is that such large organisations are not grounded in the local web of relationships that makes up community life. They find it almost impossible to be *amongst* this web, and build genuine community with it. After all, they employ professionals who usually do not come from that local place, and who have been trained to maintain their boundaries with local people.

Instead they provide services to the 'community' as a territorialised population—an object, not a subject.

The irony of this shift is that the very infrastructure people have been building for years—that creates platforms for meeting, weaving the web of relationships that enables organic support, care and 'community as hospitality'—is de-funded, or simply strangled to death by regulation, compliance and over-burdening accountabilities. People become less able to support one another and thereby more dependent on the services provided by such large organisations. Such organisations create a society in which there is plenty of 'grass' but no 'roots'; you can see all the activity, but it is not sustainable.

Structuring beyond the local

This is not to say that structuring the work must only remain oriented towards the local. In the resourcing environment described above, dialogical community development must be pragmatically trans-local. It must create new structures that tackle trans-local issues, and thereby focus on Freire's 'whole' rather than just the 'parts'. It must build structures that are trans-local but are still grounded within the multiple 'locales' where they are rooted. While the macro-level work will build a structure such as CIRA, the meta-work needs to build bridging structures that link beyond this local focus but remain grounded within the local. Manfred Max-Neef provides the following example of structuring for the meta-level work of 'beyond the local', the ECU-28 project that structured the work of peasants to address rural poverty in an Andean region of Ecuador:

> The methodology of the project was to mobilise a participatory process of *horizontal communication* between villages who rarely had the opportunity to meet together, and create a shared understanding of their problems through building a regional consciousness.
>
> The project avoided the more orthodox process of peasants from different villages talking to the 'vertical structures' of the state only as individual villages—that is, each village making its own representation about its 'village problems'. Instead, through a series of grassroots processes, supported by the project, village committees were brought to-

gether to formulate a regional analysis of their state of affairs—which they could then take to the relevant state authorities *as a whole*.

Through the process of 'provincial encounters'—which consisted of village committees meeting together, learning from one another, building a shared community analysis, they formed a *regional structure*—a Regional Peasants' Congress. Such a Congress was still rooted in the local—people represented their local villages and reported back to the whole village—yet it created a regional analysis and regional people's power-base (Max-Neef, 1992, p25-117).

This story highlights some important features and processes of building regional structures within a transformational framework:

- Building horizontal relationships between people who have similar experiences, but have not been able to share with one another.
- Strengthening these horizontal relationships to the point where people can build more formal structures.
- Maintaining clear lines of communication and accountability between the local and the newly forming regional structure.
- Nurturing participatory leadership where the emergent leaders remain committed to an ethos of on-going participation rather than accumulation of power.
- Recognising that while larger structures require some kind of role definition, the key ethos should remain relational rather than role-oriented.
- Spending time on building a strong sense of shared values and vision.

We could look at many other case studies that show how to structure transformational work beyond even the regional and provincial and move into a national and trans-national scope. For example, the work of the Indian Karnataka Farmers' Federation (Couch, 2006, p35-37), Judy Wick's work in forming the Business Alliance for Local Living Economies (BALLE) (Wicks, 2004, p25ff), South Africa's Treatment Action Campaign (Green, 2008, p242) or the International Baby Food Action Network (IB-FAN) (Eade, 1997, p156).

Closer to home, some colleagues have been building a different kind of regional structure on the Sunshine Coast of south-east Queensland. Their work is a response to the decisions of some government departments to grant funding only to regionally oriented organisations or work. The consequence for the Sunshine Coast was to threaten many years of local community effort invested in building local neighbourhood centres. Large organisations, often with no local base, were applying for and winning grant opportunities—by employing consultants to prepare swish applications—and then ironically starting to network with the local neighbourhood centres to build local contacts, understanding, and credibility. The services they provided could not build on local community life; they were not amongst the community and often the workers did not know the local people. The local neighbourhood centres in the region decided to fight back.

> In 2007 four local structures: the Caloundra Neighbourhood Centre, the Hinterland Community Development Association, the Maroochy Neighbourhood Centre and Nambour Community Centre, decided to get together and start a process of forming a regional structure that would be able to compete within the regionally oriented funding market, yet be structured in such a way as to remain grounded within the local work of the neighbourhood centres. The Sunshine Coast Community Co-op was formed; it acts not as a 'super-structure' that will swallow up each local organisation, but as an enabling structure that respects each of the organisations. Each organisation is developing capacity to engage with the issues, both in its own areas, and also in the areas of its new partner organisations (Buckley, 2007, p2).

The story of this organisation illustrates some innovative ways to structure the work so that local issues can be engaged with at a regional level, but still remain small enough for local people to participate poetically. The structures remain as people's infrastructure—built from the bottom up, drawing on horizontal relationships (between neighbourhood centres and associations) and yet able to interact with the vertical formal system (usually donors or/and government). Such a model provides an alternative pathway to the conventional practice of large NGOs simply dropping in with a ready-made 'blueprint' approach to provision of services.

Structures as people's structures, not service-oriented agents

To legitimise their work, many social structures have to demonstrate a need for some service. They become experts at creating need, and then argue that they are the experts at addressing that need—usually through their services (McKnight, 1995). While emphasising the importance of good services, we can also observe that these services have often been provided to the detriment of supporting community-based responses to local challenges.

Youth Force is a community-based organisation within New York's South Bronx. This organisation was set up by young people with the view that young people are resourceful, rather than troubled people who need more services. Their analysis was that any services provided should emerge from a broader youth-led community development approach. In 1999, Youth Force formulated the idea of a democracy multiplied zone (DMZ) to mobilise young people in the South Bronx into a youth-led movement for social change.

Their strategy was built on a particular process of youth empowerment. First, most young people struggle in silence. They start finding their voice by talking to friends or speaking publicly at meetings. Then they see suffering or injustice and try to deal with it through community service, legal education or court support. They then develop a political analysis—through education and training—and decide that power must be challenged. Then they rock the system by increasing the involvement of young people in the issue. Then they build coalitions and alliances with other organisations, to build a stronger voice and make some noise through rallies and demonstrations.

The young people in the DMZ engage in work such as: (i) outreach through forming teams and conducting street theatre; (ii) recruitment through local chapters to involve young people in organising; (iii) education and training through such initiatives as their ten-week training program in community organising ('Youth Organising 101') and the Street University workshops in political theory, organisational development and community change, electoral participation, and critical awareness of the media's depiction of young people. (Checkoway et al., 2008).

This case study involves local young people structuring their own work in mobilising participatory action groups, community organising and political protest. Such an organisation does not pathologise young people. It is not service-oriented, at least not initially.

During the 1990s many refugees within Brisbane became tired of the 'service' provided by the torture and trauma clinic based at the Mater Hospital. The focus of that service was clinical work, with strong assumptions about refugee trauma and the need for medically-oriented treatment. By the mid-1990s several leaders from Cambodian and Salvadoran refugee groups decided they had had enough of this clinically and medically oriented service, and initiated a collective process of building their own structure. Over the next couple of years these leaders engaged in the micro and mezzo levels of community work: building relationships with diverse groups, forming an action group, and conducting some community-based research. Finally after much deliberation they formed an incorporated association, called Queensland Program of Assistance to Survivors of Torture and Trauma (QPASTT), to work with refugee individuals, groups and communities within a framework that incorporated clinical, group and community work, and human rights advocacy.

QPASTT, governed by refugees, compatriot professionals and other volunteers, continues to be a vehicle for refugees to find space to heal, for refugee groups to advocate human rights and for the creation of 'community' between refugees and non-refugees. The governance of the organisation is firmly grounded within the 'co-created community' between refugees and non-refugees, rather than being the passive object of a hospital governance system. It is a people's structure.

2.5 Careful conflicting

In the process of community development work, practitioners inevitably meet different groups reflecting differing interests and positions. Given most community workers' commitments and values, conflict is inevitable. This reflection will consider ways of working with conflict that reflect a dialogical, soulful and hospitable approach to community development.

The reality of a shit-fight

Recently when walking home through my neighbourhood a woman handed me a free newspaper. She was handing hundreds of them to people as they walked home from work. I noticed that the front page headline went something like "Global Climate Change is a Fraud". I felt the inner urges of unskilled power—a need to scream at the woman, grab all the papers and throw them in the bin. I didn't. I made the choice to walk away, but feelings of anger accompanied me. I did some research and discovered that the paper is produced by a group of local businessmen.

That week whilst reading George Monbiot's book *Heat: How to Stop the Planet Burning* (2006), I was stunned to read the chapter titled 'The Denial Industry' that exposes corporations that are trying to stop us from taking action. I felt anger towards businessmen and corporations. To add to my anger, the headline of that day's *The Australian* newspaper (30 April, 2007) screamed "Rudd earns wrath of business"—on a story of how big corporations were determined to campaign against the Australian Labour Party because it wanted to restore some 'power' to unions.

Why tell this short, pithy story? Because despite our previous calls to start engaging any conflict with dialogue, we argue that many social conflicts will also require nothing less than what some Australians call a *shit-fight*. We only need to observe the behaviour of some private, and for that matter many public corporations, to conclude that these corporations are pathological in the sense described by Joel Baken in *The Corporation: The Pathological Pursuit of Profit and Power* (2004):

- Corporations are required by law to elevate their own interests above those of others, making them prone to prey upon and exploit others without regard for legal rules or moral limits.
- Corporate social responsibility, though sometimes yielding positive results, most often serves to mask the corporation's true character, not to change it.
- The corporation's unbridled self-interest victimises individuals, the environment, and even shareholders, and can cause corporations to self-destruct.
- Despite its flawed character, governments have freed the corporation from legal constraints through deregulation, and granted it ever greater power over society through privatisation.

At the end of the day it is hard to dialogue with pathological people and organisations. Sometimes a dialogical approach will not work. People will need to confront, challenge, and hold to account some corporations, while agitating and protesting against their excesses. Many corporations are geared only and ruthlessly towards profit, private speculation, economic growth and increased political power. Some are not intent on making the world or our neighbourhoods a better place to live. Sometimes sitting with our anger reminds us of Gandhi's axiom "It is better to do violence than do nothing". In a way, we are attracted to violent action as a release of our antagonism. However Gandhi went on to argue that it is better to engage in *truth-force* (non-violence) than violence, and so the challenge is to re-inhabit our better self.

Traditions of conflicting

There are many approaches to dealing with conflict that sit between the two extremes of violence and dialogue. Anthony Kelly and Sandra Sewell (1988) outline several different traditions that can be drawn upon in dealing with conflict: the Maoist, the Alinskian, the Christian, and finally the Gandhian tradition.

Each tradition has a different logic of conflict, with accompanying attitudes and actions that infuse their strategies and tactics. For the Maoist approach power lies "in the barrel of a gun". The tactics are that of guerrilla warfare—brief incursions into the territory of the enemy, quick retreat, revival and then renewed attack. Skilful use of violence, surprise, retreat and many other elements are central to the tactics.

Within the Alinskian tradition the focus is on a war of "social surgery" (Alinsky, 1969, p133)—a radical confrontation with those in power. While he uses the language of warfare, Saul Alinsky is not advocating violence. In *Reveille for Radicals* he advocates that conflict for the purposes of social goods such as better housing, economic security, or improved health programs, needs to be carried by powerful people's organisations. These organisations must fight in such a way that there will be "no violence, and yet the battle will be sufficiently dramatic to serve as an outlet for the stirred-up passions of people . . . The goal is nothing less than bloodless victory" (1969, p140). The tactics include the use of ridicule, threats—often more terrifying than the actual proposal—and constant pressure.

The Christian tradition subscribes to the power of loving one's enemies. It is an approach of "turn the other cheek". For many this might sound completely passive, but according to more historically astute interpretations of the biblical scriptures, it is actually an invitation to stand up against attempts to humiliate (Wink, 1992, p176). Within this interpretation the Christian approach requires people to stand up to those who attempt to humiliate with a statement that goes something like "try again; your first blow failed to achieve its intended effect. I deny you the power to humiliate me". The approach to conflicting is to persuade your enemy through love combined with tenacity and prevailing.

Within the Gandhian approach there is no enemy, or more accurately "the enemy is within". There are only opponents. While similar to the Christian approach—Gandhi said that he was desperate to find a Christian willing to follow the way of Christ—it is a Gandhian interpretation of Jesus' words that infuses the idea of truth-force or *satyagraha*. Within this approach of truth-force, the tactics are again of persuasion, all sorts of orthodox campaigning and civil disobedience tactics, hence the use of the word 'force'. The key to wielding truth-force is not the threat or fear of violence, but the moral power of non-violent action with truth. Some people describe it as a kind of moral jujitsu (Kurlansky, 2006, p153).

These briefly described traditions illustrate different social approaches to conflict. Each approach has a different conception of the world and opponents/adversaries/enemies. Such differences in turn govern logics, attitudes and actions that will guide us in the inevitable shit-fights that are a part of community development work.

Dialogical conflicting

We can now move away from the assumption and language of fighting to consider the need for dialogue within conflict. While a shit-fight works on the realistic assumption of antagonistic politics, which is discussed in Chapter Three, the hope is for a more idealistic dialogical politic in which people can listen, learn and move towards one another, being hospitable towards the 'other' and therefore becoming community.

It was 2001 and the Tampa Event was occurring within Australia. A Norwegian vessel called the Tampa picked up over 400 asylum seekers from a sinking fishing boat near the Australian coastline. The then Australian Prime Minister declared that no asylum seekers from the Tampa would set foot on Australian soil, and they were shipped off to the island state of Nauru. The Federal Government used a fear-promoting politic against vulnerable Afghan and Iraqi asylum-seekers fleeing war, to legitimise this exclusionary and illegal process. As a refugee advocate I was outraged and was willing to engage in campaigning—as I in fact did. However, at that time I was also a part-time lecturer. What struck me in my university classes was the unwillingness of many 'progressive' people, who supported asylum-seeker and refugee rights, to create a safe space for discussion with their fellow-students. When asking my students "what do you think of this government's campaign against asylum seekers?" some opened up and shared their fears of "being swamped by others", of "people who are different to us coming here".

The progressives in my class immediately jumped on these comments—labelling those 'other' students as racists. Instantly the room was infused by a spirit of deadly debate. People quickly felt that they had to take sides—for or against, progressive or racist, inclusive or exclusive. I was somewhat stunned by the rapid process of polarisation and the inability of people to hear each other. I struggled to restore a safe space of dialogue where people were able to remove labels and try and listen to one another, discerning the fears and needs beneath each position.

My response to that experience was to use community development method to find others that shared my concern—people's ignorance around asylum and refugee issues and lack of capacity for dialogue—and to agree together to do something. We engaged in analysis, discussed tactics and ended up initiating a project called Refugee Learning Circles which provided learning resources and resource people to facilitate public conversation around the issues.

Conflict for many is a problem: something scary and divisive. The students in the story above became alienated from one another as a result of the conflict within the classroom. Community workers are no different to most people. Conflict is often feared and purposefully avoided. Practitioners often find themselves trying to back away from conflict. We also know from hard experience that many models of conflicting in our society are not very hopeful; they adopt an adversarial stance looking for winners and losers, and they can quickly lead to violence, scape-goating and humiliation. Conflict often seems to destroy social relations. Because people are interested to avoid these negative outcomes, they tend to avoid conflict altogether.

However, conflict is an inevitable part of social relations, and so practitioners need to become adept at the social practice of *careful conflicting* in community development work. Conflict can provide the energy for constructive or generative engagement around differences of opinion and perspective. It can be a healthy expression of new-found self-confidence, autonomy or empowerment. Conflict means there is tension between different goals, some legitimate and some illegitimate, and yet within this tension there is often the potential for building new kinds of social relationships.

It is worth saying that not all conflict leads to the potential to build new kinds of relationships: it depends on a range of factors. For instance, if I am at a bus stop with a man who is drunk, and he starts to curse Aboriginal people, then I will not bother to enter into conflict. I have no re-lationship, and probably no potential relationship with this man, so I will not waste any energy engaging in conflict. It might be better to withdraw. However if he is someone I have known for some time, and he is sober, then I could call him into a conversation and ask "Why do you hold such a view?" This creates the possibility of challenging through first hearing the story and then bringing in my story.

Conflict can only be effectively resolved through dialogue when the following principles and practices are applied in combination:

i) a *commitment to truth*;
ii) a recognition that individuals only have a *relative view of the truth* about anything;
iii) an acceptance that individuals therefore need to enter into *dialogue with humility*, willing to learn from other people; and
iv) a particular type of courage, that people are *willing to suffer*: that is, they can let go of their own agendas and perspectives and suffer the process of taking on board someone else's perspective—potentially a very painful step.

This approach to dialogical conflicting invites community workers to bring our full attention to such inner dynamics. Questions can be asked such as:

• Do we have a commitment to truth or do we simply want to maintain our own blind spots, in order to win the fight?

• Are we conscious that our view of the world is relative or do we think it is absolute?

• Are we entering the process of dialogue with humility that enables us to understand the others' points of view?

• Are we even willing to be persuaded towards their view, or is dialogue our ultimate art of manipulation?

• Finally, are we willing to suffer and let go of ideas, beliefs, perspectives that we have held onto dearly—or do we only expect the other to suffer and let go?

The perspective of dialogical community development requires practitioners to practise conflict with a primary commitment to nurturing relationships. Techniques of conflict resolution and management are only secondary. People are only really willing to hear someone's story, or to engage with someone else's perspective, if they feel that someone has taken the time to hear *their* story, or to engage with *their* perspective. It is this primary hospitable process of hearing one another's stories that nurtures relationship, and it is within the crucible of such relationship that people have a better chance of accepting or resolving differences.

Deconstructive movements are also central to the process of destabilising stubborn and entrenched 'givens'—the beliefs and attitudes that blind people and stop us hearing one another. Binary ways of thinking such as right–wrong, black–white, conservationists–loggers, economy–environment, and rights–responsibilities lock people into debates that maintain conflict in an unhelpful way, blinding us from developing creative synthesis or transformative solutions. Framing conflicts with such binaries blocks the possibility of hearing people's stories and understanding each other's perspectives, even if not agreeing.

Finally, a dialogical approach to conflict also recognises that people are sometimes embedded within institutional processes, habitual patterns, and ideological positions that undermine their capacity to see afresh, and lock them into polarised interests. For example, the so-called 'left' is attached to a discourse of rights, and the so called 'right' becomes attached to the discourse of responsibility. These attachments can undermine the possibility of dialogue to the point where practitioners are obliged to practise deconstruction. As dialogical community workers we need to destabilise such binaries, support people in the ensuing state of transformative tension, and work with them towards potential synthesis. It is not that the person attached to either side of the binary is the 'enemy', but that they are blinded by their institutional position and by the patterns and processes where they are embedded.

People are also 'blinded in their seeing'. At the heart of our attitude towards conflict is the acknowledgement of ignorance. Rather than seeking power within the process of conflicting, people should primarily be seeking to overcome ignorance through pursuing an understanding of the currents of their deeper connections with one another.

Summing up

These five reflections have provided an overview of the ways in which a dialogical approach to community development can transform our social world. We have shared our understanding of the role of a skilled and soulful worker in supporting 'community' to become a vehicle for social change in which people find their own paths towards development as freedom.

The first reflection introduced what we call *method*. Method refers to a systematic way of doing dialogical community development work. We explored the methodical and rhythmic work within what can be called the micro, mezzo, macro and meta levels of a community development process. The push and pull of a gentling approach was then outlined. The implications of a commitment to solidarity and hospitality in methodical dialogical practice were also explored. Finally we considered the importance of gaining mandate within the method as a way of building trust and proving ourselves trustworthy within a community work context.

The second reflection examined the complex work of *analysis*. Within community development work analysis includes the process of thinking (what is going on, why?) and action (what to do? tactics and strategies). A process of widening analysis starts with practitioner analysis, but holds it lightly; then moves onto a group analysis (people within a place or space or base doing analysis together); then widens the process involving various 'others' moving towards a more inclusive community analysis; and finally pushes dialogue with 'others' to the point of holding unresolved tensions and contested understanding.

The third reflection unravelled the complexity of *power and empowerment* within the work. The relational practice that nurtures supportive co-responsibility is considered to be the key trigger to empowerment for people who "are destroyed by the inner conviction of uselessness" (Schumacher 1974, p161). We reflected on practices of power-with, co-operative power, and the wielding of skilful and soulful power that are critical to dialogical community development work that desires transformational outcomes.

The fourth reflection considered the complex business of *structuring* transformational work. The beauty of innovative local structures is that they do not strangle local energy and enthusiasm. We then pursue the need to build structures that are beyond the local, while remaining firmly embedded within the local. People's structures, emerging from their aspirations and impulses, are posited as an alternative to service-oriented structures delivered *at* people.

In the fifth reflection, we explored how practitioners might *carefully conflict* within their practice. Conflict is not only inevitable; it is often desirable. Escalating conflict, where necessary, might be important for transformational work. While bringing suppressed conflict to the surface might sometimes be necessary, it is important to at least try a dialogical approach to start with, and then move on to utilise various other traditions of conflicting. In saying this we have acknowledged that the dialogical approach has limits—it might not always work.

CHAPTER

Three

Practitioner analysis: current challenges and ways forward

This chapter identifies and examines several of the most significant trends that undermine a dialogical approach to community development practice, and invites practitioners to rethink their approach to community development in ways that enhance depth, hospitality and solidarity.

The reader might question why we do not explicitly address some of the big challenges of our social life such as violence and war, inequality and urbanisation, ecocide and climate change. Our only answer is that discussions about these big issues are both implicit throughout the whole book and have also been written about in many other contexts. This chapter attempts to bring attention to some more subtle, overlooked, and in our opinion, core challenges of our times. These issues are like undiagnosed cancers that eat away at our social well-being: objectification, ideological positions, disenchantment, addictive consumerism, therapeutic culture, and collusion with a garrison state. They undermine community, and provide particular challenges to a dialogical approach to community development informed by depth, hospitality and solidarity.

This chapter explores what could be called a negative analysis of 'trends against'. In some ways this stands out as a contrast to the other chapters, which all point positively and constructively towards what can be done in terms of community life and community development practice. We have purposefully put this analysis at the centre of the book because in many ways the analysis is central. As practitioners we build a way forward from an analysis of what is wrong. In this sense the whole book is informed by this central chapter.

We are not proposing that community development practitioners go into spaces and places and name these challenges in public ways. This analysis is, after all, practitioner analysis embodied within a historical moment. As discussed in Chapter Two, we would only bring such practitioner analysis into the dynamic of a community analysis in subtle ways, holding it lightly and bringing it to the conversation in a spirit of dialogue.

3.1 Objectification

One of the key contemporary challenges that undermine a dialogical approach to community life generally, and community development specifically, is the explosion of multiple processes of objectification in contemporary culture. Recalling the argument of Martin Buber, objectification refers to processes where people, creatures, the planet, and things are related to as objects within a subject-object relationship. I or We are the subject—aware of my/our own existence—but the 'other' is an object which is regarded in ways that create distance and undermine mutuality. bell hooks (2003, p128), drawing on Parker Palmer's work, illuminates how the idea of 'to put against, to oppose' is embedded within objectivist thinking; it entails an oppositional and adversarial stance and denies a deep sense of inter-connection.

It is the objectification of flora and fauna that has facilitated a relentless destruction of creatures, forests, and habitat. It is the objectification of the planet that has legitimised the rampant exploitation of planetary resources. It is the objectification of things that underpins a culture of waste. It is the objectification of people from 'other' cultures, ethnicities, races, classes, genders and sexualities that enables some to dismiss, disrespect, and destroy those people.

Such a perspective of the world is infused with a particular kind of scientific thinking and world-view which seeps deep into Western culture, but is also a part of many other cultures. Many of the reflections within Chapters One and Two explore this trend. The reflection on Welcoming Problems identifies the process of objectifying 'communities' as populations to be acted upon with processes of technical territorialisation. The discussion on problems is itself underpinned by a critique of how particular sciences objectify problems as 'out there' requiring a solution. A human connectedness to the problem and to the groups of people involved is pushed to the margins of this world-view.

Deconstruction as a tool for unravelling binaries

For philosophers such as Jacques Derrida, part of the solution to objectification lies with *deconstruction*. The deconstructive movement is a shift in thinking that requires the undoing, the unravelling, and the destabilising of dualisms and binaries embedded within objectification. Deconstruction provides a way forward—a process of destabilising binaries and a process of construction or reconstruction of new ways of perceiving, thinking, relating and being.

In a nutshell, the term deconstruction is used to describe the "process of identifying and undermining oppositions through which discourses represent things such as knowledge, identity and other social phenomena" (Healy 2005, p204). It is in this sense that Derrida's notion of deconstruction showed the dangers of assuming that the meanings of words are self-evident and that they represent, rather than construct, what we call 'the real world' or 'reality'. For example, the mind often makes pre-conceptions when hearing people talk about 'ethnic people'. Talking about ethnic people assumes there is some kind of opposition such as 'non-ethnic people'. The emerging discourse around ethnicity creates or constructs a particular reality.

Derrida also went on to demonstrate the degree to which people often rely on binary oppositions in a hierarchy of value. He unfolded the processes of construction and revealed the inherent un-sustainability of every opposition. Such hierarchies enfolded within binary oppositions ensure that people not only think in binary constructions such as black–white, or ethnic–non-ethnic, but also include a hierarchy within that binary of what is implied to be right or wrong, normal or abnormal, powerful or weak, central or peripheral.

He went on to challenge every hard boundary that is implied in language, demonstrating their artificiality (or constructed-ness) and their porosity. For example, for Derrida there was an inevitable instability within even a simple bounded notion such as 'white'—masking great diversity. This was an occasion to interrogate the artificiality of ethnic–non-ethnic. Finally, he showed how people are wedded to the metaphor of 'sight' for knowledge, with its binary opposition of 'blindness' representing ignorance, and to the parallel process of privileging reason.

Deconstruction helps avoid objectification

So what does this mean for community development? If community development is essentially about how people act together in their social worlds, then community workers must understand the processes of thinking through which people construct world-views.

Firstly, a Derridean understanding of deconstruction provides some guidance in the complex terrain of binaries through which many practitioners see the world. Consider binaries such as undeveloped-developed—with its implied understanding of 'them', the undeveloped, as objects, and us, the developed, as subjects. Some other binaries that are significant in community development include: subject–object, strong–weak, adult–youth, in–out, gay–straight, male–female, funded–unfunded, worker–client, manager–worker, traditional–modern, and customary–introduced. Many people interpret their world through such binaries, 'constructing' our shared world in ways that are limited by binary oppositions.

People also enter into dialogue holding preconceived notions of worth or desirability in these binaries. For example, 'developed country' is considered the normative benchmark for societies and 'underdeveloped countries' should apparently be trying to model themselves accordingly. Modern is good and traditional is backwards. Adults are stable, whilst youth are risky.

Within our dialogical approach, informed by deconstruction, such oppositional constructions are unsustainable and intrinsically artificial. They construct a reality that is far from the 'truth'. Why should 'developed' nations be the benchmark? What is wrong with traditional? Is not the social-political-economic world a much more nuanced, complex mixture of each of these terms? This is not to say that there are not genuine conflictual relationships between the binaries. It is rather that the binary opposition of concepts in itself is problematic for our practice. Dialogue should look to open up new ways of thinking about each issue or concern.

Secondly, deconstructive movements actually challenge some of the foundations of how we as practitioners think about our community development work. There are many other binaries embedded within contemporary community development discourse: practice–theory, process–outcome, remembering–forgetting, recognition–redistribution, rights–responsibilities, empowered–disempowered, conscious–unconscious, disadvantaged–advantaged, doing–being, public–private, strong–weak, bottom-up–top-down, and resilient–vulnerable.

Deconstruction invites consideration of the shifting ground that opens up when these binaries are undermined. True, each of these words that represent a 'reality' is useful in a limited way, but practitioners must be aware that these words and their location within a hierarchically constructed binary undermine people's capacity to hear stories, to see with different eyes, to consider the grey spaces in-between and to explore the blank spaces in some 'other' place.

Moving towards an 'other' option: an in-between space

The key antidote is a shift in thinking, away from the subject–object binary embedded within objectification and towards an orientation that seeks to find another option to those embedded within the binary. At a foundational level it requires a move from "object–subject" thinking to an understanding of inter-subjectivity.

For example, in the reflection on emplacement in Section 1.3 we discovered that it is helpful to no longer view people as subjects and land as object. There is an inter-subjective perspective, understood intuitively and acutely by many indigenous people, that sees land and people both as inter-related subjects within a co-creative process. Consider another example: deconstructing the theory–practice binary within community work. A deconstructive approach to thinking ensures that theory is no longer an object to be studied 'out there' while practice gets our daily attention. As practitioners we need to see both theory and practice as subjects, both necessary for us to do our ongoing community development work thoughtfully, reflectively and in a disciplined manner.

With a framework informed by inter-subjectivity, it is important to find the 'in-between' spaces within and between the supposed binaries, and the new 'other' options that emerge within this in-between space. Community workers shouldn't do theory at university, and practice on the street—they should find another way of doing theory–practice in daily work at either the university or the street, giving birth to notions like 'praxis' (Freire, 1972) which describe the combination of theory and practice in a way that holds the tension between them.

Issues previously considered to be 'problems' are no longer perceived as objects to be removed. A deconstructive and dialogical approach compels reconsideration of so-called problems as subjects to be related to in a new way, seeking another perspective. In Chapter Two, shadows were considered in the same way. The imperative is to relate in a new way to whatever was previously projected as 'out there': a fixed idea, a firm conviction, a strong opinion. Community workers look for a third space, an in-between place, an 'other' option. This is the wisdom of our favourite of Saul Alinsky's *Rules for Radicals:* "If you've only got two options—pick a third".

> In his work in Vanuatu, Peter constantly finds himself in a situation where many of the chiefs are arguing that they need more *respect*. Conversely women argue that they need more *rights*. The two concepts are posited as oppositions and people become firmly entrenched in either/ or camps. Within our community development work we have tried to open up a new space where we include other concepts such as *responsibility* and *relationships*. The binary-oriented respect–rights debate is broadened into a new space that discusses responsibilities–respect– rights within the context of a commitment to relationship. Within this new space the dialogical process opens up new possibilities of viewing people's needs, fears, and hopes, and of building transformative processes.

3.2 Ideological positions

Ideology plays a significant role in people's understanding of life and their intention in the social world. As Michael Freeden (2003, p2-3) says, "ideologies map the political and social worlds for us" and for many they are "a way of imposing some pattern on the world—some structure or organisation". In this appreciative understanding of the term it makes sense that we are all ideologues. People need some kind of map, pattern, structure and organisation for thinking and acting. Without such an ideology people would feel very lost. However, more attention must be given to what we call "ideological positions".

An appreciation of ideology

Viewing ideology appreciatively as community workers, we see that it can energise people, provide a sense of security, and also often provide what appears to be a clear analysis. Ideologies can provide people and groups with an agreed and uniform way of viewing the world, and such agreement can make it easier to generate a certain amount of energy. People are often mobilised and energised through commitment to a way of viewing the world, combined with a clear, agreed, and uniform rationale for action. This is one of the virtues of ideology.

Ideologies can also provide a sense of security. In a world that is becoming more and more complex and confusing—with so many political and religious options, so much information, and so many calls to loyalty—adopting a particular ideology sometimes enables people to relax. Someone has finally found the truth (although they might see it as *the* truth and the way) and it makes them feel safe and secure.

Cast in a positive light, ideology can provide useful 'windows' through which people analyse a given situation. A Marxist political ideology provides a tool to see the relationships between capital and labour in a certain situation. If someone subscribes to Marxist ideology they will have a sharp awareness of labour exploitation. In the same way, if someone subscribes to a particular feminist ideology they will have a sharp insight into gender relations. Ideologies can sharpen analysis of the world and can bring insightful perspectives to an issue.

However, ideology cast in such a positive light is in itself often also filled with shadow. Subtle shifts of understanding and intention can swing action in the direction of liberation and emancipation on one hand, or in the direction of repression and totalitarianism on the other.

The shadow of fundamentalism

For example, one of the shadow dangers of ideology is that the energy, sense of security and sharp analysis described above become captive to fundamentalism. Religious fundamentalisms arise from all traditions: the Christian 'moral majority' movement in the USA, Hindu fundamentalists emerging as a political force in India, and Islamic fundamentalism growing in many parts of the world. Political expressions of fundamentalist-oriented ideology appear in the form of neo-liberalism, and narrow interpretations of Marxist, feminist and Green political philosophies and practices. Embedded within these fundamentalist-oriented understandings of ideology are strong bounded-set positions usually underpinned by very strong binaries such as right–wrong, orthodox–unorthodox and correct–heretical. Such ideological positions give people a passion, safety and commitment that can evoke amazing energy, but at a cost to community as dialogue and hospitality.

Such bounded-set ideological positions, for all their potential positive uses, are essentially damaging to the world. This damage occurs when there is a shift from using multiple ideologies to understand a complex world, to people taking polarised ideological positions and adopting a fundamentalist stance. When this shift occurs, ideological positioning is divisive and anti-dialogical, and undermines the possibility of community.

Ideological positions as exclusive

One of the key problems with ideological positioning is that although it might be able to energise people, it does so in a way that is exclusive of 'others'. As briefly discussed above, ideological positions are often located within bounded or closed-set world-views. People are either in or out. You agree or disagree, or at least you are perceived to do so. You have claimed epistemological superiority without first giving a hearing to the alternative views.

There is a deep tension between the benefits and dangers of ideology. Ideologies often inspire a vision of the good life or a better world; yet when people make that subtle shift towards ideological positioning they will exclude those from the world who do not agree with them. Their political–economic–cultural vision underpins a social process of exclusion that might not be explicitly violent, but can hardly avoid being *implicitly* violent; social exclusion is usually felt as painful and implies some kinds of violence. The implicit ideological position is "we will not relate to you because you hold a different perspective".

Community or a community-oriented world is not built on the basis of uniformity, exclusivity or exclusion; its foundations are inter-subjectivity and pluralistic social participation. One of the most useful and yet challenging definitions of community we have encountered is "a community is a place where there is always someone you don't want to be with" (Palmer, 1980). This is the kind of "community as hospitality" that we need to keep dreaming of and extending ourselves to encounter.

To exclude those who do not share your ideological position is to invite deeper problems in the long run. Within Australia it is interesting to reflect on what happened when people from the suburbs and rural areas were excluded from 'public conversation' by the Keating government of the early 1990s. One reading of the political process is that important progressive ideals of the political left have gradually transformed into ideological positions guiding policy development around controversial issues such as rights, refugees, reconciliation and the republic. These ideological positions stabilised or ossified into bounded circles of orthodoxy and unorthodoxy. Many so-called 'ordinary' Australians felt locked out of the public conversation. John Howard and Pauline Hanson were able to exploit the 'shadow' side of this exclusionary process and eventually lead Australia into dangerous political and social territory. One ideological position gave birth to another position, one just as violent to those excluded. Within Keating's world, the excluded were regional–rural Australia, and some of the working class; in Howard's world it was indigenous Australians, refugees, single women, and other vulnerable groups more or less reliant on the welfare state.

This is not to say that people who advocate a non-ideologically motivated praxis do not subscribe to values, ideals, commitments and even confrontations. It should be clear that we as authors advocate all these things. For example, we have argued for an approach rooted in solidarity with the poor. However the crux of our argument is that the world we dream of and work for must be socially modelled in the way we attempt to get there. The process, or means, is at least as important as the outcomes, or ends. Community practitioners must be socially inclusive both of people who work in solidarity for our dream, and of those who oppose it. If community workers dream of an inter-subjective world and yet socially exclude those who are turned into "other objects", there is a deep contradiction within the praxis. Practitioners will have become stuck within their own ideological positions.

Ideologies: prescriptive in approach and limited in perspective

Ideologies may also provide useful windows through which community workers can analyse situations—helpful as part of the *practitioner analysis*—but ideological positions do not give us the capacity to be attentive, aware or imaginative within our *community analysis*. The problem with ideological positions is that they are prescriptive in approach and limited in perspective. Ideologies might give insight into a part of the problem or issue, but when one part is over-emphasised inevitably many parts are left out—the analysis becomes overtly partial. Ideological positions squeeze diverse experiences and complexity into narrow conceptual frameworks.

A dialogical approach to community development requires that practitioners develop the skills of attention, observation and engagement with people who have differing perspectives. Bringing people with differing perspectives into the process introduces many more pairs of eyes which enables community workers to look carefully at what is happening. Also, a soulful orientation adds to a dialogical approach in that it prefers to approach a problem or issue with a sense of mystery. What is happening in a given situation is a mystery that can only be unravelled through constant attention. Ideological positions often lead to arrogance—I or we are too sure, too soon, of what is happening.

As discussed earlier, ideological positions might also be useful in providing some sense of security. However, historically a politic built on the hope of security, applied either nationally or locally, does not lead to social tolerance, trust and therefore 'community', the ultimate source of security. The recent experiences of Israel and South Africa tell the story well. In Israel the politic of security based on the ideological position of statehood has left a legacy of hatred, exile and war. In South Africa the politic of security based on the ideological position of apartheid fuelled fear, violence and destruction. In both cases the ideological positions that provided the analysis of the situation, inspired the energy to exclude others, and gave some people a sense of security, actually undermined the very thing that people ultimately wanted—a safe society to live in.

Expanding conceptual frameworks and appreciating mystery

Our approach to community development requires attention to diverse experience, awareness of complexity, and use of imagination in social engagement. It is not people who accumulate ideology that inspire a truly better world, but rather those who are ready to adapt their conceptual frameworks and appreciate mystery.

An approach informed by a soulful orientation expands conceptual frameworks to engage with actual experiences. Soulful people still advocate ideals. They often subscribe to some kind of ideology, in the sense of a map, pattern, structure and organisation to help understand the world; but they do not do it arrogantly, exclusively or primarily. Their primary focus is on the *lived* present rather than an *ideal* future. Such people still inspire energy but they do it creatively, imaginatively and experimentally. They remain open to being challenged, dialogued with, and confronted. These people link action closely to reflection, ongoing analysis and strategising. An appreciation of mystery and the hope for expanded conceptual frameworks implies that we actually see more attentively than those subscribing to an ideological position could ever wish to do. It requires that community workers adopt a teachable spirit enabling them to learn about many perspectives, themes and windows of analysis that can unravel complex relationships and dynamics within social spaces.

So how do practitioners develop such an approach to community development, that recognises ideology yet inspires mystery, that understands the significance of ideology yet is committed to expanding conceptual frameworks? Firstly, community workers must thoroughly understand other people's ideological positions. If we are going to engage in a praxis that is based on inter-subjectivity then we must understand the people who come to that process with their own ideology. This will enable community workers to avoid alienating people in the early stages of their dialogue, making them sensitive to these people's non-negotiable positions.

Secondly, community workers must respect the underlying passions and fears that are the basis of people's ideological positioning. If the foundations of someone's ideological position are attacked, especially at the early stages in the building of a relationship, most certainly a lose–lose scenario will be triggered. Usually people involved in the struggle for community transformation share some similar dreams, such as safety, prosperity, and access to resources. The expression of these dreams, and the method advocated to get there, might vary widely; nevertheless, community workers can tap into the hope that people do have some common underlying aspirations and needs. It might get trickier as more contested issues are discussed, but the process can start with what people can share. Practitioners need to remember that beneath people's stated positions often lie their unstated immediate interests and feelings. Beneath even these interests and feelings are deeper needs and core values. So while community workers start a dialogue being aware of very different stated positions, they might find that some very similar needs and core values are shared (Sen, 2006). It is wise to move dialogue into this territory as quickly as possible.

Thirdly, in attempts to be sensitive, respectful and engaged, community workers must not make the mistake of not being passionate themselves. An appreciation of mystery and an attitude of openness do not imply apathy, nor do they imply that people perceive attempts in dialogue as chameleon-like. They certainly should not mean that we sit on the fence. Practitioners can be inclusive yet forthright, sensitive yet assertive, respectful yet radical, open yet sharp. In the same way that we must understand other's ideological positions, we must be clear about our own non-negotiable values. We can learn another of Gandhi's mantras: "always compromise, but never with the ideals".

3.3 Disenchantment

Max Weber used the idea of 'disenchantment' to describe the modern condition. Within his analysis, 'pre-modern' people lived in an enchanted world, one occupied by "the world of spirits, demons, and moral forces" (Taylor 2007, p26). For many people, the shift from such an enchanted to disenchanted world has been a good thing. Most of us prefer to live in a predictable world without such spirits and demons. Most of us are also glad to now live in secular societies where at least the political sphere of life has been emptied of religion. Spirits, demons and moral forces are no longer key determinants of national goals and ethical codes. We, as authors, are glad that within our own country of Australia there is a clear separation between church and state—one of the key determinants of a secular society. We are also glad that science has been able to usurp itself from the grips of religious dogma and that people are free to pursue inquiry without fear of sanctions.

However, as Charles Taylor argues, secularity doesn't mean people's lives are emptied of religious or spiritual practices. Many people continue to search for a full and meaningful life through vigorously practising religious and spiritual lives (Taylor 2007, p2). But more significantly, whatever one thinks personally about religion or spirituality, the beauty of secular societies is that people can choose what will provide such full and meaningful lives—maybe it is the vigorously pursued religious or spiritual life, maybe it is humanism, maybe it is something else altogether.

So in celebrating the beauty of secularity, what is the problem of disenchantment? Taking the Vanuatu case again:

> Peter was talking with some chiefs about the most significant challenge to their community life. His frame of reference was anticipating that

the discussion would move towards issues of land, livelihoods, young people leaving villages and so forth. However, the chiefs wanted to talk about sorcery as a significant source of conflict. This was the key challenge to their building of peaceful and co-operative communities that would enable 'development'.

A soulful approach to community development needs to be able to engage with this kind of enchanted reality. The problem with a trend towards disenchantment is not so much that people close their conceptual frameworks, as in the previous reflection on ideological positions, but that the frame of reference is simply not large enough to engage with many people's 'other' realities. And it is not only in places such as Vanuatu that people live in an enchanted world. Taylor's book presents a very strong case that many people in so-called secular societies continue to live in somewhat enchanted worlds. The question is, do we have eyes to notice?

Hegemonic secularism as ongoing disenchantment

Some current discourses of secularisation, not content with the social acquiescence of secularism, seek a complete *hegemonic* domination by rationality and a destruction of sacredness and enchantment. The tendency is not towards what Thomas Moore (1996) calls "a secular sensibility" but instead towards ideologically oriented discourses of secularism that close out 'other' ways of thinking and being. The hegemonic tendencies of such discourses of secularism objectify the religious or spiritual other, seeing it as 'enemy' and undermining any possibility of maintaining or even seeing an enchanted world.

This kind of secularism has a profound impact on how people live their lives and how they can become unaware of possibilities that lie beyond the shallow and the material. Such secularisation can literally suck the life out of everything. Trees become merely lumps of timber, hearts become pumps and brains become machines. The land becomes a resource. Within such secularist world-views, techniques and technologies become the root metaphor for dealing with our problems. To fix our hearts, all we need are trained doctors and a technique of by-pass surgery. To fix the destruction of our forests, all we need to do is plant acres and acres of pine forest.

Hegemonic secularism undermines deep engaged pluralism

Another key problem with some current discourses of secularism is that they undermine the possibilities of deep engaged pluralism. As will be discussed in Chapter Four, a key aspect of community development work is care of the 'social–cultural' sphere of community life—that is, a caring for diversity. However, to care for diversity requires an understanding of the philosophy of co-existence and cohesion. We suspect that some forms of secularism, as currently understood within public life, do not provide the foundation for pleasurable coexistence and cohesion. The current *modus operandi* of secularisation undermines religious and irreligious impulses in such ways that they become "shadow" movements. As the public discourse becomes confused and unable to deal with the kinds of diversity that people now have to coexist with, society finds itself stuck in terms of where to go. A framework that does not take into account spiritual sensibilities will undermine deep pluralism—it will not be able to engage with diverse cultural practices.

Mario Blaser and his colleagues have argued the significance of this for the undermining of indigenous people's 'life-projects' (Blaser et al., 2004). Life-projects are a way of thinking about how indigenous people can choose their own vision of life. Most indigenous people still have a framework of thinking, being and doing that links 'fullness of life' to connectedness, wholeness and spiritual well-being. Their world-view is still thoroughly enchanted. Our challenge is to not only develop conceptual frameworks that are large enough to engage with such people, but to also learn from their enchanted world-view—in the same way as was suggested in previous remarks about entering into dialogical I-Thou kinds of relationship with the land. Modernist notions of secularism are failing us, both in terms of plurality and also other dimensions of life, such as ecological sustainability. We can learn from indigenous people through understanding the wisdom embedded within their enchanted world and their life-projects.

A disenchanted development vision: a materialist outcome

Another challenge to confront is an approach to thinking about development that is *disenchanted*. Such an approach lacks the reflexive capacity to critique a hegemonic discourse of secularism, and will probably fall into the trap of supporting a materialist and economic approach to development. This shift is more likely to be subtle and implicit than obvious and explicit. Returning to Blaser's idea of a life project, a disenchanted development vision will inevitably limit the gaze to material and economic outcomes. People's imaginative literacy shrinks, and their possibilities atrophy.

Empirical studies show that at a general level "secularisation is associated with economic development and prosperity" (Peroca, 2006, p9). If development is primarily oriented towards the economic, then secularisation seems to be an inevitable necessity—both as an effect of and a stimulus to economic development. However, from an orientation of community as dialogue, development needs to be de-linked from a centring economic paradigm. Development as presented here requires a more nuanced understanding of modernity, one that avoids an *inevitable* trajectory of secularisation and economic prosperity. Fortunately there are global movements that measure 'development' through indicators much broader than economic growth; for example, the United Nations' use of the Human Development Index and more recently the New Economics Foundation's use of the Happiness Index. These movements indicate that people are starting to exercise their imaginative muscles, and that maybe the atrophy can be reversed.

Disenchantment, modernity and human waste

The trend of disenchantment is linked to the on-going 'project' of modernity. While this process has some good consequences—such as limiting the influence of religion in the public sphere (Taylor, 2007)—it is also problematic. For the philosopher Zygmunt Bauman the "spread of modernity", which accompanies disenchantment, brings significant problems. Drawing on his book *Wasted Lives* (2004) it can be argued that the spread of modernity is closely linked to the production of all kinds of waste, and human waste in particular.

Springing out of the Marxian tradition, Bauman's argument in essence is that globalising modernity, with its commitment to a particular kind of economic ordering of life, produces all kinds of human waste. These people are the economic surplus—or more accurately the surplus population, simply not needed. There is the human waste 'internal to nations' that is warehoused in ever-burgeoning prisons, relocated in ghettos of poverty, and discarded in states of redundancy—a much greater fear than unemployment: there is an echo of superfluity and irrelevance to the idea of redundancy. In some parts of the world, internally displaced people, numbering some 25 million (UNHCR, 2007), are disenfranchised within their own homeland; for example, many Congolese have had to flee their home areas but are still within the Congo. Then there is the human waste made 'external to nations', manifest in massive refugee movements, detention centres, and stateless people groups.

Historically these internal and external processes were linked. When there was an overflow of internal human waste within centres of power, as in the case where many people in parts of newly industrial modernising England during the 1800's simply became too poor to feed themselves and their families, such people were simply made 'external' after they tried to steal some food, or organise the first trade unions, and shipped to prisons in colonies like Australia. Now, however, the spread of modernity having reached its outer limits—where is there to go, other than the moon or Mars?—we can no longer ship people to other places, other than the occasional idiosyncratic 'solutions' like Nauru or Guantanamo Bay. Hence the growth industries in managing internal human waste, such as prisons.

Creating space for people's sensibilities

The way forward is to approach public politics and community development practice with a framework that balances a spiritual and secular sensibility, nurturing "mental spaces" or conceptual frameworks, and also safe social spaces that refuse disenchantment. Within these spaces we can learn to balance a sceptical and appreciative understanding of *both* spiritual and secular sensibilities.

These are more subtle signposts about how to live a full life than can be discerned from problematic secular, material, modernist or economic world-views. Direction can be drawn from these alternative and subtle signposts if we also elicit spiritual and enchanted sensibilities. One signpost is a secular sensibility. This can be understood as a perspective inviting deep plurality that resists the centring of any one moralistic religious or other moral framework, and yet refuses to become a dogmatic discourse that marginalises all religious or irreligious passions. A dialogical approach to community development is infused with a commitment to supporting both a secular and spiritual sensibility that supports a "public ethos of engagement in which wider varieties of perspectives inform and restrain one another" (Connolly, 1999, p5).

An appeal to create space for people's spiritual and religious sensibilities, alongside the secular sensibility, can also be part of a cultural defence against the trajectory of secularisation, modernity, prosperity and an all-colonising economic approach to development. Such space encourages people to exercise the creative muscles involved in expanding their imaginative literacy, informing a greater diversity of possible 'life-projects'. The trend is towards a more technocratic and economic approach to solving social problems; but community development, as a social practice, can resist this trend by creating space that elicits people's religious and spiritual sensibilities to sit alongside secular sensibilities. People's lives will be enriched by stories, myths, and dreams that enable them to collectively destabilise and deconstruct the modernistic and economic gaze.

Rediscovering spiritual traditions of wisdom

The modernist secular age did people a favour by unravelling the hegemony of religious elites—but unfortunately has now been captured by some people's desire to form a secular hegemony. Without suggesting a regression to old forms of hegemonic spirituality and religion, we propose a re-enchantment of our lives through rediscovering spiritual and sacred traditions as sources of wisdom. In turn this will help to develop new insights and wisdom for our community development work.

It is important to remember that in many places, these spiritual and religious sensibilities are still very much alive. However, our approach to community development requires practitioners to become more *attuned* to what is already alive in such places, in such ways that these resources can be utilised. Joanna Macy's study of the self-help Sarvodaya movement of Sri Lanka, as documented in the book *Dharma and Development* (1985), is an example of how religion can be a key mobilising and moral resource for development. Her framework of 'seeing' was able to discern the significance of religion in their development efforts.

The following story, told to Peter while he was living in New Delhi in the late 1980s, illustrates the significance of a spiritual and sacred sensibility that infuses community development with important warnings and lessons.

> For the past 20 years in the Indian desert state of Rajasthan all sorts of techniques and technologies have been used to try and develop modern systems for water capture and distribution. During that time, despite all the capital investment and technological innovation, there has been crisis after crisis—flood followed by drought. People were either drowning or wilting. There was always either too much or too little water. Recent research showed that the problems had not been solved by modern innovation—they had in fact grown. Prior to this plethora of modern interventions it is clear that water supply had never been plentiful but had been enough. One of the key factors was that trees and water had been considered sacred by local people: communities were only able to use resources that the "gods" deemed necessary. There was a great deal of care taken in the use of water and trees as a result of this sacred worldview, and the whole sacred system remained in balance.

Reflecting on such a story Brian Bates (1996) warns people that:

> ... For dealing with the machinations of the environment, we depend upon our scientific, head-driven paradigms. We construct cause and

effect sequences out of the stream of events; a way of apprehending and predicting life processes which lies at the heart of the empirical approach.

But linear cause and effect chains are too narrow to truly reflect the unimaginably complex interactions of event and factors in the dynamics of agriculture, nature and life. We try to broaden our understanding, paying attention to events previously thought lateral, tangential and of no consequence. But we simply cannot control enough variables even if we could identify and understand them all in order to engineer a satisfactory comprehensive analysis of the process.

We are surprised and baffled by many of the more complex ecological disasters, and can barely keep up with monitoring them, let alone developing interventions to head off their worst effects. (p52)

To ecological problems we can add social ones. We equally despair in trying to find solutions or even understand what is going on despite all our information, research and techniques.

Total disenchantment would lead us down the path of illusion. A secularist and scientific approach that lacks the balance of a spiritual sensibility will fuel a naïvety that deceives people into believing that they can understand all the social variables connected to a proposed problem and design purely 'scientific' social interventions. In contrast, an approach that is infused with a spiritual sensibility would lead to open-mindedness that can *combine* the empirical and the scientific with the mysterious and the imaginative. Practitioners need to put technology in its place, put aside the arrogance of certainty, and locate our techniques in a deeper view of their purpose and use—a view which might be better informed about the sacred.

Re-enchantment through attunement and ritual

Brian Bates (1996) provides a well-documented account of the sacred wisdom of ancient pre-Christian Europe. He gives insight into the problem of disenchantment and the importance of the practice of *attunement* when exploring the way ancient peoples engaged in living well.

The sun has an equally powerful influence in our contemporary agriculture, of course, but we tend to focus more on the human generated interventions we have introduced to modify the natural processes: fertilisers, crop-sprays, agri-business machinery, and so on. But for indigenous peoples across the earth, including our own culture 1000 years ago, the task was not one of intervention, but one of attunement. A sensitive and sophisticated knowledge of the sun and moon patterns was vital. And anything of great import, of central concern to life, was expressed not only in the material world, but in the spiritual realms too. (p52)

For Carl Jung, the way to rediscover the sacred—what we are calling "re-enchantment"—is to become attuned to the broader currents of a mysterious world through the use of *ritual*. For Jung, rituals amplify themes that are important to our sacred existence. One of the new challenges for community development workers is to invite people to participate in community rituals that facilitate attunement.

It is impossible to understand and solve all of the many social problems. They are too complex and there are many mysteries and un-knowable unknowns. However, what practitioners can do is develop rituals that inspire hope and imagination, and weave a social web of relationships in which people become attuned to their connections with one another and their world.

A community network that we were a part of in the late 80s and early 90s exemplified for us how sacred ritual could invoke community and re-energise. Every Monday morning at 6.00am people from the Waiters Union community network used to meet together. People would spend some time reflecting on a text for meditation or someone's personal story. They would sing some songs of celebration or songs that would sensitise our spirits. People would then share information about what events were happening this week. From here a couple of people would write up all the events shared, draw a couple of pictures, photocopy it and then we would distribute it to people in the neighbourhood by hand. Bundles would be given to people who represented clusters of households.

Right at the beginning it was decided that two things would be avoided: firstly writing up the newsletter using a computer; and secondly sending the newsletters by post. There was a sense that by maintaining a handwritten newsletter and using feet to distribute it, people could make a sacred thing out of the importance of the ordinary. Each newsletter maintained the character of those who had written it: their handwriting, their cut-out cartoon. And people would have to create time and space to distribute it: a simple weekly ritual of connection that meant people would drop in and drink cups of tea together, use the time to walk with a friend, and connect with life on the streets in our neighbourhood.

This is a simple example of how community workers can re-enchant community life. A secular sensibility might see this as irrational. Modernist and economically oriented worldviews would see it as madness because 'time equals money'. Computers, faxes and postal services would be more efficient; yet the people involved in this community communication strategy were attuned to the 'other' possible layers of meaning and community beneath the obvious need for communication—they were informed by a spiritual sensibility. Within this story the weekly ritual of hand-writing the newsletters and walking the letters to one another's homes attuned people to nurturing community with one another. The web of relationships woven together through this ritual also provided a key resource in working through many social problems in the neighbourhood.

3.4 Addictive consumerism

Following the previous reflection on disenchantment and its accompanying economic ordering of society, this reflection examines the impact of a contemporary culture of consumerism on our efforts to build community. The materialistic imagination has led many people to prioritise consumption over other ways of living, and therefore become addicted to a peculiarly 'modern' pattern of consumption. Contemporary Western culture in particular has managed to commercialise almost everything. People watch television advertisements that invite turning desires into wants, wants into needs, and needs into loves. People are caught in a cycle of needing–wanting–desiring more. One reading of this process is that people now live in societies in which everything is commodified, and have become addicted to consumerism. Jack Kornfield (1993), a Buddhist writer, proposes this in a more generalised way:

> Ours has been called the Addicted Society, with over twenty million alcoholics, ten million drug addicts, and millions addicted to gambling, food, sexuality, unhealthy relationships, or the speed and busyness of work . . . These addictions are the compulsively repetitive attachments we use to avoid feeling and to deny the difficulties of our lives. Advertising urges us to keep pace, to keep consuming, smoking, drinking, and craving food, money and sex. Our addictions serve to numb us to what is, to help us avoid our own experience, and with great fanfare our society encourages these addictions. (p23-24)

Many community development practitioners would agree with this proposition of multiple addictions. However, Jim Wallis, a long-time North American Christian author and activist, and member of Sojourners Intentional Community based in Washington DC, argues in his book *The Soul of Politics* (1994) that the key addiction is consumerism, a proposition that the data seems to support. Clive Hamilton presents research in his more recent book *Affluenza* (2005, p5) indicating that Australians as a rule "feel they need more", no matter how much money they have. Most people cling to the belief that their happiness is dependent on consuming more. He outlines how people engage in an inner dialogue that goes something like:

> I hoped that getting to this income level would make me feel contented. I do have more stuff, but it doesn't seem to have done the trick. I obviously need to set my goals higher. I'm sure I'll be happy when I'm earning an extra $10,000 because then I'll be able to buy the other things I want.

He goes on to argue that rich societies such as Australia are caught in the grip of a "collective psychological disorder" and that the effect of this disorder is to addict people to ever-increasing amounts of money as a way of making themselves happy.

Consumerism and belonging

Jim Wallis looks beneath the trend of consumerism and argues that the dynamic is not so much about purchasing or possessing so as to feel happy, but rather about belonging. People belong because they wear the latest clothing fashion or have seen the latest blockbuster movie—or, in Australia, have acquired the latest turbo-charged super barbecue. In this day and age, not to be able to consume *at will* means that you do not belong.

Such a thesis has a huge impact on how we as community development workers understand our work. Belonging is one of the key criteria of how people understand community, but people addicted to consumption are finding completely new ways to meet their need to belong. They bypass the sociability of speech and human interaction, intimacy and commitment. Their 'sociality' is one of spending money, wandering in shopping malls, consuming at will and with ever-increasing desires. Without trying to distinguish between authentic and inauthentic belonging, this can be named as a sociality that leads to a soulless and a-social kind of belonging. It involves little in the way of depth, attention, imagination and social commitment.

We can also draw on Zygmunt Bauman's analysis (2004, 2007) and make a case that people are addicted to consumerism because at a deeper level they fear becoming "flawed consumers". Within a producer and consumer-oriented society there is a problem when we simply do not need all the people in the world to produce all that is desired. Our economic system can produce many things now "more swiftly, profitably and economically, without keeping [them] in jobs" (Bauman, 2004 p39). For Bauman, this "surplus labour" is doomed to become flawed consumers, as people who will not have enough cash to consume enough to grow the consumer market. People are aware of this, and it creates fear—who wants to be surplus, or flawed, and not belong? However, rather than face such fears with 'soul', people allow it to feed addictive tendencies.

The right to over-consume and seek profit

Adding other dimensions to the problem is not only the need for people to consume to belong, and to flee their fears, but also the emergence of the seemingly universal right to both over-consume and to seek profit at any expense. There is a growing discourse that legitimises greed as fine and as normal. In the financial sectors of the City of London, people are now only considered wealthy if they can live off the interest of the interest of their main income source. This is nothing short of grotesque.

Meanwhile some of the more 'generous' global philanthropists, people such as George Soros and Bill Gates, are giving charitably with one hand, while taking ruthlessly with the other. This behaviour is legitimised by the rationales of 'profit at any cost' and 'the shareholders are the primary stakeholder'. These people move vast amounts of money around the globe at the press of a button, but fail to see the profound impact of these movements on peripheral economies and on the social worlds of poor people. Such over-consumption and ruthless pursuit of profit represent the systemic violence of the current economic order. But their charity (the use of the 'other hand') legitimises and hides their ruthless greed and systemic violence.

The impact of this economic violence on poorer people generally and on young people specifically is huge. It is one of the major causes of daily crime and overt violence. It is no wonder that many young people have adopted the values diffused through the mainstream media and the social and economic practices of the wealthy. The poor and young have seen through the rhetoric of religions and 'ethical stances'. They can see that status and acceptance come through wealth. People are no longer accepted as people, but as successful producers or consumers. If you are neither of these, you are seen as a dole-bludger, a loser, white-trash, surplus and a 'waste of space' as some people literally put it, with a profoundly accurate neo-liberal capitalist perspective. It is important to realise that if official and celebrated leaders model a particular set of values and priorities, then that is what poor and young people will aspire to. If they see leadership that is addicted to more, more and more, then that is what they will be addicted to as well. They are not interested in what is said, but in what is done.

The challenge of passivity

One of the most significant side-effects of compulsive consumption is passivity and a loss of vitality. Here lies one of the greatest challenges to poetic and social participation in community life. It is one of the greatest challenges because such consumption-oriented activities can seduce people into believing that they *are* participating. People end up believing "I am a loyal Australian because I consume", or "Patriotic Americans will go out and shop" (the post-September 11 mantra linking consumption directly with social participation), rather than identifying the addiction. However, an activity based on addictive consumption has its shadow; it is an activity that actually reflects passivity. This passivity sucks from people their vital capacity to imagine, take action and be intimately involved in the deeper currents of social life.

> Peter had a discussion with some male friends about why pornography, as an addiction, is becoming endemic in our society. Our analysis led us to believe that it is not only due to the commercial interests that are engaged in mass advertising but also due to a passivity that is endemic to men's sexuality. Pornography fulfils the function of eroticism for men and relieves them of the need to actually be creative within their sex lives. Why use imagination and creativity when a magazine or video movie can do it for you?

This brief reflection illustrates the role of passivity in addiction that leads to a loss of vitality, depth and imagination—the stuff of soul. The outcome might be similar, that is, the experience of erotica, but the kind of action required is very different. One action requires an act of imagination; the other requires an act of consumption.

It is certainly not our intention to become 'anti' any of these joys of life; but when people lose their personal freedom and these joys become compulsions, they are in danger of losing touch with a soulful orientation. Attention, awareness and imagination, the signs of soul, imply that people can relate to themselves with depth and imagination. Addictions exist in order to escape from ourselves.

It is worth noting that these addictions may have acted as an important protection from pain in certain parts of people's lives. Maybe compulsive work has enabled people to escape the gnawing boredom and lack of meaning in lives; maybe compulsive shopping has set people free from the concerns of their marginalised and broken experience—this is fine, as far as it goes. But if a restoration of soul and depth within a communal life is desired, the pain of boredom, loneliness, grief, and anger must be faced. People must eventually start to relate to themselves and others in a way that is non-addictive, active and contemplative.

An alternative ethic and politic of eudemonism

It is important for people to engage with their own individual and common fears, passivity, and addictions, and also to restore soul and depth into their lives. But beyond that we also advocate an alternative ethical and political program—one that is attuned to deeper impulses that create human happiness and well-being. Clive Hamilton (2003) proposes such a program, very relevant to community development workers, when considering this challenge of a society addicted to consumption. He draws on the philosophy of Aristotle to outline an ethic and politic of *eudemonism*.

Eudemonism is a philosophy "which promote[s] the full realisation of human potential through, in the first instance, a proper appreciation of sources of well-being" (Hamilton 2003, p212). Hamilton calls for a politics "that has the courage to penetrate beneath the surface of material desire, and to promise rich lives instead of lives of riches" (p209). His vision of this ethic and politic of eudemonism is situated within a 'post-growth society'—which is fundamentally at odds with capitalist systems. The addiction to consumerism is confronted head-on within this new vision because it is "the social disintegration associated with excessive consumption in the marketing society" alongside the 'loss of self' that is considered to be the key problem (p213). The possibilities of community as dialogue are thwarted by such social disintegration.

A politic of eudemonism offers a way forward by re-focusing on re-integrating the self, the *I*, and re-discovering the significance of community, the *We*. Eudemonism is a way of naming a political project that aims to build social, economic, cultural and political structures within our society that support the ethical and purposeful pursuit of community life, a rationality of community rather than of self-interest, and the re-integration of the self through aligning pursuits with deeper needs.

Without going into further discussion of such an ethical and political project, what can be said is that it offers a vision relevant to our understanding of community development. The philosophy of eudemonism invites a deeper reflection on the real sources of well-being. For those seeking a way out of passivity, the first movement is to recognise that something other than the current addiction to consumerism and the passivity it engenders is needed. The second movement is to engage publicly in a dialogical process that moves towards both an ethical stance and a genuine politic of well-being through rebuilding community and re-integrating the self into non-addictive pursuits. Of course this will not be an easy public dialogue to conduct—there will be many in opposition. People's addiction to consumerism, combined within powerful interests, is firmly entrenched.

3.5 Therapeutic culture

One of the most pervasive, and yet almost invisible trends that can undermine effective dialogical community development is the colonising process of *therapeutic culture*. Frank Furedi (2004, 2005), a British sociologist, argues that Western societies now live within such a therapeutic culture. He draws on a wide range of authors and examples to show how therapeutic culture medicalises ordinary human distress, which in turn leads to a reliance on technical and professional interventions to reduce that distress.

> Gerard recently heard from a first year university student who had a laptop computer stolen from his home. The guy was fine about it, realising that insurance cover presented an opportunity to upgrade his machine. His only concern was that he had lost work that was due in the next few days. When he rang the school, he was told that of course he would be given an extension. But he was a bit taken aback when they also insisted that he be given a routine referral to the university counselling service.

The school emailed the service, and he spent the next few days bemusedly resisting various well-meaning professionals who were insistent that he see a counsellor.

This story illustrates the way that institutions and professions increasingly make therapeutic assumptions about how to engage with people—often unhelpful assumptions, arising from immersion within a pervasive therapeutic culture. Therapy is almost as pervasive as fast food—as we go about our ordinary business we are increasingly being asked "do you want therapy with that?"

In January 2009 the mining giant BHP Billiton announced that it would be cutting 3300 Australian jobs. This is a tragedy for the families and places impacted upon. But what we saw as almost equally tragic was the government's response: to fly in counsellors to support those people losing their jobs. Three thousand households in need of an income and towns in need of a future were being offered therapy!

Furedi echoes the earlier writings of depth psychologists James Hillman and Michael Ventura, presented in their adventurous book *We've had a Hundred Years of Psycho-Therapy and the World's Getting Worse* (1993). Hillman and Ventura cite examples such as clients sitting with a therapist explaining how they are distressed about the increasing levels of noise pollution surrounding their houses. Maybe they will say something to the therapist like "it's driving me crazy". For the likes of Hillman, Ventura and Furedi, therapeutic culture orients the therapist and client to collude with each other in developing psycho-social strategies to *cope* with such distress rather than engage in socially oriented processes that transform the causes of distress. The therapist's answer will therefore be something like "how are you going to cope with the noise?" or "how will you deal with the anger and frustration you are feeling towards those making the noise?" People take the path of least resistance enabling them to "feel better".

Most people find themselves doing this all the time—they cope through putting the CDs on louder when tired of the constant noise in the neighbourhood. Hillman and Ventura argue that such a coping strategy might not be very helpful in the long run. It certainly lacks a dialogical commitment to engaging with the 'why' and 'who' of causing the noise pollution, which in turn undermines social engagement with such an issue.

The medicalisation of distress and suffering

The relevance to community development work is obvious. Within the trend towards therapeutic culture, an individual's distress or suffering is usually medicalised. People are labelled as traumatised, not-coping, or fragile, and are diagnosed with all sorts of problems. An extreme problem is post-traumatic stress disorder (PTSD), but a more common problem is currently attention deficit hyperactivity disorder (ADHD). In a parallel process, social groups experiencing distress and suffering are labelled at risk, vulnerable, needy, and problematic. Whole groups or populations of the marginalised—such as young people, the aged, refugees, Aboriginal and Torres Strait Islanders—are labelled as not-coping; the problem is located within their social body. For Furedi, such therapeutic labelling is indicative of vulnerability that legitimises technological kinds of interventions.

This discussion echoes much of what we have discussed in Chapter One: for example, the issues of problems and shadow. The therapeutic trend is intertwined with much of the modernist approach to thinking and acting that we have already explored from several perspectives. The therapeutic approach locates the problem within the social body of a community, or apparent vulnerable group within a community. This legitimises a technical solution implemented by mechanical community development technocrats, or to use the metaphor more appropriately, by doctoring community development workers.

Undermining of people's agency

One of the biggest problems with this model of human vulnerability and powerlessness, transmitted through therapeutic culture, is that it coincides with a far wider tendency to dismiss the potential for people to exercise control over their own lives. There is a decline of belief in people's agency. Concepts such as at-risk, social inclusion, target groups and special needs are indicators of this sense of diminished agency resulting from vulnerability and powerlessness.

Another indicator of such diminished social agency is the tendency for people to turn for help to professionals, particularly therapists and counsellors, instead of to friends and other community members. Community, created through the sociability of friendship, has historically provided the social space for people to be together in grieving, mourning, and therefore recovering from the distress of a range of losses. Therapeutic culture cuts across this soulful expression of community and moves towards the professionalisation and medicalisation of care.

An alternative: social processes of healing

What is needed is a reversal of the trend towards therapeutic solutions and the creation of an alternative way of thinking and acting. Instead of allowing care to be professionalised and medicalised, community practitioners need to re-socialise it. People together can re-discover and re-learn how to create community for the purposes of supporting one another through life's inevitable distress.

> When I was sixteen years old, my three-year-old brother drowned in our backyard swimming pool. My parents, my sister and I were relatively new migrants to Australia and didn't have strong social networks—our 'community' was fragile. What community we did have was unable to cope with the tragedy of my brother's death. People simply didn't know how to cope with our suffering and pain. People 'walked away'. One can only say that we entered a very dark space—a space that still lingers within my family life. The funeral was a sombre affair with little connection to others.
>
> I was recently sitting with a friend who recounted the story of a similar event that happened recently in their neighbourhood. A two-year-old child drowned in a pond of knee-deep water. The event was similar to my family's story. Grief, pain and a dark space descended. However, the profound difference was that the neighbourhood generally and the street of neighbours in particular responded with profound love. All the neighbours of the street took the day off work and gathered around

the family. Everyone held the body of the child. During the next week different people engaged in different ways. Some did research on what kind of funerals could be created by a community; others took turns to be with the family. The children of the street wanted to paint the coffin. On the day of the funeral everyone came and said goodbye to the child in the casket. Items of love were placed within the coffin.

Peter's story illuminates the potential power of community in providing the social processes for healing. Whereas many people who experience a death in the family would now turn to a professional counsellor—a therapeutic technology of healing—the second family experienced the power of community healing processes. Within the first story, of Peter's family, there is evidence of diminished social agency. People have forgotten that for centuries people grieved as communities, creating social spaces for mourning, sharing, story-telling, weeping, and laughing. People in their forgetting have turned to the professional counsellor—a therapeutic agenda becomes the 'solution'.

Another of Peter's personal stories further illustrates the potential power of community as a socially healing process.

I had come to Australia in 1981 as an English migrant boy and as part of the process of acculturation (the official stance) or assimilation (my real felt experience) I immersed myself in the world of rugby league and touch footy and lost any connection to my love for football, or soccer as it was labelled here in Australia. I had to make this transition from football to footy in order to survive the onslaught of school-based racism towards new migrant young people.

It was only ten years later, through working with refugees, that I started playing football again. I joined a team that was filled with fellow migrants or refugees, mainly from El Salvador, but also from Chile, East Timor, Papua New Guinea, Italy and Vietnam. The experience was powerful emotionally and socially. Healing was embodied in emotive feelings and a psychological experience. That is, it felt great to play soccer again; but the healing was triggered by the social process of incorporating into my social life the cultural and community resource of soccer. I gradually realised what I had lost over those ten years, and

> I became aware of a part of myself that had been submerged in the process of cultural and social loss. I became literate about my self-in-context: the context of being amongst refugees, and the context of my past-present relationship to the game of soccer, which I reclaimed as 'football'. This was a healing experience—a process of sociality that enabled me to 'perform' my heart-felt game.

In this case, Peter experienced community as fellow-footballers enabling him to feel the pain of loss embedded within the migration process, and gradually to heal. Again, the healing process was social rather than therapeutic. The challenge is to reclaim community as primary within healing processes. Therapeutic and professional counsellors, while important, should be secondary. They should only be needed when community has collapsed. The irony, as John McKnight (1995) has reminded us in *The Careless Society*, is that it is often the entry of therapeutic professionals into communities that has contributed to the erosion and collapse of social solidarity and engagement. They often purposefully—albeit unconsciously due to a lack of reflexivity—nurture a therapeutic culture which orients people away from community. Community workers need to reverse the practice of turning towards professional therapists for healing, and revitalise people's collective capacities to heal one another through the ties and processes of community. As part of that reversal it is worth also developing a deeper understanding of why people are so easily assimilated into therapeutic culture.

A deeper understanding of therapeutic culture

Consideration of therapeutic culture prompts us first to ask: why? Why these feelings of victim-hood, passivity and vulnerability? Why this willingness to accept labels of at-risk-ness and special needs, and collude with therapeutically oriented professionals?

Firstly, there is a sense that therapeutic culture enables people to gaze at the *event* of suffering rather than its causes, and therefore releases people from the need for moral reflection. This gaze articulates as "I'm in pain"; "my group is suffering". The focus is on the suffering, the pain, and the capacity to cope with them. This event-focus is much less complex than one oriented towards the increasingly complex moral issues associated with the *causes* of such suffering and pain. For example, if refugee pain is gazed at therapeutically, then the understanding of suffering is limited to the event of *being* a refugee and the suffering resultant from being a refugee. This limits our need to engage with the moral problems associated with someone *becoming* a refugee—which provoke questions such as: "Why did they have to leave their country?" and "What role is my country playing in their forced migration?" The therapeutic agenda legitimises sincerity, but undermines people's capacity to become moral and social agents of wider change.

Secondly, therapeutic culture enables people to create *identities* around the labels that focus on vulnerability. Such labels create a stable identity within a social context where people have an increasingly fragile sense of self. Aligning ourselves with the philosopher and psychiatrist Patrick Bracken (2002), it seems that the fragility of people's sense of self is a result of *post-modern anxiety*. Many people no longer have access to stable resources such as religious or philosophical stories that can give them a sense of meaning and resilient self-hood. People feel alone and confused. The task of meaning-making has become a task for the individual, and this task often feels too hard. People then find solace within the therapeutic process of group identity construction. The label is all-sufficient for the person to feel OK, absolving them from the need to engage in moral and social change processes.

Our conclusion: Resist!

Creating an alternative to therapeutic culture requires people to re-assert personal and collective agency. It means confronting feelings of victimhood, feelings of vulnerability and passivity, and labels of 'at-risk' and 'special needs'. It requires attending with analysis to the causes of people's distresses—individual or social—and identifying the structural and social dynamics at play in either causing distress or supporting people through their distress. Such analysis focuses attention on the agents and activities that are causing distress, and this attention is the pre-cursor to exercising imaginative collective agency in dealing with causes. The story about playing football is illustrative in that it alludes to tackling school-based processes of racism that prevent young people from playing their 'heart-felt' game.

3.6 Collusion with a garrison state

Over the past few years a group of colleagues have been involved in co-facilitating at least forty community-building courses called *Building Better Communities*. The participants in these courses have been young everyday residents of neighbourhoods, along with older people, refugees, migrants, Aboriginal and Torres Strait Islanders, official and informal community leaders of clubs, groups, and organisations, and local politicians. These courses have taken place in a diverse range of localities—from outer suburban caravan parks through to inner city "hoods'. In discussions about the kinds of visions and values that infuse people's hope for community, safety is almost always the group's number one hope, irrespective of the locality.

This is easy to understand. Currently both authors enjoy living in a safe place where it is possible to leave doors open during the night. We can wander the streets without fear, although it is wise to remain aware and attentive. We rest relatively easy. In contrast one of the authors has spent many years living in South Africa and has felt the anxiety and fear that come with constant concerns over safety.

Perhaps it is because of our own love of safety that we recognise serious problems associated with the current calls for safety, security and surveillance within our societies—a trend that increasingly undermines community as hospitality and dialogue.

Moving from a social to a security contract

In the same way that people collude with therapeutic culture on the basis of their feelings of vulnerability, so people feeling afraid collude with the garrison state in calling for increased security. Such collusion in turn legitimises a technical solution from the state and a lack of agency and responsibility by populations. The result is often an agreement to increase surveillance.

This dynamic is symptomatic of the erosion of what political scientists call the *social contract* and the *social state*. Historically, the social contract is an understanding between the state and citizens, in which citizens agree to give legitimacy to the state in governing aspects of their lives in exchange for provision of social needs. Within the welfare state, this has ensured that the state provides social needs such as health, education, and income security, and also acts as an arbiter of wealth redistribution. Citizens in turn allow the state to govern them and agree to pay it taxes. However, as the welfare state withers or is eroded away (some Western nations no longer even guarantee income security), the meeting of social needs has tended to become a privilege rather than a right, and increasingly the state does not guarantee other human securities. For example the social need to provide for education and health may be handed over by the state to the so-called 'market'.

However in handing over these roles of providing social needs, the state is in search for alternative forms of legitimacy. Questions arise such as "why should we allow the state to govern aspects of our lives if it does not also guarantee to meet our needs?" "Isn't the state reneging on its social contract with us?"

The answer is that increasingly the state's legitimacy is actualised through a new *security contract* rather than the original social contract. The state morphs from a social state to what Zygmunt Bauman, drawing on Henry Giroux, calls a "garrison state" (2004, p85). The state promises to protect global capital primarily and citizens secondarily. In turn people give it their allegiance and confer legitimacy. In this transition a slide from a social to a security contract can be discerned—people give up on the social state and collude with a garrison state. Behind this process is the constant diffusion of fear and anxiety and as Furedi has reminded us in *Therapy Culture* (2004), people allow themselves to become governed through an emotional sense of vulnerability. People feel fearful, afraid, 'at-risk' and so are willing to allow therapeutically oriented security professionals to soothe them through guarantees of safety.

This has significant implications and challenges for community and for community development work. Community development is in many ways connected to conceptions of social justice and empowerment—to ensuring that people, as citizens, have their needs and rights met by the state on which legitimacy is conferred. It is, after all, 'our' state—the 'people's state'. However, increasingly the state has becomes objectified and distant from the citizens. In that distance it has become an object that *provides* the citizenry with safety and security. Within such a framework, security and safety are no longer the responsibility of the people, requiring social processes of relating to one another carefully and accountably. It simply requires citizens to hand that responsibility over to the state.

There are many other manifestations of this anxiety and fear about safety and security. For example, many people see the United States as a model of society, and yet their lack of a social contract and a social state has led to them becoming one of the most violent Western societies. People's lack of income security has led to crime and violence in ways that have required the need for increasing surveillance. Prisons are proven to be ineffective in rehabilitation and yet they are still touted as a solution.

In a parallel process, Australian and British governments—often at the behest of citizens—use closed circuit television (CCTV) cameras as a way of increasing people's *sense* of safety and decreasing their levels of fear and anxiety. As a result of this process there is now an over-abundance of CCTV cameras. For example, within the UK there are now 4.2 million CCTV cameras, one for every fourteen people (BBC News, 2006). Australian evidence actually shows that such cameras do not increase safety; they only increase the capacity for policing authorities to identify and charge offenders (Wilson et al., 2006). When people are about to conduct a criminal act they do not really care about cameras being present; crime is usually spontaneous, connected to either alcohol or some other immediate need. However, people aligned to the vision of the garrison state continue to push for more cameras, obscuring the facts and creating further misunderstanding.

'Community' as a site of governance

At a local level, fears and anxieties over security and safety play out in many weird ways. Local populations need simultaneous governing and securing by the state. However, people within localities are increasingly called upon to act as the instruments of one another's surveillance to promote security and safety. Manifestations of this within Australia are telephone hot lines to dob in[3] a potential terrorist as part of the 'war on terror', and also initiatives where people are invited to dob in neighbours whom they catch breaking the increasingly severe water restrictions. Whether it is to do with water security or terrorism-related 'homeland security', 'communities' are considered to be both sites of governance and actors of surveillance. What kind of 'community' is this?

An alternative, dialogical orientation invites understanding of *why* people are involved in such crime and *what* they are doing that undermines people's sense of safety and security—the 'shadow' of people's participation, and our own collusion.[4] A dialogical approach to community development invites safety and security through social engagement, both in the invitation for participation of those involved in causing a lack of safety, and also in a deep examination of why people feel the need for such technical interventions.

Engaging socially with fear

A big part of the 'why?' has to do with *fear*. Fear of crime and violence is on the increase, even though actual crime and violence is decreasing. From a dialogical perspective, the hope of social safety requires engagement primarily with people's fears (Lee, c2007). It involves processes that make visible the agents that propagate fear—insurance firms, security firms, police, governments—and it requires reclaiming public spaces for people, not cameras. Community workers need to challenge slogans such as 'stranger danger', and invite people to rebuild community as hospitality.

There are exciting examples of such work. *Saferworld* is an international NGO working in post-conflict and war settings, some of the most unsafe places on earth. Saferworld has learned many lessons that show a

---

3   An Aussie colloquialism meaning 'identify to authorities'
4   See the discussions on shadow in Chapter One above.

more dialogical approach to creating community safety. Their approach involves community development practitioners

> . . . accompanying communities through an action-planning process which enables key actors within places to identify and address their safety concerns in collaboration with others. It is an approach that is people-focused, encouraging the engagement of marginalised, disen-franchised and sometimes cynical people, often in environments where trust between communities and power-brokers has broken down (Saferworld, 2006).

Many of the lessons learned from such work indicate that the concerns of safety, linked to issues of fear, are almost always to do with broader issues of relationship (for example, between community members and police), aesthetic (such as urban decay), and environmental design (such as street lighting). This approach invites people to *engage* with these kinds of issues rather than purchasing more CCTV cameras.

Firing back for a social state

The French sociologist Pierre Bourdieu's book, *Firing Back* (2003) argues that while dealing with people's fears socially is important, it is also imperative that practitioners actively resist the trend towards a garrison state and a security contract. Part of the goal of dialogical community development practice is to build coalitions and federations of community-oriented organisations that insist on re-building a social state that fulfils its social contract obligations. The terms of the new contract are that community workers will allow the state to govern us, we will confer legitimacy on it, we will pay it taxes—but only to the degree that it will provide for the needs of all people, and particularly those who are poor and marginalised. It is within the spheres of 'human waste'—amongst the ghettos of inner-city migrants and unemployed, refugee young people; amongst prisoners who are denied voting rights or access to a fresh start; amongst those whose only hope for living or just wages is still through joining labour unions—that lies the seed of a movement that will fire back for this social state.

Summing up

Six trends against dialogical community development work have been identified. Discussing each of them provides a rich analysis of the many challenges facing community workers who are committed to depth, hospitality and solidarity. A soulful orientation, a social practice and deconstructive movements require engagement with these trends that can inform careful, considered ways of working with others.

The first two reflections, on objectification and ideological positions, shed light on patterns of thinking that undermine a dialogical approach to community development. *Objectification* refers to thinking processes where people, creatures, land, all things, are related to within a subject-object kind of relationship. There is no chance for mutuality or dialogue. Embedded within the idea of objectification is the notion of 'objecting to'—the construction of an adversarial relationship usually built on binaries of either–or. We explored the kinds of binaries that construct much of social life and then offered a way forward through an understanding of inter-subjectivity and embracing of deconstructive movements.

In identifying *ideological positions* as a key challenge for dialogical community development we suggested that many people, in their search for security, an easy and simplistic analysis of society, and a sense of 'community', find it very hard to open up to dialogue. Ideological positions tend to emerge or be constructed from closed-set, bounded systems of beliefs with clear 'ins' and 'outs'. We offered an alternative way of thinking with an appreciative attitude towards 'other' ideals, expanded conceptual frameworks, and a delight in mystery.

While the first two sections of our analysis reflected on ways of thinking, the next four considered the challenges of people exercising social agency and of the atrophy of imagination within social life.

Our exploration of *disenchantment* considered how certain contemporary discourses of secularism undermine pluralism, fuel a limited materialistic vision of 'development', and support the expansion of modernity with its by-product of human waste. We advocated instead for a community development approach that appreciates both spiritual and secular sensibilities, and is willing to learn from sacred wisdoms.

The reflection on *addictive consumerism* explored how people increasingly substitute consumerism for the sociality of embodied community life as the primary means of meeting their need for belonging: "I belong because I can consume". Beneath such hopes for belonging is both a deep fear of becoming flawed consumers or surplus population, and a passivity which makes it easier for people simply to consume rather than engage in the more complex task of considering an ethical and political project that meets their deeper needs for well-being and happiness.

Our discussion about *therapeutic culture* argued that people and professionals increasingly collude with one another to find solutions to social problems via technically oriented therapeutic interventions. Within therapeutic culture, rather than addressing the causes of social distress—often related to moral, social and political processes—people focus on individually *coping* with the distress. In fact people often find solace and cultivate a sense of identity through ascribing a high level of significance to the story of suffering resulting from their distress. We offered a way forward through proposing an alternative model of social healing.

The final reflection on *collusion with a garrison state* considered the danger of contemporary movements away from a social state (that has a social contract with citizens) and towards a garrison state (to which citizens give legitimacy in exchange for security). Ways forward require both social engagement with our fears, and a process of fighting back for a social state.

As stated in the Introduction, we are not proposing that community development practitioners go into spaces and places and name the trends in public ways; these trends are, after all, part of the analysis that practitioners first have to internalise themselves. Many people would not be able to make sense of this practitioner analysis. The sterile ways of thinking, being and doing that result from these trends have seeped deep into people's conscious and unconscious ways of living. Community workers can only hope to enter into dialogue with people gradually, bringing a fresh and subtle perspective informed by such an analysis. Within this space of dialogue arises the possibility of new ideas, of 'in-between' ways of thinking, being and doing—and new kinds of community.

f o u r

Caring for different spheres of community life

In Chapters One and Two we explored broadly how a dialogical approach to community development can deepen our understanding of living and working in communities. Chapter Three explored our practitioner analysis of contemporary challenges to the life of communities. We now examine the different spheres of community life that practitioners need to care for: the ordinary, socio-cultural, economic, political, and ecological spheres. In many ways these spheres of life are intertwined; however we have pulled them apart for the purposes of understanding how a dialogical framework of practice is diffused within each one. We have named this everyday practice of community development as *caring*. The accumulated knowledge, skills and awareness of the community worker should never lead to a notion of professionalism that undermines a commitment and capacity to care.

Caring is a core imperative. Care can be contrasted with the notion of *cure*. Cure implies the end of trouble: if you are cured, you do not have to worry about what was bothering you any longer. In contrast, care carries a sense of ongoing attention. If an understanding of community development is informed by a paradigm of cure, then the focus will be on technique. The primary concern becomes: "What techniques will be used to remove the problem?" Such an approach undermines all the notions of the dialogical approach explored in Chapters One and Two. However, if an approach to community development is to be informed by a paradigm of caring, then 'problems' will be approached with depth, hospitality and a soulful orientation. Problems invite caring; they promote a deeper understanding of shadow, story, discourse and dynamics at work in neigh-bourhoods and nations.

Our work in community development would change remarkably if practitioners thought of it as ongoing care rather than the quest for a cure. We might take more time to watch and listen as people in spaces, places and bases gradually reveal the deeper mysteries and patterns of daily life. Problems within such spaces offer a chance for reflection that would otherwise be precluded by the swift routine of life. The approach to community development outlined here acknowledges, despite its implied paradox, that a muscled, strong-willed pursuit of change can at best actually stand in the way of substantive transformation and at worst, cause more problems.

4.1 Caring for the ordinary

In the movement towards a more sophisticated and professionalised view of community development, it is important to remember that much of the caring aspect of community-building is done through being aware of and involved in the ordinary. Such ordinary activities might include sharing a cup of tea or coffee, standing in line at the social security office in support of someone needing help, taking a stroll through the local park with someone who wishes to simply chat, or taking the afternoon off to cook up a barbecue with some friends. These everyday events work as a kind of social glue that connects ordinary people with one another, building community around the concerns of daily life: how are the kids? what's happening at school? how might the weather affect Saturday's game?

Sometimes we watch the way community development workers live (ourselves included) and get the sense that our lives as community workers are the antithesis of what we dream. We don't walk our talk. We dream of a sociability of community life in which people have time for one another, in which beauty and art are welcomed, in which the rhythms of work blend with the pleasures of recreation and friendship—in which the ordinary is considered significant. Yet the lives lived—charging around from meeting to meeting, project to project, heads full of analysis of global geo-politics and national trends—squeeze out any time or space for the ordinary life of community.

As professionals with specialised skills and knowledge, community workers should have developed an acute self-awareness and sense of personal power; but none of this should detract from the ordinary activities of caring in community. If practitioners do not have time for family, friends, and play, then they are actually undoing community while trying to nurture it. There is no space in this frenetic busyness for community as dialogue or community as hospitality.

Doing ordinary things with extraordinary love

In the whirlpool of activity that is modern life, we are reminded of Mother Theresa's words of wisdom. For her, at the heart of living is the requirement to do "ordinary things with extraordinary love" (Devananda, 1986, p65). The extraordinary activist efforts of Gandhi, in South Africa and then in India, were balanced by the ordinary simplicity of significant parts of his daily life. It could have been easy for Gandhi to forget the daily routines required of living in an ashram— working on the land, spinning yarn, preparing food, and teaching and playing with the children. However, he lived and modelled his dream at 'home'.

As community workers run around manically trying to build community, trying to build a better world, it is important to ask "what is this world, this community that is being dreamt of?" The answer is often about a nurturing, wholesome web of relationships full of wonderful ordinary living. It is about people walking in parks, drinking coffee, sharing a beer or glass of wine and chatting while picking up the kids after school. It is a soccer game, cricket or tennis match amongst friends on a Saturday afternoon; or a weekend camping trip out into the bush or meeting up at a day spa. It involves open homes; chatting at the kitchen table while cooking dinner; a cuppa at the fence; nursing mum's groups, playgroups or birthday parties creating happy, messy chaos in lounge rooms and backyards. This is community with depth—or our version of it! Do community workers have time to participate in such activities, or in their technical or instrumental commitment to building community, are they too busy to be a part of it?

Beware of our idealism

A major obstacle preventing community development workers from enjoying and participating in the ordinary is a sense of idealism. Idealism in itself is wonderful; it inspires hope, energy and action. But it also has its shadow side, often appearing as rejection of the ordinary, and neglect of the mundane. Idealism can inspire a grandiose vision of change, which can actually become an obstacle to participating in the simplicity of ordinary community life.

> We live in a classic inner-city neighbourhood, where the politics of the left is expressed through factionalism—the International Socialists vs. the Democratic Socialists vs. the Socialist Alliance—and anarchist factions beyond count. The result is that some of the most passionate and committed people in our community find it difficult to work together, let alone be inclusive of 'ordinary' garden variety neighbours who are compromised by their bourgeoisie values and mortgage.

> It all came to a head one night during Expo 88, when the community mobilised in support of a squat in some flats that had been cleared for redevelopment. About 30 of us sat against the walls of an empty lounge room, discussing the events of the day—police presence, outstanding warrants, media attention, electricity workers cutting off the power, how the squatters were travelling emotionally, and how they would feed themselves that night. At that moment the squat was on the front line of the community resistance to Expo; and many diverse people were there to offer support.

> We were discussing tactics and ethics, a debate between experienced campaigners and tough survivors of the global peace movement. The debate became tense as people disagreed and tried to persuade the group to come round to their viewpoint. The discussion got louder and angrier, and polarised around the opposing ideals of a well-known Christian pacifist and a non-violent Dutch environment activist recently returned from action in the rainforests of Borneo. Neither had the awareness to know that they were dominating the room and alienating people. Neither would back down, but we were all a bit surprised when

suddenly they both flew across the room, at one another's throats in a classic cat-fight! Neither was much of a fighter, so no-one got hurt. But what was sad was that the ordinary people who had come along to offer support—some venturing into social activism for the first time—were completely alienated, and many did not return.

Community practitioners all need to develop an awareness of the ways that idealism distracts from caring for the ordinary.

4.2 Caring for the social-cultural

In the same way that genetic diversity enables a biosphere to survive change, so socio-cultural diversity enables rapidly changing communities to not only survive but thrive. In the light of this, a core assumption of our development practice is that diversity enables people–in–places to creatively and imaginatively deal with challenging issues. A communal monoculture may lead to a lack of imagination and therefore a lack of transformational options.

It becomes one of our roles as community development workers to nurture people's capacity to welcome, rather than just tolerate diversity. In doing this we build a community's capacity to imagine and respond creatively to opportunities, problems and crises. This role is a significant challenge for community development workers in the context of increasing migration and the resulting demographic diversity, with the concurrent growing fear of the 'other' as strangers, portrayed as dangerous, destabilising and threatening.

A social ecology of diversity

Such a view of our role in this kind of community development is critical in an age where some people can say "genocide is an act of community-building" (Gourevitch, 1998). In the year 2006 there were 278 political conflicts in the world. Six of these were wars, with twenty-nine severe crises. Altogether, 118 conflicts were carried out violently (Heidelberg Institute for International Conflict Research, 2007). Many of these conflicts were legitimised in the name of 'community'—a kind of community not oriented towards hospitality, but rather the kind that for Jacques Derrida is understood through the prism of 'munitions' which shares the etymological roots of the word 'community' (Derrida in Caputo,1997).

In *Ecology and Community*, Fritjof Capra (1994) outlines the dynamics of an alternative kind of community characterised by a diverse socio-cultural ecology:

Diversity means many links, many different approaches to the same problem. So a diverse community is a resilient community. A diverse community is one that can adapt to changing situations, and therefore diversity is another very important principle of ecology . . . But it's not always a great advantage, and this is what we can learn from ecosystems. Diversity is a strategic advantage for a community if, and only if, there is a vibrant network of relationships, if there is a free flow of information through all the links of the network. Then diversity is a tremendous strategic advantage. However, if there is fragmentation, if there are subgroups in the network or individuals who are not really part of the network, then diversity can generate prejudice, it can generate friction, and as we know well from our inner cities, it can generate violence (p10).

This is why it is imperative to develop an approach to community development that has an appreciation of both the fragility and the importance of a diverse socio-cultural community ecology. Here is Peter's experience:

The work of diverse community that celebrates and loves difference is fragile. I have spent the past several years involved with diverse refugee groups in my home town of Brisbane. This involvement has made me aware of huge human diversity, the complexities of human relationship, and the challenges of community cohesion and coexistence within many of our contemporary social geographies. For example, my work in recent years with Sudanese refugees has immersed me in the complexities of coexistence:

- between ethnic groups or tribes from within Sudan—many of whom have been fighting against one another for years;
- between religious groups—Arab northern and western versus Christian southern and eastern Sudanese who have been at war for decades;

- conflicts of generation and gender;
- between Sudanese and other recently arrived groups, like those from the former Yugoslavia or from nations of the Pacific;
- between Sudanese and Australian indigenous people;
- between Sudanese and many Anglo-Australians, like the older woman from a white working class suburb who rang the police, because there were a group of young black men in the park near her home: "Are they threatening you?"

"No."

"Are they misbehaving?"

"No."

"What are they doing?"

"They are kicking a ball around."

Each of these challenges to cohesion and coexistence is also immersed within broader national and international discourses—that are currently 'anti-Arab', hostile to Muslims, and fearful of 'others who are not like us', a quote from the then Australian Prime Minister, referring to asylum-seekers who were trying to access Australian national territory.

With such a story in mind, practitioners need to address the question: how do we nurture diversity in the fragile web of social relationships that are at the heart of community?

Being hospitable to the enemy within: an ethic of plurality

We all live and work at a time when, more than ever, people need to face and love their differences. We are threatened with chaos and political disintegration. There is a tendency to project the enemy onto the other—whether it be Muslims, gays, blacks, conservatives, liberals, greens or socialists—and such a tendency will lead society in a downward spiral of endless exclusion and expanding violence. It is imperative that all people cultivate an ecological attitude that affirms diversity. The way to achieve this is to understand and practise hospitality in a way that people have rarely had to practise it before.

Learning about hospitality requires facing this enemy within ourselves, and becoming hospitable to that enemy—an enemy that demonises others. This is the challenge: a dialogical approach to community practice means a dialogue with ourselves, acknowledging the shadow parts within—acknowledging that deep inside many of us lie racist, sexist, bigoted, class-conscious selves.

A dialogical approach which reawakens love is not afraid of such selves. Cultivating a love for them enables individuals to look them in the eye and transcend them. We can be friends with the enemy within and find less need to look for the enemy 'out there'. In doing this people are free to utilise what culture and intelligence has taught: to 'be ethical' with the full knowledge of who we are. People can develop what William Connolly (1991) calls an ethic of cultivation, cultivating a deep plurality within ourselves, our neighbourhoods and our nations.

Fostering centripetal dynamics of connection

There are many centrifugal dynamics at work, pushing people apart, creating distance and disconnection. They fragment and disintegrate the possibility of community as dialogue and hospitality. Many government programs, and many 'community' groups and organisations actively work against a socio-cultural configuration that affirms diversity. They do not want to see people coming together to hear one another's stories. They see 'community' as an opportunity to build walls and gather 'munitions'.

Our role as community development workers is to oppose such distancing and disconnecting centrifugal dynamics, and instead nurture centripetal dynamics that bring people together to listen to one another, learn from one another, and creatively find solutions for living together. The challenge is to create platforms in spaces, places and bases that enable such listening and learning to take place.

Several years ago we were involved in a wonderful initiative that brought indigenous women and women from refugee backgrounds together to share stories and overcome their misconceptions of the 'other'. The initiative emerged out of a 'dialogue in healing' project whereby indigenous people and people from refugee backgrounds realised they knew little about one another. Their perceptions of the other were dominated by media images and 'politician-speak'.

The outcome of the dialogue was an agreement that a group of refugee women from various African nations, El Salvador, Columbia, and Vietnam, would spend a weekend at the Nungeena Indigenous Women's Healing Centre at Mount Beerwah—one of the Glasshouse Mountains in the Sunshine Coast area of south-east Queensland.

The women shared stories of losing country, both indigenous and refugee, their suffering and their journeys of healing. They cried, laughed and cooked together. One of the great outcomes was the decision to share recipes with one another. One indigenous woman commented how, 'I never knew they'd suffered so much. Now I know, I can heal as well'.

This gathering of people, made possible by the purposeful laying of a platform for dialogue, reversed the centrifugal dynamics that were at work within the nation, and fostered centripetal dynamics that wove meaningful relationships between people of 'difference'.

There is no utopian or perfect place, in the same way that there is no utopian or perfect bio-sphere. There will still be expressions of violence, selfishness and apathy in neighbourhoods. But when platforms for dialogue have been laid in which people of difference have come together, then places that thrive are possible—ecologically sound and balanced, full of vitality, and capable of transformation.

4.3 Caring for the economy

Another role for community development workers is that of caring for the economy. For many decades of the twentieth century, the economic debate was dominated by binary modes of thinking, focused on the either–or choice of adopting an economy based on free market principles, or developing a bureaucratic socialist economy. Neither of these dominant approaches has proved themselves to those who care for the economy in the service of a people-centred approach to development.

Current forms of growth-oriented, free-market capitalism—declared the 'winner' in a period of apparent post-politics—operate almost by definition on the basis of what is expedient, and are therefore open to question on ethical grounds. Anything so obsessed with selective advantage and profit cannot be trusted to provide either moral guidance or long-term stability. The cataclysmic economic events since 2008 have proven this to be true. Authors such as David Korten (1995) and Vandana Shiva (2005) have provided an analysis of the dangers of global capitalism—or what Shiva calls the 'death economy'. On the basis that people do not want a death economy, and that the 2008-9 economic meltdown has undermined people's commitment to 'turbo-charged capitalism', we along with many others are searching for new perspectives on care for an economy that will enhance people's lives.

Fostering human-scale relational economies

The word economy originates from the Greek word oikonomia, meaning the organisation of the house and a prudent and ethical use of its resources (Booth, 1993). Informed by this etymological understanding, our perspective is oriented towards the idea that caring for the economic sphere requires a renewed focus on the micro-level of households while also supporting locality-based, human-scale economic initiatives (Max-Neef, 1991).

For community work practitioners guided by orientations such as solidarity, economic development implies the development of a 'community economy': a relational moral economy, and a living ecological economy. Such an approach is underpinned by a moral imperative for everyone to have enough, with particular reference to the disadvantaged, and future generations. It is a people-centred approach, as opposed to corporate or state-centred approaches which are monopolistic and anti-human. A people-centred economy honours people's freedom to engage in economic transactions—an acknowledgment of the importance of the market—but also attempts to overcome the widespread failure of market mechanisms to promote social justice or ecological sustainability. Here is an example of the limits of a market-oriented economy, that provides insight into the possibilities of a more people-oriented one.

The neighbourhood we live in is a place where people love to live. It's close to the university, the river, the central business area; the amenities are fabulous. However, in recent years the rents have risen exponentially as processes of gentrification have taken hold. In this context we have watched two parallel housing economies at work.

The market economy is the more visible one. The rental contract is often mediated through the real estate industry that has a vested interest in high rents: the more the rent, the more the agencies' fees. The more vacancies the agencies create, the more re-letting fees they earn. Often local 'free' newspapers are linked to real estate industry interests, who are their biggest advertisers, and they publish constant hype about the market rental rates that could be charged. If you are a landowner in the area and read these papers you could regularly lick your lips with the taste of potential profits. On the whole this market housing economy pushes lower-income households out of the area. It is an economy of social exclusion based on the contradictory logic and mythology of the market. The logic is that the household who can pay one dollar more than any competitor gets the vacancy, while the mythology is that this is somehow a fair way to allocate roofs over people's heads.

On the other hand we know plenty of tenants living in the area who are known by their local landlords. The 'contract' between these landlords and tenants is mediated through a relationship that has some 'other' kind of meaning and connection, and therefore some scope for dialogue. Within this relational economy the rents are significantly lower than those being charged in the market. The relational economy is guided by some ethic other than profit, and enables a whole diversity of people on lower incomes to continue living in the area—it is a more inclusive economy.

Of course, individual real estate agents also bring varying levels of compassion and types of relationality to their industry, and we have heard beautiful stories of agents, usually the Greeks who have strong historical roots and social ties to the area, defying the market in ways that preserve their community.

Such a case-study illustrates the powerful potential of building relational and human-scale moral economies. Not everyone need be driven by the profit motive that is usually the focus of a narrow market orientation. In the relational economy both the relationships between landlords and tenants, and a commitment to maintaining some lower-cost rental options for people in the neighbourhood, take priority over maximising profit. This relational, living and human-scale local economy balances economic objectives with social and ecological objectives.

Building economic institutions with social objectives

Another element of our vision for community economic development is that earnings, spending, savings and investments remain primarily in localities, generating jobs for local people and furthering other local social and ecological outcomes. This kind of relational local economy focuses on building structures such as savings and loans co-operatives, local micro-credit groups, community credit unions, local industries, and social enterprises.

Co-operatives are key vehicles for building local relational economies, because they both ensure member and/or worker control of the company, and link business imperatives into a broader ethic of co-operation and other community-oriented values.[5] A little-known fact is that there are more members of co-operatives than there are shareholders in publicly-listed companies around the globe. Co-operatives need not be at the margins of the economic sphere of society, but can be vibrant economic, ecological and social contributors. " . . . through their self-help enterprises and their commitment to members and their communities, [co-operatives] generate an estimated 100 million jobs worldwide" (United Nations, 2007, p4).

We have both been members of several co-operatives. We currently both work part-time for Community Praxis Co-op Ltd—a not-for-profit workers' co-operative established in 1998 that provides training and con-

---

5   For example, see the seven principles of the International Co-operative Alliance (http://www.ica.coop/coop/principles.html)

sultancy services to non-government organisations, community-based organisations, and government. All members of the co-operative sit on the Board of Management and have a key say in the direction of the co-op. 3% of all income goes into an "ethical dividend" that we give away, to foster other co-operatives and respond to other community needs. The ratio of pay is 4:1, a relational commitment limiting greed and exploitation by ensuring that the highest-paid worker (usually someone with a doctorate on a consultancy) never earns more than four times the hourly rate of the lowest-paid worker (usually the admin. worker or a student in the role of project assistant).

Within our city are many other community co-operatives. During the past ten years Reverse Garbage has built a recycling business, employing local people who source and sell industrial and other discards, and supplying materials to household projects and artists who create recycled art works. Nundah Community Enterprises Co-op is another social enterprise that employs people with learning difficulties and health issues. This co-op runs a successful café, catering business, egg-retailing venture and property maintenance business. Such co-operatives are an integral part of the vision of re-building local economies by establishing and growing businesses that have social objectives.

We are also fond of two stories from other parts of the world that illustrate how community development practitioners can be involved in building economic institutions that focus on a relational moral economy: Mohammad Yunus' work of the Grameen Bank (1999) and Judy Wick's work of the Philadelphia White Dog Café and the accompanying Business Alliance for Local Living Economies (1998, 2004). There are huge challenges to building new legal structures that enable community-oriented people to invest in such local relational economies. Questions arise such as "How do we ensure our superannuation funds are channelled into legal structures that could invest in local work with social objectives?" or "How do we move away from an over-reliance on government or philanthropy to build such economies?" A number of colleagues are involved in experiments of building such structures.

Over many years some Brisbane colleagues have built Foresters ANA, now called Foresters Community Finance, into a viable organisation that is not dependent on government. Foresters Community Finance now has a legal and ethical structure to invest funds into work that will provide social housing, arrange premises for community organisations, and cultivate other kinds of asset bases for neighbourhoods. Foresters Community Finance specialises in supporting community development through investment and business, rather than just focusing on government funding and philanthropy. Their ethical investment fund is only one of many mechanisms that offer investment options to rebuild local living economies. They argue that we need to re-think our returns on investment and include ecological, social and community returns in our calculations.

Such structures are sometimes seen as representing a new 'fourth sector'—neither government, private or non-profit. The fourth sector is made up of hybrid structures, experimenting with business models but driven by social and ecological objectives.

Challenging greed

Caring for the economy does not simply mean that we develop our own local relational economies; it also implies that we challenge some of the 'givens' of the *current* manifestation of the market economy. Deconstructive thinking helps to destabilise the orthodoxies of many economic fundamentalisms. For example, we need to advocate a transformation in the way wages are allocated, destabilising the rationalisations used to legitimate greed. The obscene disparity of income levels between high and low-income earners is an abomination to anyone committed to an ethical, relational or community-oriented economy. A recent *Guardian* article highlighted how within some corporations the "ratio between bosses' rewards and employees' pay has risen to 98:1 . . . meaning that the work of a chief executive is valued almost 100 times more highly than that of their employees" (Finch, 2007, p41).

For many serious commentators it is this growing inequality and undermining of economic egalitarianism that will thwart much of our social progress. Studies indicate that it is people's sense of *relative* poverty that undermines their health and good will, and often provides the impetus and motivation to participate in anti-social activity and crime (Wilkinson, 2005). Within Australia the 'p-word', poverty, is unspoken. Social justice has slid from the agenda of both the powerful and the activist middle class. Social capital has replaced social justice (Everingham, 2003)—and it is the 'aspirational class', not the marginalised, that are central to politicians' gaze. The egalitarian society is now a myth!

In opposition to this kind of trend we need to develop an ethos that is committed to a decent living wage, rather than just a minimum wage, and shames those who receive disproportionately high wages. We are not talking about a 'politic of envy'—a disparaging slogan being used regularly within Australia against those who mention the dirty word 'class'—but a politic based on ethical imperatives and a reconsideration of moral economy. There is a need to reclaim a commitment to social justice that implies genuine movement towards an equal society. We need to re-develop a praxis oriented towards the politics of *enough* and *equality*, rather than simple equity—and ensure all people are guaranteed enough to live happily. This is an imperative grounded in the passion of personal experience for Peter:

> I have spent many of my days talking with people who are desperately trying to survive—young and old. I have spent time living in a shanty town of Manila; I have eaten meals with the poor of Phnom Penh and New Delhi; I have sat with families and practised my Zulu in the townships of South Africa; I have sat with young people in Vanuatu dreaming of a future despite having to support extended families of twenty people. These people live on the crumbs of the rich.
>
> Then I see a job advert linked to AusAID funding with a company such as ACIL or the equivalent private sector agent in the 'development industry' and learn of consultants earning the equivalent of three months' income of the poor in one hour. These consultants use so many rationalisations: "such high wages must be developed to keep people from moving to the private sector", or that "these people work so hard that it is deserved". I call them rationalisations—nothing more.

Such rationalisations are simply ways of legitimising rampant greed—greed that is destroying an economy that would otherwise have the capacity to genuinely care for the poor. Clive Hamilton's diagnosis of 'affluenza' accurately describes the ailment that blinds us to the possibilities of global social justice (2005).

Examining economic orthodoxy for signs of madness

Along with such rationalisations there is much economic orthodoxy that we need to challenge. We are reminded of the satirical question: "Who believes that you can grow something infinitely within a finite system?" The answer is "mad people and economists".

Current orthodoxies legitimise trading activities such as shipping apples from the UK to South Africa to be waxed and then back again to the UK for consumption. Economically it is sound: it generates trade activity and the employment of people in South Africa. However, on every other basis it is madness. Ecologically it is a disaster—think of the fuel consumption, refrigeration costs—and politically it undermines South Africa's food security: its people could be growing apples for their own consumption. But it is assumed to be permissible in the name of orthodox economic principles of comparative advantage. Some of the greatest struggles will be faced in restructuring the international trade system towards the local, and away from the kind of economic activity represented by the apples being shipped back and forth; rewarding businesses that produce and sell as locally as possible, and that only work externally when necessary with other bio-regions and nations.

Our approach to community economic development requires a certain level of economic literacy. To unravel rationalisations and unmask orthodoxies such as those mentioned in the previous paragraphs requires an awareness that is willing to cut through all the mystification of technocratic economic elitists, whether of government treasuries, chambers of commerce or the World Trade Organisation. It is important that people are able to deconstruct and destabilise the current economic discourses that legitimise speculative and shareholder-oriented economies in the name of the ever-present need for 'growth'. We must trust our intuition and yet complement it with a hard-headed analysis. Economics cannot be separated from politics. The terms 'scientific' and 'pure' economics are merely technocratic disguises for an imperfect, politically charged exercise. 'Economics' is a politically constructed view of the economy reflecting either a struggle for fairness, equality and justice, or the legitimation of greed and 'free enterprise'.

Facing our economic-selves honestly

At the same time as growing awareness awakens us to the political economy of rationalisation and so-called orthodoxies, it also challenges us to be honest with ourselves. A dialogical approach to caring for the economy points out that many of the problems encountered in current economic discourses are in fact the product of our own collective and individual shadow problems. Many of us, deep down, are committed to the *status quo* to the extent that we are unable to imagine an alternative household or human-scale economy.

The growing crescendo of voices highlighting interconnections between the economy and environmental sustainability challenge us collectively and personally. Books such as George Monbiot's *Heat* (2007) confront us more than ever about the impact of our personal decisions on the environment and the economy. For Peter, choosing to fly for holidays and also choosing a job that requires many flights—for example, to Vanuatu as part of a development partnership—has a profound impact on the environment and therefore on the lives of the poor who are most vulnerable to the impacts of human-made global warming. This impact provokes an honest look at the connections between our choices and their consequences.

Living simply that others may simply live

Many of us have seen the bumper sticker displaying the Gandhian mantra "Live simply that others may simply live". It strikes to the heart of the matter and calls us to recognise the interconnectedness we share as economic, social and ecological beings. Under-development is directly connected to over-development. We now know that global development will not take place simply through a transfer of technology and/or utilisation of more resources. Development is a matter of sustainable, just and equitable utilisation and distribution of the resources we have, and reduction of our over-consumption patterns that over-utilise limited resources. Our ethical commitments and ecological realities must inform our economic strategy.

Raff Carmen (1996, p59), in quoting Ivan Illich, unveils a key problem of modernist economics: the *paradox of scarcity*. This idea expresses the 'truth' that once people choose the option of modernist economics, there will never seem to be enough:

> Economics always implies scarcity. What is not scarce cannot be subjected to economic control. This is true of goods and services, as it is of work. The assumption of scarcity has penetrated all modern institutions. Education is built on the assumption that desirable knowledge is scarce. Medicine assumes the same about health, transportation about time. ... Being immersed in it, we have become blind to the paradox that scarcity increases in a society with the rise of GNP. This kind of scarcity which we take for granted was—and largely still is—unknown outside commodity-intensive societies.

Working in Vanuatu has made the truth of Carmen's analysis very clear to Peter. The Paramount Chief of Vanuatu and some of his colleagues expressed it in these words:

> When we first visited your country [Australia] we were amazed at the wealth. Then we realised that if we aspired to this—changing from our underdeveloped economy to yours [as a developed economy]—we were destined to always be poor. We would only be aware of our scarcity of resources and riches. We would lose our self-respect and confidence. So we turned our back on that model and started re-thinking our customary economy in which we have traditionally traded in shells, mats and other goods made and collected. We are very wealthy when our reference becomes these goods. So we are re-building our economy on this basis.

On one of these work trips, one of Peter's colleagues handed the chiefs the book *Ancient Futures: Learning from Ladakh* (Norberg-Hodge, 2000). It is a book about how some of the Ladakhi people of the Western Himalayas resisted 'development' and are returning to a human-scale, intimate, gentler, natural economy. The chiefs were astounded, and became totally absorbed with the story. For the Vanuatu chiefs here was the story of a group of indigenous people far away geographically struggling with the very same thing they were. Since then Peter has been working with the chiefs to re-build an equivalent 'life-project' (Blaser, 2004) in which the key goal for indigenous people is to develop a vision and strategy for their collective lives that is infused with their own definition and goals for life. It requires resistance to the respect-destroying version of life depicted by modernity. This vision and strategy engages with conventional development in a variety of ways, including many variations of assimilation, accommodation and resistance.

This work with the chiefs of Vanuatu has given Peter cause to stop and reflect:

It was in the context of such a conversation that I became more conscious of a lack of my own life-project. In the light of human-induced global warming I am becoming increasingly aware of my own vulnerability. Awareness grows that my work is so linked to a global cash economy and my personal food security is so deeply connected to the industrial food economy that I lack any self-sufficiency. Clearly one cannot go back to some pre-industrial age, nor am I particularly nostalgic about such an epoch; one is constantly reminded of how hard such a pre-industrial life is for many in rural Vanuatu. Yet I am gradually becoming conscious of participating in a completely unsustainable livelihood pattern. It becomes clearer that I live without a life-project that infuses me with a vision of how to live sustainably. I've become captive to the impulses of modern consumerism and addicted to an increasing amount of 'needs'.

Peter's work with the chiefs highlights the significance of a dialogical approach in that both chiefs and Peter were learning from the partnership. Development was not about a transfer of information, resources and technology from Australia to Vanuatu, but about a dialogical process of exchange in which both parties to the dialogue were opened up to new possibilities. The new possibilities opening up for Peter involved honest acknowledgment of something lacking in his development vision, and its replacement by one that incorporated a renewed vision for sustainable living and also the needs of future generations so that they might simply live.

Such awareness is an imperative enabling us to give legitimacy to a new economic development vision. It starts with us! From that start it is possible to participate in a broad voluntary movement of community-oriented citizens willing to live simply while collectively modelling an alternative household and human-scale relational economy. In a parallel process, such a movement can also challenge state and transnational governance bodies to develop polices and initiatives that enable local, national and global economic justice. The movement will consist of people able to acknowledge their own greed, selfishness and fear, and also be able to live simply and ethically enabling a global economic and ecological balance that cuts through both the under-development that is killing 'others' and the over-development that is killing us.

4.4   Caring for politics

Rebuilding community-oriented places will require a vigorous process of politicking. Dialogue does not take place in a vacuum devoid of political processes. Politicking, while not being necessarily about party politics (which is not to say that people committed to community work should not be thoroughly involved in party politics) is most certainly about engaging with issues to do with power, democracy, participation and citizenship. This is the domain of politics. This reflection on caring for politics considers the importance of democratic political processes within our dialogical approach to community work.

From private concern to public action

A key skill of community as dialogue is that of engaging with people's stories and accompanying them in the transformation of their own narratives. Dialogue requires more than just listening to people's narratives—it requires a transformation of narrative. Kelly and Burkett (2008, p39), drawing on the insights of Paulo Freire, set out how this transformation can be achieved through shifting narratives from nouns and adjectives to verbs. For example, it is more useful to think of poverty as 'poverty-making', accurately implying that there are actors involved in a complex array of activities that lead to people's experiences of being poor—and that it is not just a given state of affairs that we cannot do anything about. Our understanding of poverty changes from a *state* to a *process*.

Another example illustrates how transforming the narrative in this way can also encompass a shift from passive object to active subject. Someone describes their experience of life as loneliness—'I am lonely' or 'I am alone'. Entering into dialogue with such a person involves engaging them in the discovery that 'being alone' is a result of social processes of not connecting with others. This can be helped by shifting the narrative that uses the adjective 'I am alone' to a different narrative that uses a verb, for example 'I am not connecting with people'. This latter verb-based narrative illuminates that there is social agency involved, or lack of it—and that the state of aloneness does not just happen, but is a result of social practices. It opens up the possibility of acting to change the world; it can start a person or group on a journey that Freire calls *conscientisation*, and that Kelly and Burkett describe as the initial step in a move from private concern to public action.

The project of democratising

Democracy is a classic example of a term requiring this kind of transformation. Restating the noun democracy as the verb *democratising* exposes the social dynamics at work within any political process—usually either for or against the process of democratising. Democracy as noun is often talked about in binary terms of democratic–undemocratic, in which Australia and countries 'like us' are described as being democratic and 'other' countries as undemocratic.

The Derridean deconstructive movement destabilises this simplistic binary and invites us to rethink democracy as a 'project of democratisation' that requires constant renewal. We can transform our thinking and illuminate the contest over democracy simply by getting some verbs into it. If people are *lacking* the freedoms to engage around their concerns, we have a problem. If some people are *protecting* entrenched powerful interests or some key people are purposefully *blocking* engagement, then there is a risk that the project of democratisation will reach a state in which it has stalled. On the other hand, if people are actively *engaging* around their concerns or are *challenging* elites then the project of *democratising* is a process that has some life in it, and we are all actors who are *determining* its future.

One of the key tasks as community development practitioners is to care for politics, because one of the key imperatives is the project of democratising all our social, cultural, economic and political contexts. Democratisation is central to making the political sphere of participation meaningful. Democratisation is one of the cornerstones of an approach to community development in which people have a right to voice, can act publicly and are able to influence decision-making processes. Many significant development outcomes—those that genuinely reflect the way people want to live—are dependent on people's democratic ability to participate in the process of deciding how they should live.

Community as dialogue, informed by solidarity, is an approach in which community practitioners accompany other people, usually marginalised people, in a process of transformational change. Such transformational change often requires challenging entrenched powerful interests. It is the project of democratisation that gives legitimacy to this work.

While arguing for a 'universal project of democratisation', we recognise that the *forms* of democracy emerging from that project will be shaped differently within different social, cultural, historical and economic geographies. What *democracy* looks like within Australia will be different to that emerging in Vanuatu. *Democratisation* is however worth fighting for within any context: it is a universal desire and an instrumental imperative.

Supporting the public agora

So what does it mean to make the project of democratisation central to community practice? One of the classic essays on democracy was written by Alexis de Tocqueville, in which he used the key concept of the *agora*. Originally the market-place and meeting place of the city-states of classical Greece, the agora is used by de Tocqueville as 'the assembly' where people's concerns are discussed collectively and publicly. Bauman (1998, pp86-87) likens the contemporary idea of civil society to the concept of agora, seeing it as an interface between the public and private spheres of social life. Historically there has been an evolutionary process whereby the agora has, officially at least, been opened up to everyone. Originally in ancient Greece it was for 'citizens', defined as a particular group of men. In modern parliamentary democracy it has opened up to include almost everyone through universal suffrage.

One challenge of democratisation for community practitioners is to support people on the margins to learn about the political system and how they can use it to take what they have perceived as their private concerns into these public assemblies for discussion and dialogue. After all, feminists and others have taught us all that 'the personal is political, the private is often public'. In many ways the process of present-day community development "may be conceptualised as the late modern *agora*—as the site of political, or at least politicised, assembly of citizens . . ." (Geoghegan & Powell, 2008, p15).

In supporting people on the margins to access their right to practise democracy, we often take on a coaching role, or what we earlier called an accompanying role, walking *with* people and sharing with them what has been learned about influencing decision-making. Here are some brief examples:

In a church context, we have supported people who smell bad (we found this to be the most significant of their many marginalising personal characteristics) to attend the service, talk to the Rector, get to know the church wardens, and cope with the formalities of participating in Parish Council. In community groups we have supported people who are being scapegoated or ostracised to stand up to bullies, find their allies, and work with others towards group processes that are inclusive and respectful. One Brisbane colleague, a disability advocate who is a strident critic of community development, asks us 'why is being screwed by a local fascist any better than being screwed by a fascist system?'

In a government context, we have supported some unusual delegations to the local Member of Parliament or city councillor, or the relevant government minister. We have found that politicians love their constituents, and so-called ordinary people can be very influential. For example, at a meeting with the Housing Minister, we well-informed, politically astute, professional housing advocates found ourselves sidelined as the Minister listened deeply to the everyday experience of the tenants in the delegation, who were nervous but whose personal stories and heartfelt analysis were highly influential. In another instance, a young person who bounced up to the Mayor at a youth festival and said 'we need a youth space in our suburb' was heard—and we professionals were able to act on the thirteen consultants' reports that had argued the same case for the last seven years.

In supporting such delegations, practitioners enter into a two-way process of nurturing democracy: democratising the people, and at the same time caring for and democratising the system—preserving the health of government by asking it and supporting it to accommodate and respond to the full diversity of its constituency.

A dialogical approach to community development also orients practitioners to advocate and nurture *multiple* agoras as sites for people in dialogue and decision-making. The more human-scale agoras there are, the more the project of democratisation is working. Fiona Caniglia, a local colleague of ours, has worked with others to put two democratising grass-roots institutions into the fabric of politics in Brisbane—'Politics in the Pub' invites politicians to meet their constituents on the ground of the constituents; and the CAN Awards are an annual recognition of the value of grassroots contributions to the civic life of the city. Other colleagues at Vibewire, an Australian youth media and arts organisation, run Election Tracker—an online forum for young people to engage with candidates in Australian election campaigns.

Translating the private into the public

For community development workers, another element of caring for the sphere of politics is the work of translation, ensuring people connected as community are able to take their private concerns into the public assembly. The process is one of people working *together* as an act not only of individual but of collective citizenship.

This is complex work. Sociologists and political scientists conceptualise the difficulties in terms that they call the 'agency-structure dilemma'. Some argue that while people can exercise agency (for our purposes this means that people can act collectively as community in ways relevant to their concerns) the structures of society are all-powerful in denying or limiting the effectiveness of that agency. Many argue that structures related to class, gender, race, economic and political interests are so powerfully entrenched that it is naïve to believe that people at the grassroots can act to bring about change.

But we are buoyed by the memory of occasions when people on the margins have realised that they are not isolated and powerless, and have taken their concerns into the public agora, sometimes finding unexpected support. We saw a beautiful example in the West End of 1988.

A group of property owners and speculators calling themselves the West End Progress Association had been actively talking up the gentrification of the area and supporting property development. They began to move into the public arena, and started to get community and media support. They became bolder and more vocal and began making statements on behalf of the community.

At this point, the local indigenous community started talking about the establishment of an indigenous cultural centre in Musgrave Park, a long-time meeting place for traditional and urban aborigines, including a group who lived on the streets and slept in the park, many drinking heavily. The Progress Association called a public meeting to oppose the initiative and propose to 'clean up' the park, seeking a public mandate for their campaign.

On the evening of the meeting, hundreds of local people gathered in the auditorium at the local high school—one of the biggest local gatherings we have ever seen. The Progress Association executive was beaming from behind their tables on the stage, and opened the meeting with invited speakers against the cultural centre. People began asking questions from the floor, and it started to become clear that a lot of people had not been convinced by the case put by the speakers, and that in fact there were many in the room that liked the idea of a new cultural centre and were keen to support the aspirations of the indigenous community.

Eventually, it was Jim Bellas who exposed the sectional interests and the hidden agenda of greed at the heart of the meeting by asking one of the key speakers 'Aren't you the guy who owns several properties in the area, who opposed public housing in your street, because it would lower your property values?' There was an outcry that confirmed the dominant mood of the meeting, and a buzz grew as people realised they were far from alone in their views. It was a magical moment when people realised the potential of collective citizenship: this was a public meeting, and the will of the people was looking for a way to be expressed. The few people who were still opposed to the cultural centre started to get up and leave and the Progress Association guys on the stage moved to close the meeting.

Then Paddy Jerome, an old indigenous Anglican minister who saw the people of Musgrave Park as his flock, spoke from the back of the room 'Mr Chairman. Before you close the meeting, I believe there is one more item of business.' The auditorium hushed as he made his way down the side of the packed hall, and slowly climbed the stairs onto the stage. He stood at the lectern, and spoke very clearly and with great care 'I move that this public meeting SUPPORTS the establishment of an indigenous cultural centre at Musgrave Park.' There was a huge cheer—a near-unanimous endorsement of Paddy's courage in providing a touchstone that articulated the will of the people, and a sense of justice being done by the people themselves, in the face of those in power who had tried to manipulate the event to their own ends.

While stories like this keep us believing in the power of public expression of private concern in a democracy, it is important to develop a realistic approach to the complexities of caring for the political sphere. We need to avoid on the one hand believing that people can always (or even usually) make an easy translation of their private concerns into the public agora, and on the other hand giving up caring about such democratising processes. History has provided many cases of social transformation resulting from marginalised people's participation in decision-making processes as social and political agents. A realistic approach requires a deep care of the political process, and an even deeper—and tougher—commitment to keep trying to accompany people in their translating work while being conscious of the deep structural barriers to social change.

Community development workers, while involved in the praxis of supporting group processes of translation, also need to be committed to the broader project of democratisation. This project requires a public sphere large enough, an agora creative enough, to engender the engagement of diverse groups—even those we totally disagree with. Within a thriving politic diverse groups of people are all attempting to translate their concerns into the broader assembly (or agora). This is essentially the role of the contemporary state: to be a public institution maintaining a thriving politic of debate and discussion. As community workers we nurture this broader political project while simultaneously supporting those on the margins, who usually have limited capacity for translation, to engage fully in democratising their contexts.

Nurturing dialogue and agonistic politics

Drawing on the work of political scientist Chantal Mouffe (2005), two possible constructive processes at work within such a pluralistic agora can be identified. The first is that of public *dialogue* which involves moving towards agreement or consensus, and the second is the process of *agonistic* engagement. Within the first process, people move the dialogue towards agreement on the basis that people and parties can listen to one another, understand one another, move towards one another, and develop some public agreement that encompasses the diversity of views. In contrast, agonistic engagement implies some on-going differences that are in some way irreconcilable, and yet there is still respectful engagement within that difference and people work to maintain some conversation within the tension of disagreement.

We consider both of these as pro-social and informed by an orientation of hospitality in the sense that attention is given to the 'other' as human, and therefore as worthy of respect. In agonistic politics there is an adversarial but still respectful social relationship of me–you, us–them. It acknowledges both the legitimacy of the other's position and the legitimacy of contested ground in democracy. We do well when we foster the philosophy of Socrates, the ancient champion of dialogue, who maintained that the purpose of dialogue is to discover and do what is right, and therefore valued the experience of being corrected or becoming convinced by others more than the experience of convincing them to adopt *his* views.

However, sometimes such agonistic engagement deteriorates into a somewhat destructive *antagonistic* relationship in which the 'them' becomes not just an 'other' as adversary, but an enemy who is considered illegitimate. There is little space for respect, and by this stage political relationships and activities have lost their social foundations and maybe their soul; they are probably moving towards violence. The implications of this should be clear: nurture a body politic that maintains respect at its centre. Within the agora, community workers can hope for dialogue towards consensus, they can at least work for agonistic engagement and they can work against antagonistic dynamics.

There is another chapter in the story of the Musgrave Park cultural centre public meeting that illustrates some of the potential and limitations of agonistic dialogue.

In the weeks following the public meeting, a group of those who had connected at the meeting banded together to attend the next few meetings of the Progress Association, and attempted to continue the dialogue over the preferred future of our neighbourhood. At the first meeting the Progress Association executive sat at the front of a room facing rows of chairs. It was not long before one of the local rat-bags called on the group sitting in rows to move their chairs into a circle, and the executive to join them. Unfortunately, the Progress Association were not open to other views, were not willing to give up their power, and reacted as though this was a hostile takeover—they stopped attending their own meetings. The opportunity for dialogue was lost. The organisation faded quickly from public view. We assume they continued to pursue their own sectional interests together, but they did not seek a public mandate again.

Reflection on this story invites consideration of the need for openness from all parties in the process of agonistic engagement, the difficulty of holding sectional self-interest in dialogue, and the messiness that people bring, with their complex personalities, agendas and egos, as they engage in public processes.

The struggle over community as a paradigmatic site

Our final reflections on caring for the political sphere re-engage with the thinking of Jacques Derrida. These thoughts act as a balance to the argument made above. For Derrida, community can be understood not only as hospitality, but also as an institution, a place, or discourse that has become what he calls a *paradigmatic site*. Paradigms are linked sets of ideas, concepts or processes that provide an explanation and justification for a particular view of reality. Derrida argues that once a particular view of reality becomes dominant, then social and political processes regulate and discipline people into certain ways of ethical being, thinking and behaving that are consistent with such a view. Derrida's insight is that 'community' is becoming an important locus of struggle in the regulating and disciplining processes of ordering how people live. Community development practitioners need to be part of the struggle—contesting the meaning of 'community' when the term is used in ways that are antithetical to hospitality and solidarity.

For example, in countries such as Australia and the UK, 'community' is now being constructed as a place for 'civil people'. People are constantly told they must act and behave in particular kinds of social ways, and are called anti-social if they do not. To act 'anti-social' is perceived to be 'anti-community'—which smells of sanitised notions of community as some kind of imagined place without problems. In the UK there are Anti-Social Behaviour Orders or ASBOs, politically sanctioned punishments against those considered un-civil. There appears to be the re-establishment of a moralistic order echoing pre–1960's notions of deserving and undeserving, based on simplistic binaries such as deviance and normality.

In Australia 'community' is also now a discursive site for new kinds of 'responsible workers'. People are deemed to be pro-community if they are responsible workers and taxpayers first. Citizenship, with its accompanying rights, becomes a secondary concern. The government-sponsored *Welfare to Work* programs re-orient people's self-perception in the light of this discursive pressure. If someone is not first and foremost a responsible worker—that is, if they are unemployed—then they are not fulfilling a new social contract called 'mutual obligation'. To break that social contract means to lose income security and become a *non-citizen* of community life. Fueled by this kind of thinking 'community' becomes closely associated with its etymological roots as munitions. Within this approach, people invoking 'community' in fact mean such things as: 'get out', 'you are not welcome here', 'if you live here we have the right to engage in surveillance over your life', or 'you are to become like us'. It is the world of the gated community. It is hardly community as hospitality.

The challenge for community development workers is to care for the political sphere through entering this paradigmatic site of community with a different understanding and therefore a destabilising agenda. The agenda argued for in this book is that of community as an open site of hospitality to the 'other'—others who are different, strangers, young, non-consumers, non-producers, instrumentally non-useful, old, disabled, deviant, refugee, asylum seekers and so on. These people will often fall out of the bounded sets of so-called, self-defined 'civil people', 'workers' and 'responsible people'. Derrida's invitation is for 'communities of hospitality', 'community as hospitality', and fundamentally, 'community as ethics' (Caputo 1997, p124). In this sense community is an ethical and political project focused around the core value of hospitality towards the 'other', not exclusion.

A commitment to the project of democratisation requires caring for deep plurality and advocating for an agora open to all. However community development workers need to engage in a political struggle *against* those who might use the cherished open pluralistic agora to close out 'others'. In order to maintain inclusion and voice of 'others', practitioners may paradoxically need to limit the political influence of those who want to exclude 'others' and may even have to fight for their exclusion from political processes in which they have an anti-democratising role.

4.5 Earth care

Having considered the need to care for the ordinary, the socio-cultural, the economy and politics we now turn to what many, including ourselves, consider the be the most challenging imperative of our day: the imperative to care for the earth.

The Earth Policy Institute (Brown, 2007) has calculated that globally an investment of approximately $93 billion per year is needed to restore health to the planet. A few months ago this scale of investment may have seemed impossible, but as we go to press in early 2009, governments around the world have been pumping much more than this into rescue packages for a failing global economy. Many, including The Australia Institute (2008), are seeing the irony:

> The most interesting thing about the worldwide approach to bailing out the financial system is how pragmatic policy-makers have been. No one, from the US Treasury Secretary to Kevin Rudd, will put their hand on their heart and say they understand the full nature and extent of the problem. Nor will they look the voters in the eye and declare that, after spending

trillions of dollars to bail out banks, they are certain that the problem will be solved. On the contrary—when it comes to the world of finance, we all have to accept just how complex the systems are. We can't really expect certainty, and we can't really guarantee success. Rather, we all just have to comfort ourselves with the thought that it would be irresponsible to sit back and do nothing. It is, it seems, self-evident that we should at least try.

But not, apparently, when it comes to climate change. Even though most of our bankers can't explain the risks associated with the derivatives they have purchased over the years, our climate scientists are expected to be able to predict the weather to a high degree of accuracy in 70 years' time. Even though economists can't predict the rate of GDP growth, inflation or the exchange rate next month, those determined to do nothing about climate change demand certainty about what the price of emissions permits will be in 20 years' time.

In the last month, trillions of dollars have been found [to bail out banks]. New regulations have been introduced. And countries have all committed to work collectively in the pursuit of a common goal. Unfortunately, none of this effort has been aimed at reducing greenhouse gas emissions; it has been aimed at something far more important—sustaining the banking system as we know it. ('Some crises are more equal than others', *Between the Lines*, 22 October 2008).

The investment advocated by the Earth Policy Institute would enable work on projects such as reforestation, stabilising water tables, protecting biological diversity, restoring fisheries, restoring rangelands and protecting topsoil on croplands. Such an investment is deeply connected to our previous concerns about caring for the economy, politics and the social-cultural. Current economic models have destroyed the earth, and now the earth needs restoration. More human-scale, people-centred, and relational economics are required. The current political stasis has resisted effective translation of these concerns into the public agora. Governments around the world, in collusion with corporations, have ignored the plight of our whole life support system—they are in denial (Homer-Dixon, 2006).

The dark spectre that sits behind this possible collapse of the earth is of course human-induced global warming, watered down in name by governments and other stakeholders as 'climate change'—giving the impression that human activity is not the primary cause of the change. Here the interface between a truly global issue and local places is made most clear. The impact of the global on local places is profound. In the Pacific there is the rapidly approaching need of environmental refugees from places such as Kiribati, with the President travelling to New Zealand in 2008 looking for a new home for his nation. In Asia, consider Aceh and its vulnerability when the 2004 Boxing Day Tsunami struck, and large areas of Bangladesh that are under threat of disappearing should ocean levels continue to rise. In Africa, Ethiopia is experiencing more famine as weather patterns make sustainable agriculture more difficult. In Australia increasing ferocity of drought and fire make life tenuous in both cities and the bush. Earth care is the arena in which the biggest challenge is to act locally *and* globally, avoiding the binary of either–or.

Working locally and globally

People working together as communities can act, both locally and globally. As noted previously, the word economy is closely connected to the notion of household, which is also the starting place of earth care. Household action is the initial base for taking responsibility. We have already mentioned George Monbiot's book *Heat* (2007), as a treatise on how to make significant changes at the household level. The permaculture movement has shown how we can all grow food within households and local neighbourhoods, and how appropriate technologies can be utilised to enhance local food production. Earth care does not imply a Luddite anti-technological stance.

However, the household is not the only level of involvement in earth care. The caring imperative is to utilise community development, as a social practice, in mobilising people to participate in these issues at every level of the public agora. People with a vision for earth care need to be involved in local councils, regional organisations, national initiatives and of course global alliances. To put it bluntly, we all need to scale up household-like action in a massive way to make the kind of ecological impact required to restore any semblance of health to the planet.

Alternative institutions

In participating in this multiple-level agora it is important to be clear about strategy. Joanna Macy (1998) provides a useful framework for conceptualising strategic options. She sees three key ways forward. The first strategy involves "analysis of structural causes and creating of alternative institutions" (1998, p19). This strategy requires understanding the dynamics of the current industrial growth system. Macy poses questions such as "What are the tacit agreements that create obscene wealth for a few, whilst progressively impoverishing the rest of humanity?" "What interlocking causes indenture us to an insatiable economy that uses our larger body, Earth, as supply house and sewer?" We explored these and other similar questions in the reflection on challenging economic orthodoxies.

However, as practitioners we are challenged to not only tackle the causes of the problems, but also create new institutions that reflect the 'dreams' of new ways of consuming, growing, producing, commuting, working, and travelling. At a local level the dream is created and modelled through community initiatives such as re-localisation work, transition town initiatives, community gardens, city farms, community supported agriculture (CSA), permaculture demonstration sites, bicycle and car co-operatives, local energy production, new public transport systems, and bikeways. The work then needs to be structured through macro and meta levels of organisation into coalitions, federations and networks of groups and organisations that have the capacity to scale up such work on a much broader level.

> The Northey Street City Farm in Brisbane continues to be a source of inspiration in modelling an alternative mode of production. Local people come together and work in the gardens, learning about sustainable urban agriculture. The farm brings refugee groups together to grow their own kinds of food. It fosters awareness and celebration of earth cycles with annual harvest and equinox festivals. It supplies organic

plants, food and seeds through the markets and nursery. However, it has also become a hub for diffusing ideas and building a network of community gardens across the city.

The building of such a network is an example of a scaling-up process, enabling local work to connect to broader social processes of change.

Changing hearts and minds

Macy's second strategy calls for a "change to hearts and minds". This requires careful and honest dialogue with ourselves and with 'other' people around the concern of earth care. Dialogue must be gentle so as to draw people in, enabling them to overcome fear, apathy, selfishness and ignorance. There is a sense of urgency here because people committed to earth care might not have much time to challenge themselves and to persuade others to change their behaviour. For Macy (1998, p21) such dialogue is aimed at shifting "perceptions of reality, both cognitively and spiritually."

Initiatives such as the *Roots of Change* study circles developed by the International Society for Ecology and Society show how people-in-places can structure up strategies for changing hearts and minds. Conversation groups, coffee circles, reading groups, and Politics in the Pub are all ways that we can engage in the gentle but critical work of changing people's hearts and minds. In the south-east Queensland region the Ethos Foundation focuses on learning as an essential condition for positive change. Their mission is to "cultivate effective new thinking, values and action for positive, ecologically sustaining futures." The Ethos Foundation has learnt that people learn best in groups within either their neighbourhoods or organisations, sharing their experiences and common concerns.

One of the key challenges is to embark on these difficult conversations with people who do not currently share the same concern. The planet seems to be at an ecological tipping point. People's consciousness about the issues and urgency is shifting in such a way that what Macy calls 'The Great Turning' might be occurring. However plenty of people are still not convinced that we face ecological catastrophe, or if they are convinced, are simply unable to act purposefully to bring change in their lives or neighbourhoods. Rather than engage such people through disseminating more information, community workers have the skills to make a critical contribution by opening up new conversations infused with the practice of dialogue, creating spaces and platforms for ordinary people to reveal their fears, come to terms with their doubts, and gradually to embrace alternatives. Within these conversations, practitioners need to be equipped with stories of alternatives—models of how people can live a new life in their local neighbourhoods—and stories of how people have bonded and banded together to challenge corporate and governmental power that is blocking such change.

Holding actions

Macy's final strategy is that of 'holding actions' in which some people mobilise around the issue of protecting environmental sites that others are still trying to utilise in unsustainable ways. This strategy requires still more radical action, which will probably mean confrontation. Although within this book we have advocated dialogue before moving to confrontation, we recognise the strategic value of more visible and dramatic public actions.

Macy's framework provides a useful way of thinking about the diverse strategies of the everyday practice of earth-care. They clarify the multiple and parallel work required, no one strategy being more important than the others.

In conclusion it might be useful to remember that for many people around the world, earth care does not just represent issues of conservation—it is about survival. Many people in the world live off the bountiful supply of the 'global commons', but this commons is increasingly being fenced in by the colonising actions of corporations in collusion with governments. For example, national parks are formed that marginalise tribal people from their livelihoods; corporations over-fish areas that destroy the fishing commons for local villages; and forests are logged as export crops, destroying local commons food sources and water tables.

At the core of a commitment to earth care in community practice is a commitment to the local and global commons. Modernity encloses all spaces within a profiteering economic grasp. The practice of guarding some local and global spaces from this encroachment is becoming ever more critical.

Summing up

Words such as *critical* and *imperative* have echoed through Chapter Four. These words have not been chosen lightly. They are infused with passion, belief, and hope. They have been chosen to highlight the importance of community development impacting on these key spheres of community life.

The first reflection explored caring for the *ordinary life* of community: valuing the mundane, the commonplace, and the everyday events that are the social glue connecting ordinary people with one another. As workers, we probably need to be less busy, less idealistic, and attend to the challenge to do ordinary things with extraordinary love.

The second reflection looked at caring for the *socio-cultural sphere* of community life, by nurturing diversity in the fragile web of social relationships that are at the heart of community. We argued for an approach to community development oriented towards an appreciation of both the fragility and the importance of a diverse socio-cultural community ecology. The practice of being hospitable to the enemy within, requires cultivating an ethic of plurality and fostering centripetal dynamics of connection that bring people together.

The third reflection considered the impact of growth-oriented, free-market capitalism on communities, and explored the building of alternative, local, human-scale, *relational economies* with social and ecological objectives. At the same time as we build these economies, we need colleagues to be challenging the state and trans-national governance bodies to develop polices that enable local, national and global economic justice. A movement is needed of people who acknowledge their own greed, selfishness and fear, and yet choose to live simply and ethically. This would promote a global economic and ecological balance that cuts through both the under-development that is killing others and the over-development that is killing us.

The fourth reflection considered the importance of democratic *political processes* within community work. People begin the process by transforming their understanding of the world so that it enables agency, moving from private concern to public action. This is the beginning of a wider project of democratising all our social, cultural, economic and political contexts. We reflected on the need to support the public *agora*—different 'people's assemblies'; and the work of *translation*—ensuring that people connected in community are able to collectively take their private concerns into the public assembly. In this context, we care for politics by nurturing both dialogue towards agreement, and dialogue in the tension of disagreement; and by defending democracy through resistance to antagonistic and exclusionary politics.

The fifth reflection considered the urgent and imperative need to *care for the earth*. Governments around the world, in collusion with corporations and populations, have ignored the plight of our whole life-support system on planet earth—they are in denial. People working together as communities can act both locally and globally. To put it bluntly, we need to scale-up our action on a massive scale to make the kind of ecological impact required to restore any semblance of health to the planet. Joanna Macy's (1998) three key ways forward were considered: (i) "analysis of structural causes and creating of alternative institutions"; (ii) changing of hearts and minds; and (iii) 'holding actions' in which some people mobilise to protect environmental sites that modernity encloses within a profiteering economic gaze, claiming them as the local and global commons.

Recently Peter heard someone say "What's economics got to do with community development?" We imagine different people asking the same question in relation to any of the spheres of community life discussed above: "What's politics got to do with community development?" and so forth. We hope you are now convinced of their relevance.

five

Training for transformation: the possibilitators

Chapter Two considered how a dialogical approach is diffused into transformational community work processes. This chapter goes further to explore *transformational training* as a way of engaging people in community development work. We have drawn on Anne Hope and Sally Timmel's (1984) classic handbook *Training for Transformation*, again within the Freirean tradition of community development. We have also appropriated Martin Buber's term of 'possibilitator' to describe the kind of change agents that are to be supported through transformational training. Drawing on the Italian revolutionary Antonio Gramsci, such possibilitators are imagined to be the 'organic intellectuals' of community life. They are people who dare to think and act differently in the face of the hegemony that determines how much of our current social life is perceived and lived.

An elicitive approach to training

Dialogical community development requires dialogue with everyone, but it particularly requires entering into a purposeful dialogue, with consent, with those people who are potential change agents in their communities. As practitioners we envisage our work as engaging in dialogue with people in rings of concentric circles. The poor and marginalised are within the first ring. An approach informed by solidarity requires engagement with them as a primary task. Possibilitators sit within the next ring; they can become our comrades in the journey of social transformation. Finally, everyone else as 'other' is in the outermost ring, for we are open to the stranger, the intruder, and even our enemy or opponent.

For some, the notion of change agent reflects a modernist and ultimately colonial approach to development. They question why special people or outside knowledge is needed to bring change and development. For many people, the idea of an education or training role implies that someone 'knows better'. As trainers we are very appreciative of this critique and recognise the potential dangers of change agents in many cases—that of easily slipping into colonial or neo-colonial thinking and practices.

However, as Miles Horton and Paulo Freire argue within their book *Conversations on Education and Social Change* (1990), it is important to develop an approach to education and training that *both* respects people and honours their knowledge—avoiding colonial approaches to practice—and yet can 'move' people into new understandings of their world. Social change requires new ways of thinking and acting. Over many years of practice we have learnt that 'elicitive' training is an approach that achieves both respect for people's knowledge and movement of these people into new social territory, a requirement of most community development practice. In this training approach, the content is elicited from the context and experiences of the participants, and the journey forward is a mutual dialogical journey of educator–trainer and participants in co-discovery (Lederach, 1995). The key principles for this kind of elicitive training are:

- People in their setting are a key resource, not passive recipients.
- Indigenous or local knowledge is a pipeline to discovery, meaning, and appropriate action.
- Participation of local people in the process is central.
- Building from available resources encourages self-sufficiency and sustainability.
- Empowerment involves a process that fosters awareness of self-in-context and validates discovery, naming, and creation through reflection and action.

This kind of transformational training is part of our dialogical community development approach. Training does not sit separately from praxis—it is embedded within the work.

The role of possibilitators in social transformation

Part of our strategy for a just world is to build a network of people that we have called possibilitators, who are skilled up to be key catalysts for social transformation. In our work we have realised that the key to community development is not lots of money; neither is it buildings and infrastructure—clinics, schools, roads, or water. It is the quality and creativity of people who dream of a better world for their neighbourhoods and want to take some form of public, communal, transformational action. Such people are possibilitators: change agents, organic intellectuals in their communities. Community development workers have a key role in providing a training space, enabling these people to develop transformational skills and strategies.

These change agents can model a new attitude, a new caring, and a new vision. They are people who can bring a fresh energy and who can facilitate the awakening of awareness, imagination and powerful action. They are people who can create a fresh dialogue and hold it open with integrity, hospitality, depth, respect and solidarity. They are the possibilitators who can bring fresh hope and a sparkle of transformation to the places where they live, work and play.

In our experience some of the most exciting work has happened when a cadre of such possibilitators has come together with the intention of defending a locality, transforming a sociality, or prosecuting a cause. There is great camaraderie in the shared work. There is great resource in the soulful stories and hard-earned life experiences of any group of diverse and committed people.

This chapter presents some simple signposts to re-thinking community development work in training such possibilitators. These signposts include: education as a spacious soulful imagining; texts and stories as resources for sparking re-imagination; the exchange of inspiration, not information; educating as deconstructive conversations; and finally, the logic of wishing, willing and action.

In our approach to facilitating learning we use processes both of training (focused on learning and practising skills) and education (a broader process focused on building understanding). It is helpful to make the distinction between the two. We can make it clear by way of an example. Imagine your child–favourite nephew–father–maiden aunt or partner is going to sex education. Now imagine they are going to sex training. You can easily imagine the difference. With the former you would be fine; with the latter you would probably be hesitant, to say the least!

5.1 Space to re-imagine

One way of understanding the context for training possibilitators is as a failure of the imagination of modernity. Such a failure of imagination means that most people can no longer imagine a community or society based on anything other than *what is*. The media has dominated people's dreams; formal education systems have dominated people's minds; our heads are so busy with the information superhighway that we have lost the capacity to imagine a world that might be different. There is little space to dream; little space to articulate alternative models of living; little space to re-imagine community— altogether too little space to create a society in which we care for the earth, economy and *polis* in a new way. There appear to be no other possibilities.

The worlds we take for granted are an imaginative construct

It is a key assumption of our community work practice that the worlds taken for granted in the economic, political, cultural, ecological and social spheres are an imaginative construct. As constructs, these worlds can be imagined differently from another perspective. It follows then that such imaginative constructs can be challenged, and counter-givens entertained. Recognition of these processes of challenging and entertaining is central to our goal of re-thinking training within a dialogical approach to community development. We suggest that people can gain new imaginative literacy with the nurturing of an appropriate kind of transformational training space. Such spaces are explored below.

It should also be noted that the goal is not to create a new hegemony in terms of what *should be*, but to create a transformational training space that enables participants and possibilitators-in-dialogue with others to imagine new possibilities for our world.

Creating space for imaginative literacy

A young, highly intelligent, and most accomplished young student wished to have an audience with the Grand Master. The young student sat down and the Master asked if he wished to have a drink of tea. The student said yes, and the Master started to pour. He poured the tea until the glass was full, and then continued to pour until the glass was overflowing, and still kept on pouring. The student jumped up, startled by the tea flooding over the table top and down onto his legs, 'Master, the cup is full to overflowing!' The Master continued to pour, the tea spilling out onto the table and floor. 'As you are,' the Master replied.

The story illustrates a problem that many people have, being so preoccupied with progress and development within the parameters defined by the current 'given', that there is very little space to begin imagining a new world. To nurture imaginative literacy, space and silence is needed; or to work with the metaphor, we need to stop pouring tea into a full glass and find another glass. In Peter's life there is a reoccurring dream that reminds him of this lack of space:

In the dream I am usually trying to do something or go somewhere. I am racing for a plane or a taxi and I am trying to fill my bag or pack. I always have problems filling my bag—some items fall out or refuse to remain attached. I often miss the plane or taxi. In my dream I am then presented with an alternative; usually it is someone, a friend or relative, who is sitting silently or walking up into the mountain to meditate.

For Peter the dream has become a story, an image that presents options for living. One way is *doing*—the way of the activist; the other is that of *being*—retreat, silence and attention to our surroundings. Neither option in isolation is the correct way; there is the Buddhist middle path. This middle path enables both engagement with the world and time taken out to imagine and re-imagine a new world.

Creating spaces that support imaginative literacy

This co-creative training work of re-imagining can be nurtured almost anywhere. We have sat in caravan parks in the suburbs, in garages beneath community organisation offices, and under huge trees in Vanuatu and Papua New Guinea. These are people's spaces. We are not advocating a training approach that creates spaces disconnected from people's realities, or removed from their everyday world. It is best if possibilitators are not removed from their lived settings, so that the process of re-gaining imaginative literacy is connected to their daily endeavours.

Emotionally, the spaces need to be safe. A safe space does not mean that boundaries are not pushed, or that 'givens' are not destabilised. Training for transformation can well be painful. Nevertheless the training setting must be a space in which people do not feel that they will be coerced or attacked.

Intellectually, the space must be alive with the dynamism of dialogue where ideas can be tested, assumptions deconstructed, alternatives considered, critical feedback exchanged and proposals interrogated—but with a commitment to respectful dialogue rather than debate. Vulnerability is critical to re-imagining new ways of being, living and working in our world; but debate will only lead people into defending known territory and old ways of imagining. Dialogue can facilitate deep listening, the letting go of non-essentials, and the appreciative consideration of new ideas. This is the kind of space in which possibilitators imagine new ways of transforming their worlds.

5.2 Stories for sparking re-imagination

Within this reflection we consider the role of *stories* as the vital resources for an education in re-imagination. They provide the models, images and pictures that enable people to imagine a different kind of world. Two kinds of stories are explored: authors and books as *written* stories, and people, groups and organisations as *lived* stories.

Written stories that ignite imagination

As young community development workers, our reading of religious stories sustained us as texts that inspired the imagining of an alternative world. There is something soothing for the soul when reminded through such wisdom that everyone dies and no-one can take their wealth and riches with them. There is also something enriching for the soul when challenged to live by the ethic of the 'golden rule', common to most spiritual traditions: *do unto others as you would have them do unto you.* Such ancient texts also ignite possibilities that seem beyond contemporary realities. They inspire a hope and evoke a memory that within the stories of history the apparently impossible comes true. Who would have ever dreamt that the repressive regime in the Philippines under President-Dictator Marcos could have been removed so quickly? Or that the Berlin Wall would so suddenly be dismantled? Miracles occur—and they often fly straight into the face of a despairing reality.

Such stories are important within learning and education; it is often the power of story that unlocks imagination. Note that when talking of texts and stories we are not referring to textbooks. Textbooks are often too dry and technical to inspire imagination; they tend to simply prescribe ideological positioning. In contrast to textbooks, the texts we use for sparking re-imagination in possibilitators are full of story, narrative, and real people. In these texts, story connects with people's reality. Readers can locate themselves within a story and identify with characters and events—this is the source of their power.

For those of us who wish to sustain a lively imagination that also inspires the building of a community-oriented world, it is important to collect stories that inspire efforts and feed our soul. The collection of such stories as a resource for education is critical when it comes to sparking the imagination of possibilitators. People are constantly being fed stories through newspapers and television, and many of these stories tell of a world that we do not wish to replicate. Transformational trainers must provide soulful, alternative stories that engage people's imaginative faculties. We turn to *storytellers* and *poets* who write with depth, integrity, passion and insight: people such as Tim Winton, Michael Leunig, Margaret Atwood, Ben Okri, Frank Moorhouse, Jeannette Winterston, Allen Ginsberg, Pablo Neruda, Leonard Cohen and Salman Rushdie. We also enjoy introducing our trainees to thoughtful *essayists* who reflect in critical and imaginative ways on contemporary society, such as Clive Hamilton, Amanda Lohrey, Peter Singer, George Monbiot and Alain de Botton.

Other important stories for those involved in community work are the stories and writings of *author–activists* who articulate different dimensions of practice wisdom, and fuel the various global traditions of community development. They are not ideological textbooks, but writings that reflect on experience and are informed by certain values, perspectives, praxis and imagination. They are essential as education tools because they invite learners of community development to consider differently imagined worlds.

Examples of such author–activists that have greatly influenced our lives and community development practice traditions have been, among others, Mahatma Gandhi, Jayaprakash Narayan, Fritz Schumacher, Dom Helder Camara, Frantz Fanon, Jacques Ellul, Paulo Freire, Martin Buber, Manfred Max-Neef, Miles Horton, Sheila Rowbotham, Aung San Suu Kyi, Satish Kumar, Joanna Macy, Saul Alinsky, Parker Palmer, bel hooks, Henri Nouwen, Jean Vanier, Steve Biko, Desmond Tutu and Nelson Mandela. These author–activists have stood the crucial test of practical action. Their actions were inspired by new ways of imagining how their communities could be. They often challenge the 'given' world of the powerful—whether colonial powers, nuclear interests, and dictatorships, patriarchal leaders, domesticating educators or warmongers. Their written stories initiate us into their struggle to live and build alternatives built on principles of self-reliance, non-violence, peace, democratisation, gender equality, liberating education and fair trade.

Living stories that inspire imagination

The second types of story that we use in training for transformation are the living stories of people, groups and organisations. Many people who are not great readers, or who are 'hands-on' learners, can be transformed through meeting and experiencing people, groups and organisations that *model* alternative values, commitments and worlds. This implies the importance of documenting the lives of such individuals and the case studies of groups and organisations—they tell stories that people need to hear. However, the reading of such stories should not imply that we set out to imitate those people, groups or organisations. A dialogical approach will draw energy and imagination from others' stories, but it will integrate what is learnt from them and develop its own story.

Paulo Freire talks about literacy as learning to read both the word and the world. Within this tradition of literacy, learning is not simply about acquiring the function of reading text—a function of learning the word; it is also about the process of becoming conscious that illiteracy is a key symptom of powerlessness. Illiterate people become aware that their lack of knowing the word is intimately connected to their marginal place in the world. Within this Freirean tradition of literacy, the 'reading' of stories described above can be conceptualised as acquiring literacy of our imaginative lives.

The reading of lived stories as text is primarily about people gaining some power over their own imaginations, and thereby over the range of possible presents and potential futures. The goal is not imitation of others' imagined and lived worlds, but a gaining of power to make choices about how to imagine and live present and future lives. This process of gaining imaginative literacy destabilises previous solidified imaginary tapestries. A key goal in training possibilitators is the deconstructive movement of destroying 'old' imagined worlds fed by meaningless infotainment, and creating new processes of imagining communities infused with depth, soul, hospitality and solidarity.

Stories of people's lived experiences

As community development practitioners we continue to gain inspiration and fresh imagination from people of all walks of life. Many of the refugees we work with in Brisbane have challenged us and called us to imagine a world of peace, solidarity and hospitality. We have been deeply touched by their exposure to the harsh realities of brutality and irrationality, and their resilience in the face of alienation and exile, as Gerard relates.

> My son Ciaron knows the story that his first visitor in the world, the first of our friends to appear in the maternity ward of the local hospital after his birth, was a refugee from Peru who was a member of the Sendero Luminoso—the Shining Path guerrilla movement. Ciaron has no memories of being nursed by this guy as he opened up more and more

about his experiences of torture, violence and imprisonment in a world far from our comfortable inner-urban home. He moved out of his flat and out of our lives before Ciaron could walk. But when I have recalled his story around the table over the years my voice has carried an echo of his passionate belief that any price was worth paying for the struggle against oppression. His story is embedded in Ciaron's identity, his way of imagining the world.

So is the story that he was named not after, but at a time that we were getting to know Ciaron O'Reilly—a West End local who has become an international peace activist imprisoned for disarming bombers at American air force bases in the USA and Ireland. Now these stories inspire Ciaron as a young physicist to take an expansive view of his place in the world, and of the possibilities that could unfold over a lifetime.

The stories of our refugee colleagues are gifts that constantly destabilise the 'given' world. They remind us of the interconnections between a supposedly peaceful Australia and a world at war. The traces of chaos and the tentacles of globalising forces deconstruct our imagined safe, moral, relaxed and comfortable, fortress Australia. Through their stories, we are challenged to re-imagine Australia as a country that not only extends hospitality to the refugee, but also engages morally and peacefully with the causes of refugee movements.

Along with refugees, many of the young people we have worked with in Australia, KwaZulu Natal/South Africa, Papua New Guinea, the Philippines and Vanuatu invoke hope within us. Many of their lives are incredibly difficult. Their futures are precarious. For many of them the rural life is impoverishing and no longer the vehicle for their growing aspirations. They flock to the cities—to peri-urban or inner-urban shanty towns. We find ourselves despairing for their future. Yet they seem to have hope, and through their hope they inspire hope in us. They make music, they create small enterprises, they enjoy football or basketball, they take care of one another, they work hard for meagre money, they pay for education, they create groups that get involved in their neighbourhoods, holding clean-up days, health days, and fun days. Sometimes they get involved in the criminal economy, or turn to the ever-growing security industry; sometimes this is their only hope. The point is that they continue to imagine a world that has a place for them despite the difficult 'given reality'.

A cadre of possibilitators also need to share their stories with one another in ways that inspire and sustain their work together. There is great resource in the soulful stories and hard-earned life experiences of any group of diverse and committed people. Often our task as transformational trainers is to watch the group process and pick the right moment to create space for learning experiences, to tell our own stories in ways that reflect on the work, and to draw others into sharing their stories and the insight they offer.

Groups and organisations that keep the dream alive

Many groups in our neighbourhood inspire us to keep on dreaming and living a hopeful life. These include groups of activists; reading and learning circles; collectives building alternative economic realities such as Local Economic Trading Schemes (LETS), the Justice Products Shop, Community Supported Agriculture Schemes (CSA) and savings and loans circles; and groups focusing on solidarity and service, refugee support groups and indigenous reconciliation groups. These are just a few local groups amongst many that model a living story invoking alternative presents and futures.

Organisations also provide an essential tool in empowering possibilitators to imagine and work for a new world. They do this by modelling new patterns of thinking, acting and structuring work into the socio-political fabric of our civil society. Part of our role as trainers is to link people with such organisations in a way that will enable them to sustain their imagination and their work as possibilitators. As trainers for transformation it is important for us to look out for, participate in and nurture organisations that provide a culture, a tradition, a spirit and a structure that is alternative to the assumed 'given'. They can be organisations focusing on anything from local to global development. They may be corporations, associations, or networks, but they have one thing in common: they inspire us and possibilitators to imagine and work for a community-oriented world.

In our city there are many organisations that inspire hope and renewed imagination. Here are just a few of our favourites:

- Jabiru Community, Youth and Children Services: standing up for families, young people and children within particular neighbourhoods,
- Foresters Community Finance: working and resourcing alternative economic systems;
- Food Connect: supporting alternative food sources to big agribusiness and monopoly food stores;
- New Farm and Sandgate Neighbourhood Centres: modelling alternative local planning processes;
- Community Living Program: working with young people, people with disabilities and many others
- The Australian Centre for Peace and Conflict Studies (ACPACS): nurturing global alliances imagining a peaceful world;
- The Queensland Program of Assistance to Survivors of Torture and Trauma (QPASTT): working with refugees and asylum seekers within our city; and
- The Waiters Union: taking action as a catalyst for community-building within our neighbourhood.

Around the world we continue to be inspired by organisations such as the Highlander Research and Education Centre in the United States, the Community Development Resource Association (CDRA) in South Africa, the Development Alternatives Centre (CEPAUR) in Chile and the Self-Employed Women's Association (SEWA) of India.

The cadre of possibilitators need to be able to connect with these kinds of activities and organisations mentioned above, that embody an alternative spirit and work pattern. These organisations are the nodes and hubs within a web of organisational relationships that continue to energise us when we feel despair, keeping the dream alive and modelling the structuring of change.

5.3 Inspiration, not information

Information is not empowerment

Information has become the key exchange in a world understood as 'the information society'. It is often assumed that information provides power. In our experience this is a fallacy.

For four years Peter was working in South Africa with an initiative called the Better Life Options Program. This initiative was aimed at supporting adolescent girls around issues of sexuality, reproductive health and reproductive rights. A key part of the initiative was education and training, through adult-initiated and also peer-oriented processes. In the early days of the program we tended to mimic similar initiatives which focused on providing information to young girls: ensuring they "knew" about HIV, sexually transmitted diseases, their bodies, and so forth.

However, after some time and through a deeper listening to young girls' experiences, we realised the issues were more about power and poverty than about information. Young girls were getting pregnant because some teachers would only exchange good marks for sex; or young men in the community would demand sex as a ritualised part of a boyfriend/girlfriend relationship; or young men would refuse to use a condom; or police ignored their reports of rape. We learned that any useful and transformational education strategy could not be limited to an exchange of information. In this case the education needed to focus on empowerment strategies appropriate to the girls' diverse experiences: assertiveness skills (able to negotiate a "No"), accessing female condoms, advocacy towards local police, peer support groups of girls, and economic activity to lift them out of poverty. Selling condoms to their friends worked for them and for us.

In this story, while the explicit focus became gaining skills of assertiveness, the implicit exchange was about empowerment. The young girls needed to feel inspired enough to be involved in processes of social change that related to their real, lived experiences; and they needed to *believe* that change can happen and that they can make it happen. No matter what their culture or situation, marginalised and powerless people must experience the same inspiration or belief in order to become empowered.

As the vast experience of the Highlander Research and Education Centre demonstrates, empowerment requires that education processes start with 'where people are at' and then, through dialogue, move people into new spaces of thinking, analysing, making sense of their world and acting (Horton et al., 1991).

Resisting the seduction of content-focused technologies

The overuse of content-focused technologies such as computer-based slide presentations is one of the contributors to the domestication of education. The seductive power of this technology ensures that lots of information can be provided to students and learners with ease. It is a seduction that destroys the role of dialogue within any learning space. Peter reflects on his more recent experience in Vanuatu, illustrating the significance of Marshall McLuhan's (1964) maxim that "the medium is the message":

> Within my work in Vanuatu I often work in outer islands where the learning spaces are under trees, in traditional huts and on grassy knolls. There is rarely electricity. I love going to these places with a roll of butcher's paper and big felt-tip pens, ready to sit in circles with the people. However, I am stunned by the amount of times other "community development" professionals ask if they can see the computer presentations or posters that I am using within the training. In reply, I ask them whether they think such use of computer technologies could possibly be experienced as empowering and inspiring to people who do not have the on-going use of such technologies. I remind them that with the use of such technologies it would be easy to go and share lots of information; it would be easy to provide a "shock and awe" display of wealth and technology; but it would be very difficult to enter into a dialogue about the concerns and resources related to their experiences of their places.

Peter's analysis implies that such a content-centred approach would not inspire possibilities of a new world; it could only create either a sense of deficit in terms of what they do not have in the villages, or yearnings to head to the city or Australia—that is, to leave the villages. What really inspires people are stories—stories of how other communities are tackling the same kinds of challenges they are experiencing. In this sense the learning space facilitates empowerment, not through the depositing of information and the utilisation of content-oriented technologies, but through the exchange of inspirational stories.

Inspiration: taking new ideas and energy into ourselves

Inspiration as a word implies taking something in, hence the 'inspire', which quite literally means 'breathing in'. In the reflection above, it is the stories of other communities that can be 'taken in' and become inspiring. Inspiration leads to greater confidence, hope, and animation. Inspiration becomes an educational metaphor for taking new ideas and new stories with their accompanying new energy deep into ourselves so as to be a resource during the hard times. A critical part of the transformational training process is that people take something *in* that leads to transformation of self, which is a key catalytic process for community transformation. Possibilitators need plenty of this inspiration, and it is our job within training settings to ensure people have 'breathed in' enough stories and to be 'at hand and in heart' when needed. This poem by Robert Theobald (1997, p15) explores these themes of information, inspiration and transformation.

> *Information*
> *Is the bludgeon*
> *Of the expert*
>
> *"I know"*
> *She says*
> *And leaves*
> *The citizen*
> *Gasping*

Striving for language
Which will convey
Their tentative Strivings
Towards clarity
Of desires
And Hopes

Meaning is not found in information
We will find it in personal connections,
In the unexpected resonances
Which emerge from silences.

5.4 Deconstructive conversation

Many who have been involved in transformational struggle end up confronted by the need for healing. Renewed imagination awakens people to the hope of a new world, and often people are then inspired to be part of a transformational process, only to be tripped up by inner contradictions. In our experience good social practice teaches us to be attentive, and in that outer-oriented attentiveness we become conscious about aspects of our inner selves that need a deeper exploration. Our shadow-selves become ever-present. Many activists and community development workers end up seeing therapists or counsellors at some stage of their life journey.

The personal journey of deconstruction

In becoming more socially aware, people also become aware of the layers of resistance within themselves. As practitioners or possibilitators we end up having to engage many of the contradictions that have become ingrained from our socialisation and biological make-up. It is one thing to advocate a world without the divisions of race, gender, age, sexuality and class; it is another thing to live without expressing them in daily life. Many of us dream of a non-violent world, yet our night dreams are sometimes full of violence. We dream of a community-oriented world, but often we want to withdraw into our private space and avoid the inevitable conflict and pain of difficult relationships. We find ourselves caught up with parts of our complex self that we cannot understand or even relate to.

Many forms of therapy have assigned themselves the task of unravelling the contradictions of the many parts of our self that make a very complex 'us'. The therapeutic challenge is to learn to welcome, relate to, even befriend the many parts of the self, and explore a richer texture of self than we may have known existed before.

When people start in therapy, they often subscribe to a way of viewing themselves, a relatively stuck perception of who they are. This view of self essentially becomes *the story* (one could imagine it as a fictional story as opposed to fact) of how we imagine ourselves to be and how we describe ourselves to others. We could call it our own *mythos*. It is not a story or myth based on facts, but only on perception—a memory of our lives, filtered through all sorts of lenses. In response to this the therapeutic task is to 'broaden' the myth, "open up the presented story" (Gibney, 2003, p120), to fill it out, creating what psychologists like Carl Jung and James Hillman (1983) have called a *healing fiction*.

The therapeutic task is to awaken imagination in such a way that people do not limit self-perception to the realm of old stories, often stories imposed by damaged parts of ourselves or inherited from others; this can lead to tension. However if people can hold an on-going dialogue with the emergent stories—the other parts of self—then a more creative, dynamic and whole person can emerge.

The social journey of deconstructive conversation

This therapeutic task is in some ways similar to the deconstructive task for possibilitators within a transformational training framework. However, it is not so much about engaging with the contradictions of the psyche, but about engaging with the contradictions of the social worlds. The task is to initiate a deconstructive conversation that destabilises the given mythos that participants–as–possibilitators have assigned to their reading of the social, cultural, ecological, economic and political worlds. This deconstructive process requires both a destructive process, as people let go of the 'givens', and a reconstructive process as people open up the presented story and re-imagine alternative worlds. Four stages within this potential-ly transformative process of deconstructive conversation can be identified and described:

(i) Acknowledging different possibilities

Everyone comes to the training space with an imagined social, economic, cultural, ecological and political world—a story, a myth of how it is; and usually how they see it *should* be. These stories in no way reflect the com-plex reality of what is or could be. They reflect an individual's *one* reality. The story has been informed through parental and educational socialisa-tion, through the lens provided by gender, race, and class locations, as well as by media and political propaganda.

Stage One of the transformational learning process requires partici-pants to recognise this: to recognise that as an individual "I do not really know the truth", that "my given reality is just one reality". It requires what Arjen Wals and Fanny Heymann (2004, p134ff) call 'frame aware-ness'. The shift begins when participants are invited to become aware of *difference*—often through simply listening to others.

We often facilitate a simple training exercise in which the whole group listens deeply to one another's stories of their personal journeys. In some contexts, we then follow this with the task of stepping out into the neigh-bourhood, beginning a conversation with a stranger who is very different from them, and listening deeply to their stories of their experience of the place. This awareness is a critical process in 'destroying' the narrowly im-agined world, the 'de–' part of the deconstructive conversation.

(ii) Imagining new possibilities

In the light of this awareness of difference and the 'destruction' of a nar-rowly imagined world, stories of an alternative world can then be explored. These stories, mentioned above as written and lived stories, broaden the mythos and unravel the old stories—they present options for 'reframing' (Wals & Heyman 2004, p135). They do not give any 'true' story; they sim-ply broaden and increase the possibilities of embracing new stories. We often use an educative process of reflecting on the work at hand through considering insightful writing, visiting innovative organisations, or interviewing gifted practitioners. This process introduces the cadre of possibilitators to many ways of seeing the world—or seeing many worlds. In Freirean terms, they regain or at least refresh their imaginative literacy.

(iii) Creating space for dilemma and struggle: which possibility?

The third transformational training stage requires the nurturing of a space for internal struggle in which a dialogue around these stories, perspectives, and multiple imagined worlds can occur. Old stories are evaluated alongside new ones; some myths are broadened; others are narrowed. There are many tensions and dilemmas, and it is important to encourage one another to engage with these stories with honesty and courage. In moments like these we can find support for our choices in the stories of our heroes, like Oscar Romero:

> Many before us have struggled to make the choice to engage with the marginalised in a struggle for genuine community and justice. Oscar Romero's classic moment of internal struggle in the desert of El Salvador is an example. In the desert he knew that he had a choice: either to back off from the soul demands of solidarity and struggle and accept the world as given by the Salvadoran government and US allies; or to dig deep and find the courage to push on, imagine the world as different, advocate another truth in opposition to the government and stand alongside the poor in a struggle for justice.

It is hard to manufacture these kinds of 'conflict spaces' in a training room. They usually occur in the crucible of engagement. It is not a romantic or abstract task; it usually requires getting 'hands dirty' through involvement in the ordinary.

(iv) Transformation or regression: new possibilities

Finally there is a stage of either transformation or regression. People either give up the struggle and remain content with a given reading of the world that they brought to the training, or they embark on the transformative journey to live a life that engages with the ever-critical work of social solidarity through a re-framed reading of the social, cultural, economic, ecological and political world. In doing this people become committed to the process of on-going action-reflection that reshapes the way they frame their understanding of the world. We often use a training exercise in which we ask people to articulate as simply as possible their own personal framework of practice and then reflect on it some months later, in the light of their subsequent experience.

This is an iterative process. As soon as people stabilise a certain my-thos of the world that is decided to be somewhat 'real'—that is, the frame through which the world and its experiences are viewed—then from the perspective of deconstruction, they have become somewhat stuck. In sta-bilising a frame people can become unaware and un-attentive. It is impor-tant to maintain an on-going deconstructive conversation that destabilises any entrenched or habitual mythos and ensures the on-going develop-ment of imaginative literacy. In doing this people enter the territory of uncertainty and ambivalence in which they become 'un-sure'—and yet we would argue this is paradoxically the place from which people can develop a deep commitment to the struggle for a socially just world.

Warning: seek a mandate before deconstructing!

A final cautionary note, echoing our discussion about 'mandate' within Section 2.1: implicit within this approach to transformational training is also the need to have gained a mandate to *do* training. This simply means talking with people honestly, openly and lovingly; being clear about the process of deconstructive conversation; acknowledging that it might shake them up a bit; offering support; and then gaining their explicit as-sent before proceeding. It ensures that people freely enter into the process of dialogue with full awareness and consent. Gerard will never forget the woman he met at a Ministerial Advisory Committee who was the chair of a state-wide housing advocacy group. He asked how she got into this line of work:

> I was an ordinary single mum living in a run-down house in an inner
> Brisbane suburb. This bloke just came around one day, and knocked
> on the door, and we started talking about the way the neighbourhood
> was changing. Pretty soon there were other people coming over, and

the kitchen table was full of documents and plans. Then I was going to more bloody meetings and got elected chair and ended up spending most of my days at it. But I honestly didn't know what I was getting myself into at the start. I didn't even know I was being bloody 'community developed'! I certainly didn't ask to be.

Her reply provides a warning: be careful, ask permission, and gain a mandate to engage in this kind of deconstructive conversation.

5.5 The logic of wishing, willing and acting

David Yalom (1980, p286-350) has theorised the therapeutic links between the concepts of wishing, willing and acting. This discussion connects these concepts for the purposes of transformational training with possibilitators. Awareness about the possibility of a new world, a new kind of community, is not enough. Awareness does not bring social change, even though it is a key starting place. Yalom has illuminated the steps between awareness and action in ways that we find useful as facilitators of learning for transformational purposes.

The first key step in moving towards action involves reclaiming the ability to *wish*. It is not so much that people have an inability to wish, but rather they distrust or suppress their wishes. Deep down, many people desire a different kind of community, a different kind of relationship with their neighbours, a different kind of economic order. However many people also seem content with the world as it is, so it can become easy to simply distrust our desires.

At the heart of our proposition is the idea that if people do not want something, or do not trust their wanting, then they will go nowhere—more colloquially, will simply 'go with the flow'. Gerard remembers the axiom that expressed this for him: "Even a dead dog can swim with the current". Therefore at the initial stage of transformational training it is important to engage with people's stories in ways that re-awaken imagination—particularly in enabling people to express their desire or wish for a new kind of world, challenging the 'given', or re-trusting their dreams and heartfelt desires.

Unlocking our willingness that is captive to despair

The second step to consider is that reclaiming an ability to wish usually requires a process of re-claiming feeling. While Yalom considers the re-claiming of feeling as a therapist, we have found it helpful to incorporate Joanna Macy's observation (1983, 1998) that many people lose the imaginative capacity to wish for a better world because they *despair*. The task of engaging with despair is central to reclaiming a capacity to wish for a better world.

For Macy, despair is both a result and cause of separation, disempowerment and supposed apathy. However despair is also the key to regaining power, change and possibility. Repression and denial lead to self-damaging patterns of psychic numbing. Part of the transformational training agenda is therefore to unlock this despair, for which Macy provides five principles:

- Acknowledging that feelings of pain for our world are natural and healthy.
- Being clear that this pain is only morbid if denied.
- Understanding that information alone is not enough.
- Being conscious that unblocking repressed feelings releases energy and clears the mind.
- Recognising that unblocking our pain for the world reconnects us with the larger web of life (Macy, 1983, p22-23).

In following Joanna Macy's principles, transformational training creates spaces that loosen such despair, enabling people to re-sense their wishes and dreams for a better world. In those loosening and enabling processes, people reclaim feeling, which is a key engine room for imaginative capacity.

Asserting our response-ability through action

The final step in Yalom's proposition is that of reclaiming a sense of choice and responsibility. With a renewed trust of dreaming for a better world, people are then faced with the raw fact of responsibility. No social change can happen unless people choose to participate in the change process—unless they have the will to participate. We are face to face with the stark reality of decision that we referred to as either 'transformation' or 'regression' in the previous reflection.

Decision is the bridge between wishing and action—it is the test of willingness. However, as Macy has remarked, this is not a purely rational decision-making process, but often a hard choice that is also infused with deep feeling. It is this infusion with feeling that can galvanise people to act, moving from a sense of moral responsibility towards an enthusiastic *response-ability*. There is energy within, acquired through this inner working of imagination and inspiration, that evokes, motivates and enables action.

This logic of wishing, willing and acting is woven into the elicitive training processes we design in our community work practice. The modalities of thinking, feeling, infusing, and enthusing are central to effective learning for social change. Imagining a new world is a creative place to begin. Wishing for a new world opens up the possibilities of change. However, action and response-ability actually make the change.

Summing up

This chapter has presented our vision for a cadre of change agents and organic intellectuals as 'possibilitators' in every locality and community of interest. They will be the catalysts in transforming their communities. In this framework of dialogical community development, the training of such possibilitators is a central task.

The first reflection on *space to re-imagine* started with an observation that the failure of the imagination of modernity means that most people can no longer imagine a community or society based on anything other than what is. The media has dominated people's dreams, and there is too little space to create a society in which people devise new ways to care for earth, politics, economies, the socio-cultural and the ordinary. In the light of this domination we reflected on the work of creating space for imaginative literacy, and creating spaces that support imaginative literacy.

The second reflection identified *stories* as a vital resource for education in re-imagination. Stories provide the models, images and pictures that ignite imagination, and provide a soulful counter to modern infotainment. Trainers need to provide soulful, alternative stories that engage the imaginative faculties of possibilitators; so we turn to contemporary storytellers who write with depth, integrity, passion and insight; thoughtful essayists who reflect in critical and imaginative ways on contemporary society; and author-activists who articulate the practice wisdom of the global traditions of community development. Imagination is also fired by living stories—both people's ordinary and extraordinary lived experiences, and those of groups and organisations that keep the dream alive and model the structuring of change.

The third reflection argued for a training focus on *inspiration not information*. The fallacy that information is power is exposed. We argued that for people to experience empowerment they need to feel inspired to be involved in processes of change that relate to their real, lived experiences; and they need to believe that change can happen and that they can make it happen. It becomes important to resist the seduction of content-focused technologies such as presentation software, which are destroying the role of dialogue within any learning space.

The fourth reflection explored education and training as processes of *deconstructive conversation*. The reflection began with the personal journey of deconstructing ourselves, and went on to explore the social journey of deconstructive conversation, preferably shared by a cadre of colleagues, as the mythos of our social, cultural, ecological, economic and political worlds is destabilised. Mandate was then considered—a process ensuring people freely enter into the process of a training dialogue with full awareness and consent.

The final reflection argued that the learning process is a failure if it does not inspire action. The journey from *wishing*, to *willing*, to *acting* involves regaining the ability to wish for a better world, unlocking willingness that is captive to despair; and asserting response-ability through action.

Conclusion

Enfolding dialogical community development within a tradition of solidarity

Re-imagining community development as a vocation of solidarity seems to be a good way to draw together some of our most important arguments. A vocation of solidarity invites consideration of whose interests, sympathies and aspirations we as practitioners connect with. It calls for a stand with the most disadvantaged, marginalised and vulnerable people in spaces, places and bases. It invites people into a tradition of practice wisdom that infuses community work with love, humility, courage and passion. It challenges practitioners to maintain a vision that brings life, energy and depth to practice, and to cultivate a 'passion of not knowing' that is hospitable to dialogue.

To maintain a dialogical tradition rather than become mere technicians, it is important for us to understand ourselves as practitioners of solidarity first, and community development workers second. Community development as a practice, a profession, and an approach to social change needs to be enfolded within the broader tradition of solidarity, which invites thinking of the work as a vocation. We love working alongside people who are oriented towards soul rather than role. The soul is oriented towards a vocation, which is much more valuable than a professionally ascribed role. Together we embrace a primary calling of *solidarity* that infuses our vocation with love, humility, courage and passion.

A question we often consider is: do we connect with the aspirations of the profession, or the interests of the organisations we work for, or the sympathies of a vocation which calls us to work with the poor and marginalised? Another way of framing the question is: does our community of solidarity coincide with a community of 'professionals' (professionally oriented practitioners), or the community of work colleagues, or a diverse web of relationships that are calling forth community as dialogue and hospitality?

This is not to say that practitioners should not develop a network of colleagues who can support one another to work in a professional and disciplined way, or that practitioners will not value the organisation that employs and deploys them. But it is crucial that this professional or organisational 'community' does not become the primary interest group. That would take us in the direction Ivan Illich warns against in *Disabling Professions* (1977).

Solidarity with the most disadvantaged and marginalised

The notion of solidarity challenges with other difficult questions. Are we, as practitioners, on an upward career ladder within a profession, or are we on a downward journey connecting to spaces, places and bases where the most disadvantaged and marginalised reside? Solidarity calls for a movement alongside and engaged with the most vulnerable people in places where they live—invisible, unsafe, distant, uncomfortable places. It invites a movement out of comfort zones and engagement with fears, selfishness and greed. The notion of solidarity can be viewed as an invitation to enter into a journey of companionship with the poor, invisible, vulnerable and marginalised. It is not about just giving time, mobilising resources, and utilising skills. It is also about giving friendship to the 'other'—those who we would not usually choose as friends.

The story below illustrates what often happens in contemporary community development work, where the focus is on role not soul, and there is an accompanying loss of any deep sense of solidarity with the marginalised.

> For a couple of years Peter was working on a community development initiative within a caravan park in suburban Brisbane. The people living in the park were generally long-term unemployed caught in a poverty cycle. While the workers associated with our organisation (Community Praxis Co-op) would go and 'hang out' in people's caravans, we discov-

ered that in some other caravan parks community workers had been instructed to only go into such places if they were in pairs. In fact some workers were told, "You cannot go into the parks—it is too risky. People will have to come and see you in your offices". Risk management frameworks ensured that these workers could never engage in a genuine work of solidarity, or experience the hospitality of the park dwellers. The 'other' was constructed as dangerous and risky. The professionals were more concerned about themselves than the 'other'.

This is what can happen when a practitioner's community of solidarity becomes overly associated with professional roles and organisational obligations. There is a loss of solidarity towards the marginalised. The story also demonstrates a need to reclaim the idea of risk from its contemporary understanding—one in which risk is associated with 'bad'—and reconfigure its meaning to that of 'taking a chance', with all the accompanying sense of adventure and possibility (Furedi, 2005). A vocation of solidarity is risky in daily practice—an adventure infused with possibilities. Peter again reflected on this recently as he flew to a remote island in Vanuatu.

> There is no electricity, minimal health care, and a lack of any substantial communication or transport infrastructure. I feel anxious. It feels risky. But I remind myself that solidarity calls us to take such risks.

A vocational understanding of the work that is oriented primarily towards solidarity with 'others' who are poor. comes at a price. For many badly paid community practitioners it is easy to focus on the financial cost of a vocation of solidarity. We can see friends accumulating houses, cars and boats. Often we read of politicians and managers earning salaries beyond our comprehension. It is easy to start thinking that the deep sadness, the loneliness, that sense of depression or *ennui* is a result of *not having*. At the same time we might feel tired of the poor—their relentless requests, their insistent demands. We start imagining a retreat to the countryside or another country where all this could be escaped. While many community practitioners could do with a holiday, most people involved in community development do not wish to escape. The path was originally chosen because the vocation had a heart, and deep down the work inspired soul.

In fact the nature of calling is what some Taoists call "choice-less aware-ness". What else could we do?

In struggling to maintain a vocational orientation of solidarity, we would like to reflect on three realities of life and work that we propose are keys to maintaining a clear perspective on these dilemmas.

(i) Being attentive to our own mortality

The first key is related to feelings and fears, and the need to locate them within the perspective of a broader picture than we usually do. A vocation of solidarity calls people to be attentive to and aware of everyone's mortality. For most people, facing our mortality ultimately confronts us with the hollowness of the illusions and delusions that we were so easily sucked into believing. No one can leave this world with anything.

Drawing on a long tradition of authors and philosophers such as Tol-stoy and Heidegger, David Yalom points out in *Existential Psychotherapy* (1980, p31) that it is the honest facing of death that "makes it possible for us to live in an authentic fashion". Living from the impulses of greed and selfishness will ultimately gain nothing. A soulful orientation reminds us that to give our lives to the vocation of solidarity does not mean that we ultimately miss out on anything of great significance. A vocation and practice of social solidarity is a calling of great significance that can beau-tifully express attentiveness to mortality.

(ii) Anchoring our solidarity within a tradition

The second key is that for a sense of solidarity to have depth, it is im-portant to anchor ourselves within the context of a tradition. We have referred to the need to understand community development work not as technique but within a tradition. Many people have gone before us who have practised solidarity within their communities. At times of our greatest despair, the thing that picks us up and inspires us to keep going is to spend time with other community workers, or to read the story of someone who has gone before us in the struggle for com-munity and justice. We find that we speak the same language, share the same concerns and values, struggle with the same frustrations and confusions. We might be from different countries and different cultures, we might have studied in different educational institutions, but we are acutely aware that we come from the same kind of tradition. As comrades in the same struggle, we are sustained by the resonance of hard-earned, tried and tested practice wisdom that speaks to our souls.

(iii) Maintaining our solidarity with a vision

Finally, it is important to do everything within our powers to maintain a vision. All of us are bombarded with images of despair and stories of violence. We become used to the same discursive rhetoric and ideology. Our views of what is possible become narrow, limited and shallow—there is a shrinking of our literary imagination. Maybe you sit in the dust of a remote village, hearing the stories of failed development, and ask yourself "What difference can I make?" Without vision there can be no soul. Ancient spiritual traditions teach the wisdom that "where there is no vision the people perish" (King James Bible: Proverbs, 29:18). Vision brings life, energy and depth. Our hope is that this reflection on a dialogical approach to community development contributes to a renewed vision for the world, neighbourhoods and professional practice.

A passion of not knowing

We invite our readers to cultivate a "passion of not knowing" (Caputo, 1997). Modernist thinking loves to understand and explain, to provide the final word and to work out what technique is required. Some approaches to community development have become captive to such thinking, with the resultant 'cookbook approach' to solving problems. To ensure that practitioners do not become captive to this tendency of having the 'final word', it is critical to cultivate a passion of not knowing that keeps us searching for on-going dialogue and depth. We advocate a willingness to open up to mysteries and to unmask any illusions about a final word, employing what Paulo Freire (1997, p100) called epistemological curiosity.

Although such a willingness and curiosity could lead to potential chaos for some, it ensures that practitioners remain inquisitive, humble and open, regaining the ability to wish for a better world through losing a sense of security and assuredness.

It is tempting to lose curiosity when practitioners present ready-made answers, when they claim to have worked out what a community problem is, what a solution is, and what the method or technique is to bring the solution. Conversely it is very hard to lose curiosity if practitioners have a perspective underpinned by the acknowledgment that 'I don't know'. We are indebted to Henri Nouwen (1975) for the counter-intuitive insight that poverty of mind makes a good host. A professional expression of certainty can disempower the people we are working with. However, a hospitable expression of uncertainty shifts us towards the 'other'—into a shared space of mutual un-sureness. Only 'we' can work this out together. So the onward journey is infused with ownership and mutuality, expressed through statements such as "I'm not sure either, but I'm confident *we* can work through this together".

The notion of hospitality has been a central theme of this book. Embedded within the idea of hospitality is a stance that constantly welcomes the intruder—in this case the unknown. If such an idea of hospitality is combined with the passion of not knowing, then the only possible trajectory for community development practice is more dialogue. Practitioners can only remain curious and more passionate about community, development, and their practice, opening up space for mystery, possibility, and imagination.

A passion of not knowing ensures practitioners maintain a restless heart. At times this might mean feeling a little lost, somewhat confused, but this keeps practice in good stead. Not knowing is often the impetus for passion, because once people feel that they know something, they are at great risk of becoming mediocre and enter the dangerous zone of routinised and rote performance. Maintaining a passion of not knowing invites a constant wondering, a new inquisitiveness and a deep commitment to join with others to enhance the possibility of more knowing.

Invitation to dialogue and dissent

As stated in the Introduction, we hope readers will engage with us in a dialogue. Our final words are to reiterate this hope. Welcome to the dialogue. We invite dissent.

References

Alexander, C., Ishikawa, S., & Silverstein, M. (1977). *A Pattern Language: Towns, Buildings and Construction.* New York: Oxford University Press.

Alinsky, S. (1969). *Reveille for Radicals.* New York: Vintage Books.

Anderson, R., Cissna, K. & Arnett, R. (eds.) (1994). *The Reach of Dialogue: Confirmation, Voice, and Community.* New Jersey: Hampton Press.

Andrews, D. (2007). *Living Community.* Community Praxis Co-op and Tafina Press.

Andrews, D. (1992). *Can You Hear the Heartbeat.* Hodder & Stoughton.

Antoniades, A. (1992). *Poetics of Architecture: Theory of Design.* USA: John Wiley & Sons.

Appiah, K. A. (2008). *Experiments in Ethics.* USA: Harvard University Press.

Arnett, R., & Arneson, P. (1999). *Dialogic Civility in a Cynical Age: Community, Hope, and Interpersonal Relationships.* USA: State University of New York Press.

Arnett, R., Fritz, J. M. H. & Bell, L. M. (2009). *Communication ethics literacy: Dialogue and Difference.* Los Angeles: SAGE Press.

Baken, J. (2004). *The Corporation: The Pathological Pursuit of Profit and Power.* New York: Free Press.

Bates, B. (1996). *The Wisdom of the Wyrd.* Ryder Press.

Barringham, N. (2003). *Structuring without Strangling: The Story of the Community Initiatives Resource Association 1993-2003—An experiment in doing more with less.* Self-published.

Bauman, Z. (1998). *Globalisation: The Human Consequences.* Cambridge: Polity Press.

Bauman, Z. (2003). *Liquid Love.* Cambridge: Polity Press.

Bauman, Z. (2004). *Wasted Lives: Modernity and its Outcasts.* Cambridge: Polity Press.

Bauman, Z. (2005). *Liquid Life.* Cambridge: Polity Press.

Bauman, Z. (2007). *Consuming Life.* Cambridge: Polity Press.

BBC News (2006). *Britain is 'surveillance society'.* Retrieved on 1 January 2009 at http://news.bbc.co.uk/go/pr/fr/-/1/hi/uk/6108496.stm.

Blaser, M., Feit, H.A., & McRae, G. (2004). *In the Way of Development: Indigenous Peoples, Life Projects & Globalization.* London: Zed Books.

Bohm, D. (1980). *Wholeness and the Implicate Order.* London: Routledge.

Bohm, D. (1996). *On Dialogue.* New York: Routledge Press.

Booth, W. (1993). *Households: On the Moral Architecture of the Economy.* Cornell Press. Ithaca.

Bourdieu, P. (2003). *Firing Back: Against the Tyranny of the Market.* London: Verso Press.

Botes, L. & Rensburg, D. (2000). 'Community participation in development: nine plagues and twelve commandments', *Community Development Journal,* Vol. 35. No. 1, p41-58

Bracken, P. (2002). *Trauma, Culture, Meaning & Philosophy.* England: Whurr Publishers.

Brown, L. (2007). 'Costing the Earth' in *The Guardian Weekly,* 4 May 2007

Buber, M. (1947). *Between Man and Man.* London and New York: Routledge Classics (2002 edition)

Buber, M. (1958). *I and Thou.* New York: Charles Scribner's Sons.

Buckley, H. (2007). *The Development of a Community Cooperative on the Sunshine Coast: A Building Links Project.* Community Praxis Co-op Ltd.

Butcher. H., Banks, S., Henderson, P. & Robertson, J. (2007). *Critical Community Practice.* Bristol: Policy Press.

Capra, F. (1994). *Ecology and Community.* The Centre for Ecoliteracy, California.

Caputo, J. D. (ed.) (1997) *Deconstruction in a Nutshell: A Conversation with Jacques Derrida.* New York: Fordham University Press

Carmen, R. (1996). *Autonomous Development: Humanizing the Landscape.* London: Zed Books

Chambers, R. (2005). *Ideas for Development.* London: Earthscan

Checkoway, B., Figueroa, L. & Richards-Schuster, K. (2008). 'Youth Force in the South Bronx', in Flynn, M. & Brotherton, D. (eds.). *Globalising the Streets: Cross-Cultural Perspectives on Youth, Social Control, and Empowerment.* New York: Columbia University Press.

Connolly, W. (1999). *Why I am not a Secularist*. London & Minneapolis: University of Minnesota Press.

Couch, J. (2006). 'Global Rotters versus Resistance All Stars: Neo-liberalism has touched down in rural India and a new "glocal" movement is fighting back'. *New Community Quarterly*. Vol. 4. No. 4.

Craig, G. & Mayo, M. (1995). *Community Empowerment: A reader in participation and development*. London: Zed Books.

Dasgupta, S. (1968). *Social Work & Social Change: A Case Study in Indian Village Development*. USA: Extending Horizons Books.

Day, C. (1990) *Places of the Soul: Architecture and Environmental Design as a Healing Art*. London: Thorsons, an imprint of HarperCollins.

Derrida. J. (2001). *On Cosmopolitanism and Forgiveness*. New York: Routledge.

Derrida, J. (1997). *Politics of Friendship*. London & New York; Verso.

Devananda, A. (1986). *Mother Teresa: contemplative at the heart of the world*. India, Fount Collins.

Eade, D. (1997). *Capacity Building: An Approach to People-Centred Development*. UK: Oxfam.

Ellul, J. (1965). *Propaganda: The Formation of Men's Attitudes*. New York: Vintage Books.

Ellul, J. (1965). *The Technological Society*. London: Cape.

Ellul, J. (1990). *The Technological Bluff*. Michigan: Wm. B. Eerdmans Publishing Co.

Esquivel, L. (1989). *Like Water for Chocolate*. UK: A Black Swan Book, Doubleday.

Esteva, G. (1987). "Regenerating People's Space". *Alternatives*, Vol. 12, No. 1.

Everingham, C. (2003). *Social Justice & The Politics of Community*. USA: Ashgate.

Finch, J. (2007). "Bonanza in British Boardrooms". *The Guardian Weekly*, 7 September 2007.

Flynn, M. & Brotherton, D. (eds.) *Globalising the Streets: Cross-Cultural Perspectives on Youth, Social Control, and Empowerment*. New York: Columbia University Press.

Forester, J. (1999). *The Deliberative Practitioner: Encouraging Participatory Planning Processes*. USA: Massachusetts Institute of Technology.

Freeden, M. (2003). *Ideology: A Very Short Introduction*. Oxford: Oxford University Press.

Freire, P. (1972). *Pedagogy of the Oppressed*. UK: Penguin Books.

Freire, P. (1997). *Pedagogy of the Heart*. New York & London: Continuum.

Fromm, E. (1957). *The Art of Loving*. London: Thorsons, HarperCollins.

Furedi, F. (2004). *Therapy Culture: Cultivating Vulnerability in an Uncertain Age*. London and New York: Routledge.

Furedi, F (2005). *Politics of Fear: Beyond Left and Right*. London & New York: Continuum.

Geoghegan, M. & Powell, F. (2008). 'Community development and the contested politics of the late modern *agora*: of, alongside or against neoliberalism'. *Community Development Journal*. Advanced Access published July 14, 2008.

Gibney, P. (2003) *The Pragmatics of Therapeutic Practice*. Australia: Psychoz Publications.

Gourevitch, P. (1998). *We wish to inform you that tomorrow we will be killed with our families: stories from Rwanda*. New York: Farrar, Straus, and Giroux.

Green, D. (2008). *From Poverty to Power: How Active Citizens and Effective States can Change the World*. Oxford: Oxfam International.

Gupta, U. D. (ed.) (2006). *Rabindranath Tagore: my life in my words*. New Delhi: Penguin Books India.

Habermas, J. (1976). *Legitimation Crisis*. London: Heinemann Press.

Hamilton, C. (2003). *Growth Fetish*. Allen & Unwin.

Hamilton, C. (2005). *Affluenza*. Allen & Unwin.

Hamilton, C. (2006). 'What's Left? The death of social democracy'. *Quarterly Essay*, Issue 21. Melbourne, Australia: Black Inc.

Hamilton, C. (2007). *Scorcher: The Dirty Politics of Climate Change*. Melbourne: Black Inc. Agenda.

Heald, S. (2008). 'Embracing marginality: place-making vs. development in Gardenton, Manitoba'. *Development in Practice*, Vol. 18, No, 1.

Healy, K. (2005). *Social Work Theories in Context: Creating Frameworks for Practice*. UK & USA: Palgrave Macmillan.

Heidelberg Institute for International Conflict Research, (2007). *Conflict Barometer 2006*.

Henderson, P. & Thomas, D. (2002). 'Forming and Building Organisations' in *Skills in Neighbourhood Work*, 3rd edition. London: Routledge.

Hillman, J. (1983). *A Healing Fiction*. Woodstock, Connecticut: Spring Publications, Inc.

Hillman, J. & Ventura, M. (1993). *We've had a Hundred Years of Psycho-Therapy and the World's Getting Worse*. New York: HarperCollins Publishers.

Homer-Dixon, T. (2006). *The Upside of Down: Catastrophe, Creativity and the Renewal of Civilization*. Australia: The Text Publishing Company.

hooks, b. (1994). *Teaching to Transgress: Education as the Practice of Freedom*. Routledge Press.

hooks, b. (2003). *Teaching Community: A Pedagogy of Hope*. Routledge Press.

Hope, A. & Timmel, S. (1984). *Training for Transformation: A Handbook for Community Workers*, Volumes 1-3. Zimbabwe: Mambo Press.

Horton, M, & Freire, P. with Bell, B., Gaventa, J. & Peters, J. (ed.) (1990). *We Make the Road by Walking: Conversations on Education and Social Change*. Philadelphia: Temple University Press.

Ife, J. (2006). *Community Development: community based alternatives in an age of globalisation* (3rd edition). Australia: Pearson Press.

Illich, I. (1977). *Disabling Professions*. London: Salem & Boyars.

Isaacs, W. (1999). *Dialogue and the Art of Thinking Together: A Pioneering Approach to Communicating in Business and Life*. Doubleday.

Kapuscinski, R. (2008). *The Other*. London & New York: Verso.

Kelly, A & Sewell, S. (ed.) (1986). *People working together: Volume two*. Brisbane, Australia: Boolarong Publications.

Kelly, A & Sewell, S. (1988). *With Head, Heart and Hand: Dimensions of Community Building*. Brisbane, Australia: Boolarong Publications.

Kelly, A., Morgan, A. & Coghlan, D. (1997). *People working together: Traditions and best practice*. Brisbane: Boolarong Press.

Kelly, A. (2008). *People Centred Development: Development Method*. Australia: The Centre for Social Response.

Kelly, A. & Burkett, I. (2008). *People Centred Development: Building the People Centred Approach*. Australia: The Centre for Social Response.

Kornfield, J. (1993). *A Path With Heart*. USA & Canada: Bantam Books.

Korten, D. (1995). *When Corporations Rule the World*. Kumarian Press.

Korten, D. (2000). *The Post-Corporate World: Life After Capitalism*. Australia: Pluto Press.

Kropotkin, P. (1902). *Mutual aid: a factor of evolution*. London: Heinemann.

Kumar, Satish (2002a). *You are Therefore I am*. Devon, UK: Green Books Ltd.

Kumar, Somesh (2002b). *Methods for Community Participation: A Complete Guide for Practitioners*. London: ITDG Publishing.

Kureshi, H. (2008). *Something to Tell You*. London: Faber & Faber

Kurlansky, M. (2006). *Non-Violence: A History of a Dangerous Idea*. London: Jonathan Cape.

Lederach, J. P. (1995). *Preparing for Peace: Conflict Transformation across Cultures*. New York: Syracuse University Press.

Lederach, J. P. (2005). *The Moral Imagination: The Art and Soul of Building Peace*. Oxford: Oxford University Press.

Ledwith, K. (2005). *Community Development: A critical approach*. Bristol: Policy Press.

Lee, M. (c2007). *Inventing fear of crime: criminology and the politics of anxiety*. Cullompton, Portland, Ore: Willan Publishing.

Levinas, E. (c1999). *Alterity and transcendence*. New York: Columbia University Press.

McKnight, J. (1995). *The Careless Society: Community and its Counterfeits*. USA: Basic Books.

McLuhan, M. (1964). *Understanding Media: The extensions of man*, New York: Mentor.

Max-Neef, M. (1991). *Human Scale Development: Conception, Application and Further Reflections*. New York & London: The Apex Press.

Max-Neef, M. (1992). *From the Outside Looking In: Experiences in Barefoot Economics*. London & New Jersey: Zed Books.

Macy, J. (1983). *Despair and Personal Power in the Nuclear Age*. Philadelphia: New Society Publishers.

Macy, J. (1985). *Dharma and Development: Religion as a Resource in the Sarvodaya Self-Help Movement*. USA: Kumarian Press.

Macy, J. & Brown, M. Y. (1998). *Coming Back to Life: Practices to Reconnect Our Lives, Our World*. Canada: New Society Publishers.

Mayo, P. (1999). *Gramsci, Freire & Adult Education: Possibilities for Transformative Action.* London: Zed Books.

Monbiot, G. (2007). *Heat: How to Stop the Planet Burning.* London: Allen Lane, an imprint of Allen & Unwin.

Moore, T. (1992). *Care of the Soul: How to Add Depth and Meaning to Your Everyday Life.* London: Judy Piakkus Publishers Ltd.

Moore, T. (1996). *The Re-Enchantment of Everyday Life.* Australia: Hodder & Stoughton.

Morgan, B. (2006). *I Celebrate Myself: The Somewhat Private Life of Allen Ginsberg.* USA: Viking Penguin.

Mouffe, C. (2005). *On The Political: Thinking in Action.* London & New York: Routledge.

Norberg-Hodge, H. (2000). *Ancient Futures: Learning from Ladakh.* Australia: Random House.

Nouwen, H.J.M. (1975). *Reaching Out: The three movements of the spiritual life.* New York: Doubleday.

Palmer, P. (2004). *A Hidden Wholeness: The Journey Toward An Undivided Life—Welcoming the Soul and Weaving Community in a Wounded World.* San Francisco: Jossey-Bass

Parker, P. (1980). *The Promise of Paradox: A Celebration of Contradictions in the Christian Life.* USA: Ave Marie Press.

Pecora, V. P. (2006). *Secularization and Cultural Criticism: Religion, Nation and Modernity.* Chicago & London: The University of Chicago Press.

Peile, C. (1994). *The Creative Paradigm: insight, synthesis and knowledge development.* Avebury, Sydney.

Rabino, P. (1984). *The Foucault Reader.* UK: Penguin Books.

Rihani, S. (2002). *Complex Systems Theory and Development Practice.* London: Zed Books.

Rose, D. B. (1997). "Rupture & the Ethics of Care in Colonized Space" in Bonyhady, T. (ed.). *Prehistory to Politics: John Mulvaney, the humanities and the public intellectual.* Carlton, Victoria: Melbourne University Press.

Rose, D. B., D'Amico, S., Daiyi, N., Deveraux, K., Daiyi, M., Ford, L. & Bright, A. (2002). *Country of My Heart: An Indigenous Australian Homeland.* Canberra: Aboriginal Studies Press.

Rose, N. (1999). *Powers of Freedom: Reframing Political Thought*. Cambridge: Cambridge University Press.

Rose, N. (2004). 'Governing the Social' in Gane, N. *The Future of Social Theory*. London & New York: Continuum.

Saferworld (2006). *Creating Safer Communities: Lessons from South Eastern Europe*. Balkan Youth Union, Centre for Security Studies and the Civil Forum for Civil Initiatives—Saferworld.

Schumacher, E. F. (1974). *Small is Beautiful: A Study of Economics as if People Mattered*. London: Abacus.

Sen, A. (1999). *Development as Freedom*. Oxford: Oxford University Press.

Sen, A. (2006). *Identity and Violence: The Illusion of Destiny*. London & New York: W.W Norton & Company.

Shields, K. (1991). *In the Tiger's Mouth: An Empowerment Guide for Social Action*. Australia: Millennium Books.

Shiva, V. (2005). *Earth Democracy: Justice, Sustainability and Peace*. London: Zed Books.

Studdert, D. (2005). *Conceptualizing Community: beyond the State and the Individual*. Palgrave Macmillan.

Taylor, C. (2007). *A Secular Age*. Cambridge, Massachusetts, & London: The Belknap Press of Harvard University Press.

The Australia Institute (2008) 'Some crises are more equal than others'. *Between the Lines*, 22 October 2008.

Theobald, R. (1997). *Reworking success: new communities at the millennium*. USA: New Society Publishers.

Turton, D. (2004). "The Meaning of Place in a World of Movement: Lessons from Long-term Field Research in Southern Ethiopia". *Working Paper Series*. Refugee Studies Centre: University of Oxford.

UNHCR. (2007). Internally Displaced People. Switzerland: UNHCR. Retrieved on 1.6.08 at http://www.unhcr.org/basics/BASICS/405ef8c64.pdf.

United Nations. (2007). *Cooperatives in Social Development: Report of the Secretary-General*. UN General Assembly, 26 July 2007.

Vanier, J. (1979). *Community and Growth*. NSW: St. Paul Publications.

Vonnegut, K. (2005). *A Man Without Country*. New York, London, Melbourne & Toronto: Seven Stories Press.

Wallis, J. (1994). *The Soul of Politics*. New York: New Press & Orbis Press.

Wals, A. E. J. & Heymann, F. (2004). 'Learning on the Edge: Exploring the Change Potential of Conflict in Social Learning for Sustainable Living' in Wenden, A. (ed.). *Educating for a Culture of Social and Ecological Peace*. New York: State University of New York Press.

Watson, L. (1995). *Dark Nature*. UK: Hodder & Stoughton.

Weil, M. (ed.) (2005). *The Handbook of Community Practice*. Thousand Oaks: Sage Publications.

Wicks, J. (2004). *Good Morning Beautiful Business. Twenty-Fourth Annual E.F. Schumacher Lectures*. USA: E.F. Schumacher Society.

Wicks, J. & Klause, V. K. (1998). *White Dog Café Cookbook: Multicultural Recipes and Tales of Adventure from Philadelphia's Revolutionary Restaurant*. Philadelphia: Running Press Book Publishers.

Wilkinson, R. (2005). *The Impact of Inequality: How to make sick societies healthier.* London & New York: Routledge

Wilson, P., Wells, H., & Allard, T. (2006). 'Crime and CCTV in Australia: Understanding the Relationship'. *Bond University: Humanities & Social Science Papers*.

Wink, W. (1992). *Engaging the Powers: Discernment and Resistance in a World of Domination*. Minneapolis: Fortress Press.

Yalom, I. D. (1980). *Existential Psychotherapy*. USA: Basic Books.

Young, J. (1999). *The Exclusive Society: Social Exclusion, Crime and Difference in Late Modernity*. Newbury Park, CA: Sage Press.

Yunus, M. (1999). *Banker to the Poor: The Story of the Grameen Bank*. London: Aurum Press.

About the Authors

Peter Westoby

Peter originally hails from the UK but now loves living in Highgate Hill, Brisbane. He is currently a Lecturer in Community Development within the University of Queensland School of Social Work and Human Services, and a Research Associate with the Australian Centre for Peace and Conflict Studies (ACPACS). He is also a director/consultant with Community Praxis Co-op.

His experience includes work in South Africa, PNG, the Philippines, Vanuatu and Australia. His interests are in refugee related work, youth work practice and community development. He is passionate about running, reading, good coffee, hanging out at his local AVID reader book shop, bushwalking and travelling. His current greatest dilemma is how to align his love of travel with carbon emissions.

Peter can be contacted at peter@communitypraxis.org

Gerard Dowling

Gerard was born in North Queensland, a descendent of Irish-English folk who came looking for gold in the 1870's and ended up scratching for tin and wrangling packhorses in the bush.

Since 1987 he has lived in the inner Brisbane suburb of West End, where he has shared a home with Lyn, raised Ciaron and Jack, and (much to his surprise) fulfilled Ciaron's naïve childhood dream of growing a rainforest in the backyard of a humble rented cottage on a little sixteen-perch block.

He's done twenty years in various community development roles, including housing work with the Tenants' Union, prisons work with the Catholics, and collaborative community planning consultancies with Community Praxis Co-op. He currently organises youth projects for Brisbane City Council, exploring creative ways to engage young people in youth space, urban design, multicultural community, sustainability, active travel, social enterprise, and e-citizenship - with a great crew of young and young-at-heart colleagues in an innovative local government context.

Gerard can be contacted at gerard@communitypraxis.org

CPSIA information can be obtained at www.ICGtesting.com
Printed in the USA
BVOW06s0223300816

460586BV00025B/271/P